The Haynes
Ford Automatic Transmission Overhaul Manual

by Jeff Killingsworth and John H Haynes
Member of the Guild of Motoring Writers

Models covered:

C3, C4, C5, C6 and AOD Rear Wheel Drive Transmissions

ATX/FLC and AXOD Front Wheel Drive Transaxles

Does not include the electronic versions of the AOD (AODE) or AXOD (AXODE)

ABCDE
FGHIJ
KLMNO
PQRST

AUTOMOTIVE PARTS & ACCESSORIES ASSOCIATION MEMBER

Haynes Publishing Group
Sparkford Nr Yeovil
Somerset BA22 7JJ England

Haynes North America, Inc
861 Lawrence Drive
Newbury Park
California 91320 USA

Acknowledgements

We are grateful to B&M Racing and Performance Products for allowing us to photograph some of the transmission overhaul procedures at their facility. Thanks to Automotive Transmission Parts Inc. for providing us with some of the parts used in the repair and modifications chapters.

Special thanks to Brian Applegate, Randy Cannon and Jim Rose of B&M Racing and Performance Products for their help, cooperation and technical expertise provided in producing this manual.

Special thanks to Craig Calkins and Todd Otis of CRC Performance Transmissions in Thousand Oaks, CA and to Jeff Watson and Jim Rose of Champion Transmissions of Thousand Oaks, CA for their help, cooperation and technical expertise in producing this manual.

Also contributing to this manual were Mike Forsythe, Eric Godfrey, Bob Henderson and Jeff Kibler.

A book in the Haynes Automotive Repair Manual Series

Printed in the U.S.A.

ISBN 1 56392 424 2

Library of Congress Catalog Card Number 95-80973

01-288

Contents

Notes

Chapter 1 Introduction

How to use this repair manual

The manual is divided into Chapters. Each Chapter is sub-divided into Sections, some of which consist of consecutively numbered Paragraphs (usually referred to as "Steps", since they're normally part of a procedure). If the material is basically informative in nature, rather than a step-by-step procedure, the Paragraphs aren't numbered.

The first six Chapters contain material on tools and equipment, identification, theory and fundamentals of automatic transmissions, as well as troubleshooting and in-vehicle repairs. Chapters 7 and 8 cover the specifics of the overhaul procedure, beginning with removing the transmission from the vehicle. Chapter 9 discusses simple transmission modifications you can perform at home.

The term "**see illustration**" (in parentheses), is used in the text to indicate that a photo or drawing has been included to make the information easier to understand (the old cliché "a picture is worth a thousand words" is especially true when it comes to how-to procedures). Also, every attempt is made to position illustrations directly opposite the corresponding text to minimize confusion. The two types of illustrations used (photographs and line drawings) are referenced by a number preceding the caption. Illustration numbers denote Chapter and numerical sequence within the Chapter (i.e., 3.4 means Chapter 3, illustration number four in order).

The terms "**Note**," "**Caution**," and "**Warning**" are used throughout the text with a specific purpose in mind - to attract the reader's attention. A "**Note**" simply provides information required to properly complete a procedure or information which will make the procedure easier to understand. A "**Caution**" outlines a special procedure or special steps which must be taken when completing the procedure where the "**Caution**" is found. Failure to pay attention to a "**Caution**" can result in damage to the component being repaired or the tools being used. A "**Warning**" is included where personal injury can result if the instructions aren't followed exactly as described.

Even though extreme care has been taken during the preparation of this manual, neither the publisher nor the author can accept responsibility for any errors in, or omissions from, the information given.

What is an overhaul?

A transmission overhaul involves restoring the internal parts to the specifications of a new transmission. During an overhaul, the clutches, bands, bushings, seals and gaskets are routinely replaced. The parts needed for a typical overhaul are generally included in overhaul kits available from transmission parts manufacturers. Additionally, all other parts in the transmission are carefully inspected for damage and excessive wear. Any marginal parts must be replaced. Generally, the torque converter is replaced as well, since it's usually in less-than-perfect condition at this point.

It's not always easy to determine when, or if, a transmission should be completely overhauled, as a number of factors must be considered.

High mileage is not necessarily an indication that an overhaul is needed, while low mileage doesn't preclude the need for an overhaul. Frequency of servicing is probably the most important consideration. A transmission in a vehicle that's been driven normally and had frequent fluid and filter changes, as well as other required maintenance, will most likely give many thousands of miles of reliable service. Conversely, a neglected and abused transmission may require an overhaul very early in its life. Slippage and noises often indicate serious transmission problems, but could also have simple remedies. A low fluid level can often give symptoms just like those of a failing transmission. Before determining your transmission needs an overhaul, refer to the troubleshooting information in Chapter 5.

Before beginning the transmission overhaul, read through this entire manual to familiarize yourself with the scope and requirements of the job. Overhauling a transmission isn't particularly difficult if you have the correct equipment; however, it is time consuming. Plan on the vehicle being tied up for a minimum of two weeks, especially if parts must be ordered or reconditioned. Check on availability of parts and make sure that any necessary special tools and equipment are obtained in advance. Most work can be done with typical hand tools, although precision measuring tools are required for inspecting parts to determine if they must be replaced. Also, special tools such as those for compressing clutch packs are usually required. Chapter 2 contains information on special tools.

Buying parts

Commonly replaced transmission parts such as clutches, bands, seals and bushings are produced by aftermarket manufacturers and stocked by retail auto parts stores and mail order houses, usually at a savings over dealer parts department prices. Many auto parts stores and mail order houses offer complete transmission overhaul kits, often at a considerable savings over individual parts. Don't buy gaskets separately. A good-quality complete gasket set will save you money and the needless hassle of buying individual gaskets.

Less-commonly replaced items such as planetary gearsets, drums and transmission cases may not be available through these same sources and a dealer parts department may be your only option. Keep in mind that some parts will probably have to be ordered, and it may take several days to get your parts; order early.

Wrecking yards are a good source for major parts that would otherwise only be available through a dealer service department (where the price would likely be high). Transmission cases, planetary gearsets, etc. are commonly available for reasonable prices. Although, you must be very careful when selecting used parts. Running changes are often made during the model year and a newly designed component from a transmission of the same type may not be compatible with your transmission. To insure the used part will be an exact match, select a used transmission for your parts source with the same identification code as the one you're rebuilding. Then as a final precaution, visually compare the replacement part with the damaged component to make sure they are identical. The parts people at wrecking yards have parts interchange books they can use to quickly identify parts from other models and years that are the same as the ones on your transmission.

Chapter 2
Tools and equipment

A place to work

Establish a place to work. A special work area is essential. It doesn't have to be particularly large, but it should be clean, safe, well-lit, organized and adequately equipped for the job. True, without a good workshop or garage, you can still service and repair transmissions, even if you have to work outside. But an overhaul or major repairs should be carried out in a sheltered area with a roof. The procedures in this book require an environment totally free of dirt, which will cause wear or failure if it finds its way into the transmission.

The workshop

The size, shape and location of a shop building is usually dictated by circumstance rather than personal choice. Every do-it-yourselfer dreams of having a spacious, clean, well-lit building specially designed and equipped for working on everything from small engines on lawn and garden equipment to cars and other vehicles. In reality, however, most of us must content ourselves with a garage, basement or shed in the backyard.

Spend some time considering the potential - and drawbacks - of your current facility. Even a well-established workshop can benefit from intelligent design. Lack of space is the most common problem,

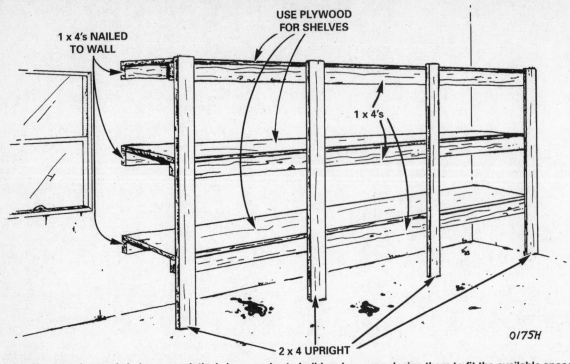

2.1 Homemade wood shelves are relatively inexpensive to build and you can design them to fit the available space

but you can significantly increase usable space by carefully planning the locations of work and storage areas. One strategy is to look at how others do it. Ask local repair shop owners if you can see their shops. Note how they've arranged their work areas, storage and lighting, then try to scale down their solutions to fit your own shop space, finances and needs.

General workshop requirements

A solid concrete floor is the best surface for a shop area. The floor should be even, smooth and dry. A coat of paint or sealant formulated for concrete surfaces will make oil spills and dirt easier to remove and help cut down on dust - always a problem with concrete.

Paint the walls and ceiling white for maximum reflection. Use gloss or semi-gloss enamel. It's washable and reflective. If your shop has windows, situate workbenches to take advantage of them. Skylights are even better. You can't have too much natural light. Artificial light is also good, but you'll need a lot of it to equal ordinary daylight.

Make sure the building is adequately ventilated. This is critical during the winter months, to prevent condensation problems. It's also a vital safety consideration where solvents, gasoline and other volatile liquids are being used. You should be able to open one or more windows for ventilation. In addition, opening vents in the walls are desirable.

Storage and shelves

Once disassembled, a transmission occupies more space than you might think. Set up an organized storage area to avoid losing parts. You'll also need storage space for hardware, lubricants, solvent, rags, tools and equipment.

If space and finances allow, install metal shelves along the walls. Arrange the shelves so they're widely spaced near the bottom to take large or heavy items. Metal shelf units are costly, but they make the best use of available space. And the shelf height is adjustable on most units.

Wood shelves **(see illustration)** are sometimes a cheaper storage solution. But they must be built - not just assembled. They must be much heftier than metal shelves to carry the same weight, the shelves can't be adjusted vertically and you can't just disassemble them and

take them with you if you move. Wood also absorbs oil and other liquids and is obviously a much greater fire hazard.

Store small parts in plastic drawers or bins mounted on metal racks attached to the wall. They're available from most hardware, home and lumber stores. Bins come in various sizes and usually have slots for labels.

All kinds of containers are useful in a shop. Glass jars are handy for storing fasteners, but they're easily broken. Cardboard boxes are adequate for temporary use, but if they become damp, the bottoms eventually weaken and fall apart if you store oily or heavy parts in them. Plastic containers come in a variety of sizes and colors for easy identification. Egg cartons are excellent organizers for small parts like bolts, springs and O-rings. Old metal cake pans, bread pans and muffin tins also make good storage containers for small parts.

Workbenches

A workbench is essential - it provides a place to lay out parts and tools during repair procedures, and it's a lot more comfortable than working on a floor or the driveway. The workbench should be as large and sturdy as space and finances allow. If cost is no object, buy industrial steel benches. They're more expensive than home-built benches, but they're very strong, they're easy to assemble, and - if you move - they can be disassembled quickly and you can take them with you. They're also available in various lengths, so you can buy the exact size to fill the space along a wall.

If steel benches aren't in the budget, fabricate a bench frame from slotted angle-iron or Douglas fir (use 2 x 6's rather than 2 x 4's) **(see illustration)**. Cut the pieces of the frame to the required size and bolt them together with carriage bolts. A 30 or 36 by 80-inch, solid-core door with hardboard surfaces makes a good bench top. And you can flip it over when one side is worn out.

An even cheaper - and quicker - solution? Assemble a bench by attaching the bench top frame pieces to the wall with angled braces and use the wall studs as part of the framework.

Regardless of the type of frame you decide to use for the workbench, be sure to position the bench top at a comfortable working height and make sure everything is level. Shelves installed below the bench will make it more rigid and provide useful storage space.

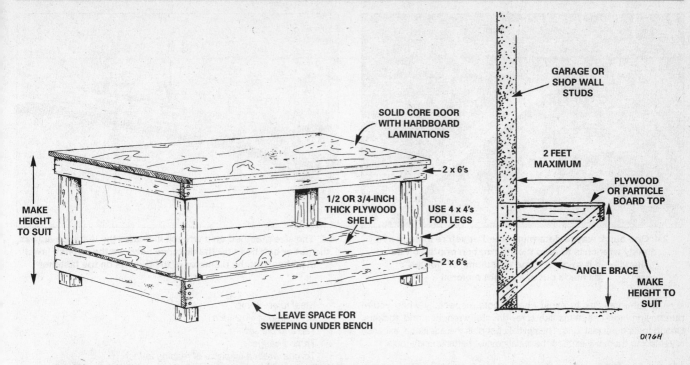

2.2 You can build a sturdy, inexpensive workbench with 4 X 4s, 2 X 6s and a solid-core door with hardboard laminations - or build a bench using the wall as an integral member as shown

2.3 Only a few hand tools are necessary to overhaul automatic transmissions. The tools shown here, along with the special tools discussed later in this Chapter, are all we needed for the overhauls themselves

Tools and equipment

For some home mechanics, the idea of using the correct tool is completely foreign. They'll cheerfully tackle the most complex overhaul procedures with only a set of cheap open-end wrenches of the wrong type, a single screwdriver with a worn tip, a large hammer and an adjustable wrench. Though they often get away with it, this cavalier approach is foolish and dangerous. It can result in relatively minor annoyances like stripped fasteners, or cause catastrophic consequences. It can also result in serious injury.

A complete assortment of good tools is a given for anyone who plans to overhaul transmissions. If you don't already have most of the tools listed below, the initial investment may seem high, but compared to the spiraling costs of routine maintenance and repairs, it's a deal.

Besides, you can use a lot of the tools around the house for other types of mechanical repairs. We've included a list of the tools you'll need and a detailed description of what to look for when shopping for tools and how to use them correctly. We've also included a list of the special factory tools you'll need for transmission rebuilding.

Buying tools

There are two ways to buy tools. The easiest and quickest way is to simply buy an entire set. Tool sets are often priced substantially below the cost of the same individually priced tools - and sometimes they even come with a tool box. When purchasing such sets, you often wind up with some tools you don't need or want. But if low price and convenience are your concerns, this might be the way to go. Keep in mind that you're going to keep a quality set of tools a long time (maybe the rest of your life), so check the tools carefully; don't skimp too much on price, either. Buying tools individually is usually a more expensive and time-consuming way to go, but you're more likely to wind up with the tools you need and want **(see illustration)**. You can also select each tool on its relative merits for the way you use it.

You can get most of the hand tools on our list from the tool department of any large department store or hardware store chain that sells hand tools. Blackhawk, Cornwall, Craftsman, Lisle, KD, Proto and SK are fairly inexpensive, good-quality choices. Specialty tools are available from mechanics' tool companies such as Snap-On, Mac, Matco, Kent-Moore, Hayden, OTC, etc. These companies also supply the other tools you need, but they'll probably be more expensive.

Also consider buying second-hand tools from garage sales or used tool outlets. You may have limited choice in sizes, but you can usually determine from the condition of the tools if they're worth buying. You can end up with a number of unwanted or duplicate tools, but it's a cheap way of putting a basic tool kit together, and you can always sell off any surplus tools later.

Until you're a good judge of the quality levels of tools, avoid mail order firms (excepting Sears and other name-brand suppliers), flea markets and swap meets. Some of them offer good value for the money, but many sell cheap, imported tools of dubious quality. Like other consumer products counterfeited in the Far East, these tools run the gamut from acceptable to unusable.

2.4 One quick way to determine whether you're looking at a quality wrench is to read the information printed on the handle - if it says "chrome vanadium" or "forged", it's made out of the right material

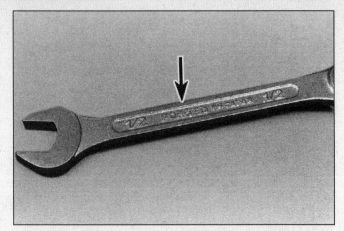

2.5 The size stamped on a wrench indicates the distance across the nut or bolt head (or the distance between the wrench jaws) in inches, not the diameter of the threads on the fastener

In summary, try to avoid cheap tools, especially when you're purchasing high-use items like screwdrivers, wrenches and sockets. Cheap tools don't last long. Their initial cost plus the additional expense of replacing them will exceed the initial cost of better-quality tools.

Hand tools

A list of general-purpose hand tools

Adjustable wrench - 10-inch
Allen wrench set (1/8 to 3/8-inch or 4 mm to 10 mm)
Ball peen hammer - 12 oz (any steel hammer will do)
Box-end wrenches
Brass hammer
Brushes (various sizes, for cleaning small passages)
Bushing remover and installer
Combination (slip-joint) pliers - 6-inch
Center punch
Cold chisels - 1/4 and 1/2-inch
Cape chisel - 1/2-inch
Combination wrench set (1/4 to 1-inch)
Dial indicator
Extensions - 1-, 6-, 10- and 12-inch
E-Z out (screw extractor) set
Feeler gauge set
Files (assorted)
Floor jack
Gasket scraper
Hacksaw and assortment of blades
Impact screwdriver and bits
Locking pliers
Micrometer(s) (one-inch)
Phillips screwdriver (no. 2 x 6-inch)
Phillips screwdriver (no. 3 x 8-inch)
Phillips screwdriver (stubby - no. 2)
Pin punches (1/16, 1/8, 3/16-inch)
Pliers - lineman's
Pliers - needle-nose
Pliers - snap-ring (internal and external)
Pliers - vise-grip
Pliers - diagonal cutters
Ratchet (reversible)
Scribe
Socket set (6-point)
Soft-face hammer (plastic/rubber)
Standard screwdriver (1/4-inch x 6-inch)
Standard screwdriver (5/16-inch x 6-inch)
Standard screwdriver (3/8-inch x 10-inch)
Standard screwdriver (5/16-inch - stubby)

Steel ruler - 6-inch
Straightedge - 12-inch
Tap and die set
Thread gauge
Torque wrench (capable of reading in-lbs)
Torx socket(s)
Universal joint
Wire brush (large)

What to look for when buying hand tools and general purpose tools

Wrenches and sockets

Wrenches vary widely in quality. One indication of their quality is their cost: The more they cost, the better they are. Buy the best wrenches you can afford. You'll use them a lot.

Start with a set containing wrenches from 1/4 to 1-inch in size. The size, stamped on the wrench **(see illustration)**, indicates the distance across the nut or bolt head, or the distance between the wrench jaws - not the diameter of the threads on the fastener - in inches. For example, a 1/4-inch bolt usually has a 7/16-inch hex head - the size of the wrench required to loosen or tighten it. However, the relationship between thread diameter and hex size doesn't always hold true. In some instances, an unusually small hex may be used to discourage over-tightening or because space around the fastener head is limited. Conversely, some fasteners have a disproportionately large hex-head.

Wrenches are similar in appearance, so their quality level can be difficult to judge just by looking at them. There are bargains to be had, just as there are overpriced tools with well-known brand names. On the other hand, you may buy what looks like a reasonable value set of wrenches only to find they fit badly or are made from poor-quality steel.

With a little experience, it's possible to judge the quality of a tool by looking at it. Often, you may have come across the brand name before and have a good idea of the quality. Close examination of the tool can often reveal some hints as to its quality. Prestige tools are usually polished and chrome-plated over their entire surface, with the working faces ground to size. The polished finish is largely cosmetic, but it does make them easy to keep clean. Ground jaws normally indicate the tool will fit well on fasteners.

A side-by-side comparison of a high-quality wrench with a cheap equivalent is an eye opener. The better tool will be made from a good-quality material, often a forged/chrome-vanadium steel alloy **(see illustration)**. This, together with careful design, allows the tool to be kept as small and compact as possible. If, by comparison, the cheap tool is thicker and heavier, especially around the jaws, it's usually because the extra material is needed to compensate for its lower

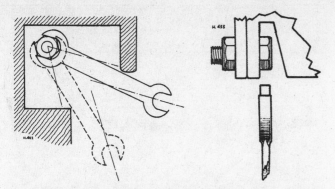

2.6 Open-end wrenches can do several things other wrenches can't - for example, they can be used on bolt heads with limited clearance (above) and they can be used in tight spots where there's little room to turn a wrench by flipping the offset jaw over every few degrees of rotation

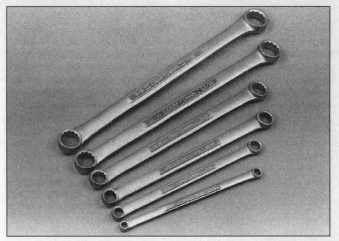

2.7 Box-end wrenches have a ring-shaped "box" at each end - when space permits, they offer the best combination of "grip" and strength

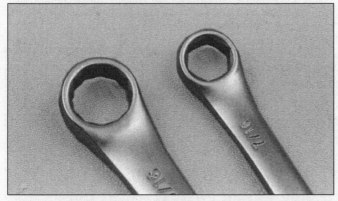

2.8 Box-end wrenches are available in 12 (left) and 6-point (right) openings; even though the 12-point design offers twice as many wrench positions, buy the 6-point first - it's less likely to strip off the corners of a nut or bolt head

quality. If the tool fits properly, this isn't necessarily bad - it is, after all, cheaper - but in situations where it's necessary to work in a confined area, the cheaper tool may be too bulky to fit.

Open-end wrenches

Because of its versatility, the open-end wrench is the most common type of wrench. It has a jaw on either end, connected by a flat handle section. The jaws either vary by a size, or overlap sizes between consecutive wrenches in a set. This allows one wrench to be used to

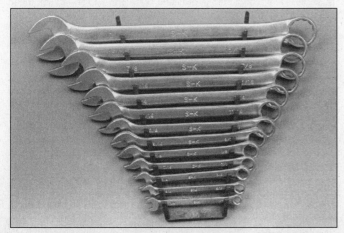

2.9 Buy a set of combination wrenches from 1/4 to 1-inch or from 8 to 22-mm

hold a bolt head while a similar-size nut is removed. A typical fractional size wrench set might have the following jaw sizes: 1/4 x 5/16, 3/8 x 7/16, 1/2 x 9/16, 9/16 x 5/8 and so on.

Typically, the jaw end is set at an angle to the handle, a feature which makes them very useful in confined spaces; by turning the nut or bolt as far as the obstruction allows, then turning the wrench over so the jaw faces in the other direction, it's possible to move the fastener a fraction of a turn at a time **(see illustration)**. The handle length is generally determined by the size of the jaw and is calculated to allow a nut or bolt to be tightened sufficiently by hand with minimal risk of breakage or thread damage (though this doesn't apply to soft materials like brass or aluminum).

Common open-end wrenches are usually sold in sets and it's rarely worth buying them individually unless it's to replace a lost or broken tool from a set. Single tools invariably cost more, so check the sizes you're most likely to need regularly and buy the best set of wrenches you can afford in that range of sizes. If money is limited, remember that you'll use open-end wrenches more than any other type - it's a good idea to buy a good set and cut corners elsewhere.

Box-end wrenches

Box-end wrenches **(see illustration)** have ring-shaped ends with a 6-point (hex) or 12-point (double hex) opening **(see illustration)**. This allows the tool to fit on the fastener hex at 15 (12-point) or 30-degree (6-point) intervals. Normally, each tool has two ends of different sizes, allowing an overlapping range of sizes in a set, as described for open-end wrenches.

Although available as flat tools, the handle is usually offset at each end to allow it to clear obstructions near the fastener, which is normally an advantage. In addition to normal length wrenches, it's also possible to buy long handle types to allow more leverage (very useful when trying to loosen rusted or seized nuts). It is, however, easy to shear off fasteners if you're not careful, and sometimes the extra length impairs access.

As with open-end wrenches, box-ends are available in varying quality, again often indicated by finish and the amount of metal around the ring ends. While the same criteria should be applied when selecting a set of box-end wrenches, if your budget is limited, go for better-quality open-end wrenches and a slightly cheaper set of box-ends.

Combination wrenches

These wrenches **(see illustration)** combine a box-end and open-end of the same size in one tool and offer many of the advantages of both. Like the others, they're widely available in sets and as such are probably a better choice than box-ends only. They're generally compact, short-handled tools and are well suited for tight spaces where access is limited.

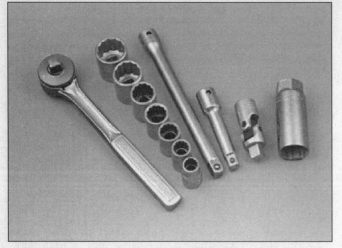

2.10 A typical ratchet and socket set includes a ratchet, a set of sockets, a long and a short extension, a universal joint and a spark plug socket

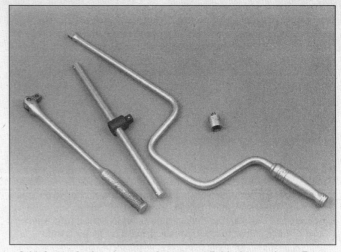

2.11 Lots of other accessories are available for ratchets; From left to right, a breaker bar, a sliding T-handle, a speed handle and a 3/8-to-1/4-inch adapter

2.12 Deep sockets enable you to loosen or tighten an elongated fastener, or to get at a nut with a long bolt protruding from it

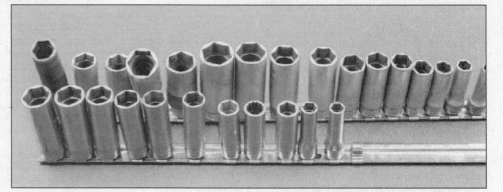

Ratchet and socket sets

Ratcheting socket wrenches (see illustration) are highly versatile. Besides the sockets themselves, many other interchangeable accessories - extensions, U-drives, step-down adapters, screwdriver bits, Allen bits, crow's feet, etc. - are available. Buy six-point sockets - they're less likely to slip and strip the corners off bolts and nuts. Don't buy sockets with extra-thick walls - they might be stronger but they can be hard to use on recessed fasteners or fasteners in tight quarters.

Buy a 1/2-inch drive for work on the outside of the transmission. It's the one you'll use for removing the transmission and most of the parts attached to the transmission. Get a 3/8-inch drive for overhaul work. It's less bulky and its easier to use. Later, you may want to consider a 1/4-inch drive for little stuff like valve body bolts and screws.

Interchangeable sockets consist of a forged-steel alloy cylinder with a hex or double-hex formed inside one end. The other end is formed into the square drive recess that engages over the corresponding square end of various socket drive tools.

Sockets are available in 1/4, 3/8, 1/2 and 3/4-inch drive sizes. A 3/8-inch drive set is most useful for transmission repairs, although 1/4-inch drive sockets and accessories may occasionally be needed.

The most economical way to buy sockets is in a set. As always, quality will govern the cost of the tools. Once again, the "buy the best" approach is usually advised when selecting sockets. While this is a good idea, since the end result is a set of quality tools that should last a lifetime, the cost is so high it's difficult to justify the expense for home use.

As far as accessories go, you'll need a ratchet, at least one extension (buy a three or six-inch size) and maybe a T-handle or breaker bar. Other desirable, though less essential items, are a speeder handle, a U-joint, extensions of various lengths and

adapters from one drive size to another (see illustration). Some of the sets you find may combine drive sizes; they're well worth having if you find the right set at a good price, but avoid being dazzled by the number of pieces.

Above all, be sure to completely ignore any label that reads "86-piece Socket Set," which refers to the number of pieces, not to the number of sockets (sometimes even the metal box and plastic insert are counted in the total!).

Apart from well-known and respected brand names, you'll have to take a chance on the quality of the set you buy. If you know someone who has a set that has held up well, try to find the same brand, if possible. Take a pocketful of nuts and bolts with you and check the fit in some of the sockets. Check the operation of the ratchet. Good ones operate smoothly and crisply in small steps; cheap ones are coarse and stiff - a good basis for guessing the quality of the rest of the pieces.

One of the best things about a socket set is the built-in facility for expansion. Once you have a basic set, you can purchase extra sockets when necessary and replace worn or damaged tools. There are special deep sockets for reaching recessed fasteners or to allow the socket to fit over a projecting bolt or stud (see illustration). You can also buy screwdriver, Allen and Torx bits to fit various drive tools (they can be very handy in some applications) (see illustration).

Torque wrenches

Torque wrenches (see illustration) are essential for tightening critical fasteners like valve body bolts, oil pump bolts, case bolts, etc. Attempting a transmission overhaul without a torque wrench is an invitation to oil leaks, distortion of the case, damaged or stripped threads or worse.

There are several different types of torque wrenches on the

2.13 Standard and Phillips bits, Allen-head and Torx drivers will expand the versatility of your ratchet and extensions even further

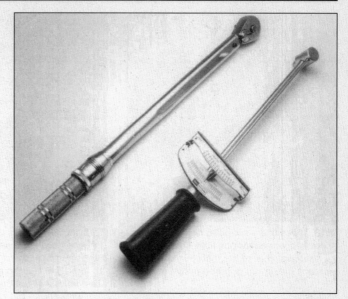

2.14 Torque wrenches (click-type on left, beam-type on right) are the only way to accurately tighten critical fasteners like valve-body bolts, oil pump bolts, etc.

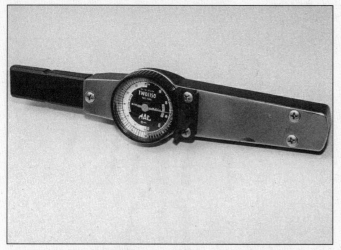

2.15 The 1/4-inch dial-type torque wrench is the most accurate for inch-pound settings - just tighten the fastener until the pointer points to the specified torque setting

2.16 "Click" type torque wrenches can be set to "give" at a pre-set torque, which makes them very accurate and easy to use

market. The most common are; the "beam" type, which indicates torque loads by deflecting a flexible shaft and the "click" type **(see illustrations)**, which emits an audible click when the torque resistance reaches the specified resistance. Another type is the "dial" type; torque is indicated by a needle on a dial, similar to a dial indicator. Dial types are very accurate down to the inch-pound range.

Torque wrenches are available in a variety of drive sizes, including 1/4, 3/8 and 1/2 inch. Torque ranges vary for particular applications, for transmission rebuilding, you will need two types. You'll need an inch-pound torque wrench, such as the "beam" type or "dial type", for tightening small fasteners like valve body bolts and a 0 to 150 ft-lbs "click" type torque wrench for larger fasteners. Keep in mind that "click" types are usually more accurate than the "beam" type (and more expensive).

Impact drivers

The impact driver **(see illustration)** belongs with the screwdrivers, but it's mentioned here since it can also be used with sockets (impact drivers normally are 3/8-inch square drive). As explained later, an impact driver works by converting a hammer blow on the end of its handle into a sharp twisting movement. While this is a great way to jar a seized fastener loose, the loads imposed on the socket are excessive. Use sockets only with discretion and expect to have to replace damaged ones on occasion.

2.17 The impact driver converts a sharp blow into a twisting motion - this is a handy addition to your socket arsenal for those fasteners that won't let go - you can use it with any bit that fits a 3/8-inch drive ratchet

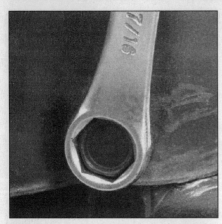

2.18 Try to use a six-point box wrench (or socket) whenever possible - it's shape matches that of the fastener, which means maximum grip and minimum slip

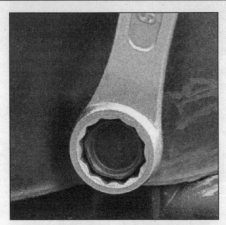

2.19 Sometimes a six-point tool just doesn't offer you any grip when you get the wrench at the angle it needs to be in to loosen or tighten a fastener - when this happens, pull out the 12-point sockets or wrenches - but remember; they're much more likely to strip the corners off a fastener

2.20 Open-end wrenches contact only two sides of the fastener and the jaws tend to open up when you put some muscle on the wrench handle - that's why they should only be used as a last resort

Using wrenches and sockets

Although you may think the proper use of tools is self-evident, it's worth some thought. After all, when did you last see instructions for use supplied with a set of wrenches?

Which wrench?

Before you start tearing a transmission apart, figure out the best tool for the job; in this instance the best wrench for a hex-head fastener. Sit down with a few nuts and bolts and look at how various tools fit the bolt heads.

A golden rule is to choose a tool that contacts the largest area of the hex-head. This distributes the load as evenly as possible and lessens the risk of damage. The shape most closely resembling the bolt head or nut is another hex, so a 6-point socket or box-end wrench is usually the best choice **(see illustration)**. Many sockets and box-end wrenches have double hex (12-point) openings. If you slip a 12-point box-end wrench over a nut, look at how and where the two are in contact. The corners of the nut engage in every other point of the wrench. When the wrench is turned, pressure is applied evenly on each of the six corners **(see illustration)**. This is fine unless the fastener head was previously rounded off. If so, the corners will be damaged and the wrench will slip. If you encounter a damaged bolt head or nut, always use a 6-point wrench or socket if possible. If you don't have one of the right size, choose a wrench that fits securely and proceed with care.

If you slip an open-end wrench over a hex-head fastener, you'll see the tool is in contact on two faces only **(see illustration)**. This is acceptable provided the tool and fastener are both in good condition. The need for a snug fit between the wrench and nut or bolt explains the recommendation to buy good-quality open-end wrenches. If the wrench jaws, the bolt head or both are damaged, the wrench will probably slip, rounding off and distorting the head. In some applications, an open-end wrench is the only possible choice due to limited access, but always check the fit of the wrench on the fastener before attempting to loosen it; if it's hard to get at with a wrench, think how hard it will be to remove after the head is damaged.

Using sockets to remove hex-head fasteners is less likely to result in damage than if a wrench is used. Make sure the socket fits snugly over the fastener head, then attach an extension, if needed, and the ratchet or breaker bar. Theoretically, a ratchet shouldn't be used for loosening a fastener or for final tightening because the ratchet mechanism may be overloaded and could slip. In some instances, the location of the fastener may mean you have no choice but to use a ratchet, in which case you'll have to be extra careful.

Never use extensions where they aren't needed. Whether or not

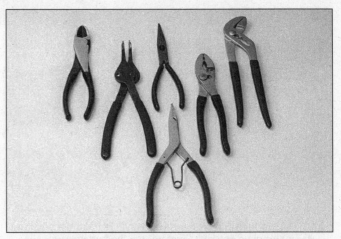

2.21 A typical assortment of the types of pliers you'll need for transmission work - from the left; diagonal side cutters, internal snap-ring pliers, needle-nose pliers, slip-joint pliers, groove-joint pliers and at the bottom, external snap-ring pliers

an extension is used, always support the drive end of the breaker bar with one hand while turning it with the other. Once the fastener is loose, the ratchet can be used to speed up removal.

Pliers

Some tool manufacturers make 25 or 30 different types of pliers. You only need a fraction of this selection **(see illustration)**. Get a good pair of slip-joint pliers for general use. A pair of needle-nose models is handy for reaching into hard-to-get-at places. A set of diagonal wire cutters (dikes) is essential for electrical work and pulling out cotter pins. Vise-Grips are adjustable, locking pliers that grip a fastener firmly - and won't let go - when locked into place. A full set of snap-ring pliers are also essential to any transmission overhaul.

Internal snap-ring pliers have extended tips that lock into the snap rings, allowing you to expand or contract the snap ring for removal **(see illustration)**. This type of snap-ring pliers can be purchased with removable tips and reversible handles.

External snap-ring pliers remove snap-rings by expanding them away from the piece they are recessed in **(see illustration)**. Typically they are heavy-duty as compared to the internal type. A good pair of external snap-ring pliers will have a notch in each end to hold the

2.22 Snap-ring pliers lock into the holes of the snap-ring

2.23 External snap-ring pliers have flat, notched blades - they expand external rings, like the one shown here

2.24 To adjust the jaws on a pair of locking pliers, grasp the part you want to hold with the jaws, tighten them down by turning the knurled knob on the end of one handle and snap the handles together - if you tightened the knob all the way down, you'll probably have to open it up (back it off) a little before you can close the handles

2.25 If you're persistent and careful, damaged fasteners can be removed with locking pliers

snap-ring in place. When buying any type of snap-ring pliers, make sure the jaws can't twist. If they can, you will have a tough time removing strong snap-rings.

Locking pliers, such as Vise-Grips (a brand name), come in various sizes; the medium size with curved jaws is best for all-around

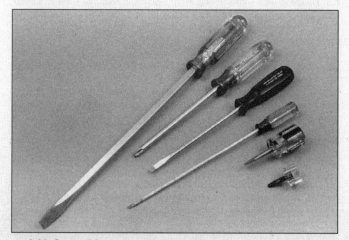

2.26 Screwdrivers come in myriad lengths, sizes and styles

work. However, buy a large and small one if possible, since they're often used in pairs. Although this tool falls somewhere between an adjustable wrench, a pair of pliers and a portable vise, it can be invaluable for loosening and tightening fasteners - it's the only pliers that should be used for this purpose.

The locking pliers jaw opening is set by turning a knurled knob at the end of one handle. The jaws are placed over the head of the fastener and the handles are squeezed together, locking the tool onto the fastener (see illustration). The design of the tool allows extreme pressure to be applied at the jaws and a variety of jaw designs enable the tool to grip firmly even on damaged heads (see illustration). Locking pliers are great for removing fasteners that have been rounded off by badly-fitting wrenches.

As the name suggests, needle-nose pliers have long, thin jaws designed for reaching into holes and other restricted areas. Most needle-nose, or long-nose, pliers also have wire cutters at the base of the jaws.

Look for these qualities when buying pliers: Smooth operating handles and jaws, jaws that match up and grip evenly when the handles are closed, a nice finish and the word "forged" somewhere on the tool.

Screwdrivers

Screwdrivers (see illustration) come in a wide variety of sizes and price ranges. Reasonably priced brands of good quality are available at department stores, auto parts stores and specialty tool stores, but don't buy "bargain-priced" low-quality screwdriver sets at discount tool stores. Even if they look exactly like more expensive brands, the metal tips and shafts are made with inferior alloys and aren't properly heat treated. They usually bend the first time you apply some serious torque.

**2.27 Pocket screwdrivers are very handy when
removing small parts**

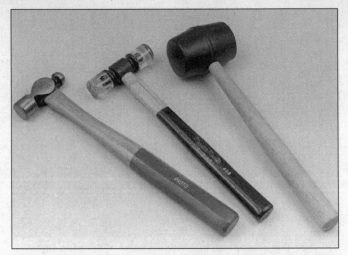

**2.28 A ball-peen hammer, soft-face hammer and rubber mallet
(left-to-right) will be needed for various tasks (any steel hammer
can be used in place of the ball peen hammer)**

A screwdriver consists of a steel blade or shank with a drive tip formed at one end. The most common tips are standard (also called straight slot and flat-blade) and Phillips. You will use the standard blade screwdriver the most in an overhaul **(see illustration)**. The other end has a handle attached to it. Traditionally, handles were made from wood and secured to the shank, which had raised tangs to prevent it from turning in the handle. Most screwdrivers now come with plastic handles, which are generally more durable than wood.

The design and size of handles and blades vary considerably. Some handles are specially shaped to fit the human hand and provide a better grip. The shank may be either round or square and some have a hex-shaped bolster under the handle to accept a wrench to provide more leverage when trying to turn a stubborn screw. The shank diameter, tip size and overall length vary too. As a general rule, it's a good idea to use the longest screwdriver possible, which allows the greatest possible leverage.

If access is restricted, a number of special screwdrivers are designed to fit into confined spaces. The "stubby" screwdriver has a specially shortened handle and blade. There are also offset screwdrivers and special screwdriver bits that attach to a ratchet or extension.

The important thing to remember when buying screwdrivers is that they really do come in sizes designed to fit different size fasteners. The slot in any screw has definite dimensions - length, width and depth. Like a bolt head or a nut, the screw slot must be driven by a tool that uses all of the available bearing surface and doesn't slip. Don't use a big wide blade on a small screw and don't try to turn a large screw slot with a tiny, narrow blade. The same principles apply to Allen heads, Phillips heads, Torx heads, etc. Don't even think of using a slotted screwdriver on one of these heads! And don't use your screwdrivers as levers, chisels or punches! This kind of abuse turns them into bad screwdrivers quickly.

Hammers

Resorting to a hammer should always be the last resort. When nothing else will do the job, a medium-size ball peen hammer, a heavy rubber mallet and a heavy soft-brass hammer **(see illustration)** are often the only way to loosen or install a part.

A ball-peen hammer has a head with a conventional cylindrical face at one end and a rounded ball end at the other and is a general-purpose tool found in almost any type of shop. It has a shorter neck than a claw hammer and the face is tempered for striking punches and chisels. A fairly large hammer is preferable to a small one. Although it's possible to find small ones, you won't need them very often and it's much easier to control the blows from a heavier head. As a general rule, a single 12 or 16-ounce hammer will work for most jobs, though occasionally larger or smaller ones may be useful.

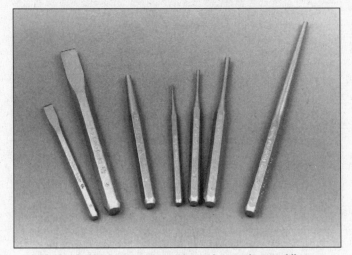

**2.29 Cold chisels, center-punches, pin punches and line-up
punches (left-to-right) will be needed sooner or
later for many jobs**

A soft-face hammer is used where a steel hammer could cause damage to the component or other tools being used. A steel hammer head might crack an aluminum part, but a rubber or plastic hammer can be used with more confidence. Soft-face hammers are available with interchangeable heads (usually one made of rubber and another made of relatively hard plastic). When the heads are worn out, new ones can be installed.

Check the condition of your hammers on a regular basis. The danger of a loose head coming off is self-evident, but check the head for chips and cracks too. If damage is noted, buy a new hammer - the head may chip in use and the resulting fragments can be extremely dangerous. It goes without saying that eye protection is essential whenever a hammer is used.

Punches and chisels

Punches and chisels **(see illustration)** are used along with a hammer for various purposes in the shop. Drift punches are often simply a length of round steel bar used to drive a component out of a bore or the equipment it's mounted on. A typical use would be for removing or installing a bearing or bushing. A drift of the same diameter as the bearing outer race is placed against the bearing and tapped with a hammer to knock it in or out of the bore. Most manufacturers offer special installers for the various bushings and bearings in a

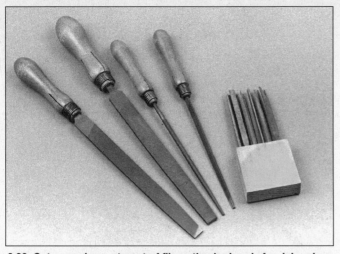

2.30 Get a good assortment of files - they're handy for deburring, marking parts, removing rust, filing the heads off rivets, restoring threads and fabricating small parts

2.31 Using a flat file to deburr a manual shaft prevents possible damage to the case on removal

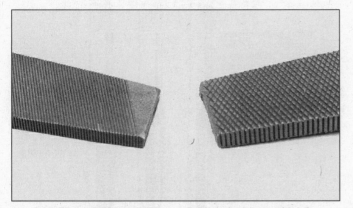

2.32 Files are either single-cut (left) or double-cut (right) - generally speaking, use a single-cut file to produce a very smooth surface; use a double-cut file to remove large amounts of material quickly

particular transmission. For bushing removal and installation, it's best to buy a universal bushing driver kit containing assorted size bushing removers and installers. If nothing else is available it's possible to use a socket of the appropriate diameter to tap the bushing or bearing in or out; an unorthodox use for a socket, but it works.

Smaller diameter drift punches can be purchased or fabricated from steel bar stock. In some cases, you'll need to drive out items like corroded transmission mounting bolts. Here, it's essential to avoid damaging the threaded end of the bolt, so the drift must be a softer material than the bolt. Brass or copper is the usual choice for such jobs; the drift may be damaged in use, but the thread will be protected.

Punches are available in various shapes and sizes and a set of assorted types will be very useful. One of the most basic is the center punch, a small cylindrical punch with the end ground to a point. It'll be needed whenever a hole is drilled. The center of the hole is located first and the punch is used to make a small indentation at the intended point. The indentation acts as a guide for the drill bit so the hole ends up in the right place. Without a punch mark the drill bit will wander and you'll find it impossible to drill with any real accuracy. You can also buy automatic center punches. They're spring loaded and are pressed against the surface to be marked, without the need to use a hammer.

Pin punches are intended for removing items like roll pins (semi-hard, hollow pins that fit tightly in their holes). You'll need a small pin punch to remove the roll pins retaining the valves in the valve body. Pin punches have other uses, however. You may occasionally have to remove rivets or bolts retaining the crossmember by cutting off the

heads and driving out the shanks with a pin punch. They're also very handy for aligning holes in components while bolts or screws are inserted.

The primary use of the cold chisel is rough metal cutting - this can be anything from sheet metal work (uncommon on transmissions) to cutting off the heads of seized or rusted bolts or splitting nuts. A cold chisel is also useful for turning out screws or bolts with damaged heads.

All of the tools described in this section should be good quality items. They're not particularly expensive, so it's not really worth trying to save money on them. More significantly, there's a risk that with cheap tools, fragments may break off in use - a potentially dangerous situation.

Even with good-quality tools, the heads and working ends will inevitably get worn or damaged, so it's a good idea to maintain all such tools on a regular basis. Using a file or bench grinder, remove all burrs and mushroomed edges from around the head. This is an important task because the build-up of material around the head can fly off when it's struck with a hammer and is potentially dangerous. Make sure the tool retains its original profile at the working end, again, filing or grinding off all burrs. In the case of cold chisels, the cutting edge will usually have to be reground quite often because the material in the tool isn't usually much harder than materials typically being cut. Make sure the edge is reasonably sharp, but don't make the tip angle greater than it was originally; it'll just wear down faster if you do.

The techniques for using these tools vary according to the job to be done and are best learned by experience. The one common denominator is the fact they're all normally struck with a hammer. It follows that eye protection should be worn. Always make sure the working end of the tool is in contact with the part being punched or cut. If it isn't, the tool will bounce off the surface and damage may result.

Files

Files **(see illustration)** come in a wide variety of sizes and types for specific jobs, but all of them are used for the same basic function of removing small amounts of metal in a controlled fashion. Files are used mainly for deburring, marking parts, removing rust, filing the heads off rivets, restoring threads and fabricating small parts. You'll occasionally need a flat file for removing nicks and burrs **(see illustration)**.

File shapes commonly available include flat, half-round, round, square and triangular. Each shape comes in a range of sizes (lengths) and cuts ranging from rough to smooth. The file face is covered with rows of diagonal ridges which form the cutting teeth. They may be aligned in one direction only (single cut) or in two directions to form a diamond-shaped pattern (double-cut) **(see illustration)**. The spacing of the teeth determines the file coarseness, again, ranging from rough to smooth in five basic grades: Rough, coarse, bastard, second-cut and smooth.

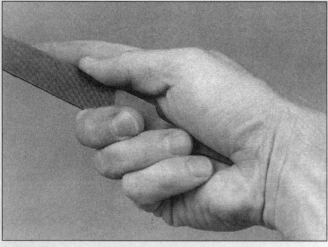

2.33 Never use a file without a handle - the tang is sharp and could puncture your hand

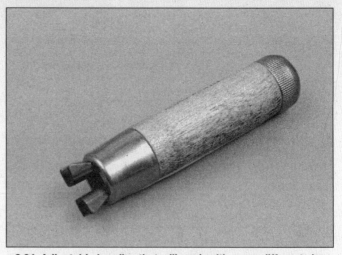

2.34 Adjustable handles that will work with many different size files are also available

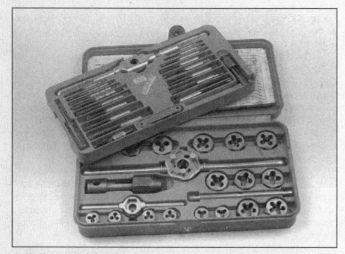

2.35 Tap and die sets are available in inch and metric sizes - taps are used for cutting internal threads and cleaning and restoring damaged threads; dies are used for cutting, cleaning and restoring external threads

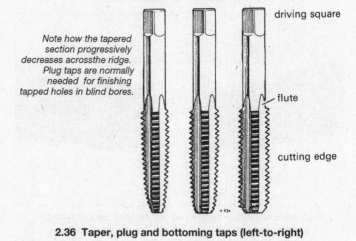

Note how the tapered section progressively decreases acrossthe ridge. Plug taps are normally needed for finishing tapped holes in blind bores.

driving square

flute

cutting edge

2.36 Taper, plug and bottoming taps (left-to-right)

You'll want to build up a set of files by purchasing tools of the required shape and cut as they're needed. A good starting point would be flat, half-round, round and triangular files (at least one each - bastard or second-cut types). In addition, you'll have to buy one or more file handles (files are usually sold without handles, which are purchased separately and pushed over the tapered tang of the file when in use) **(see illustration)**. You may need to buy more than one size handle to fit the various files in your tool box, but don't attempt to get by without them. A file tang is fairly sharp and you almost certainly will end up stabbing yourself in the palm of the hand if you use a file without a handle and it catches in the work-piece during use. Adjustable handles are also available for use with files of various sizes, eliminating the need for several handles **(see illustration)**.

Exceptions to the need for a handle are fine Swiss pattern files, which have a rounded handle instead of a tang. These small files are usually sold in sets with a number of different shapes. Originally intended for very fine work, they can be very useful for use in inaccessible areas. Swiss files are normally the best choice if you need to try and clean or deburr a valve from the valve body in the transmission.

The correct procedure for using files is fairly easy to master. Hold the file by the handle, using your free hand at the file end to guide it and keep it flat in relation to the surface being filed. Use smooth cutting strokes and be careful not to rock the file as it passes over the surface. Also, don't slide it diagonally across the surface or the teeth will make grooves in the work-piece. Don't drag a file back across the work-piece at the end of the stroke - lift it slightly and pull it back to prevent damage to the teeth.

Files don't require maintenance in the usual sense, but they should be kept clean and free of metal filings. Steel is a reasonably easy material to work with, but softer metals like aluminum tend to clog the file teeth very quickly, which will result in scratches in the work-piece. This can be avoided by rubbing the file face with chalk before using it. General cleaning is carried out with a file card or a fine wire brush. If kept clean, files will last a long time - when they do eventually dull, they must be replaced; there is no satisfactory way of sharpening a worn file.

Taps and Dies

Taps

Tap and die sets **(see illustration)** are available in inch and metric sizes. Taps are used to cut internal threads and clean or restore damaged threads. A tap consists of a fluted shank with a drive square at one end. It's threaded along part of its length - the cutting edges are formed where the flutes intersect the threads **(see illustration)**. Taps are made from hardened steel so they will cut threads in materials softer than what they're made of.

Taps come in three different types: Taper, plug and bottoming. The only real difference is the length of the chamfer on the cutting end of the tap. Taper taps are chamfered for the first 6 or 8 threads, which makes them easy to start but prevents them from cutting threads close

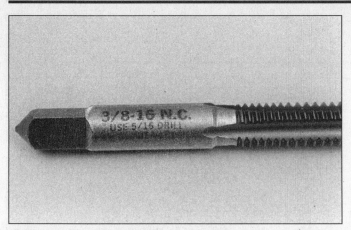

2.37 If you need to drill and tap a hole, the drill bit size to use for a given bolt (tap) size is marked on the tap

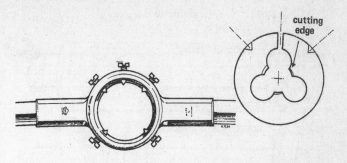

2.38 A die (right) is used for cutting external threads (this one is a split-type/adjustable die) and is held in a tool called a die stock (left)

2.39 Hex-shaped dies are especially handy for mechanic's work because they can be turned with a wrench

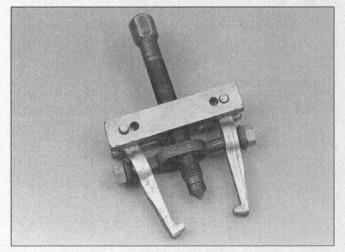

2.40 A two or three-jaw puller will come in handy for many tasks in the shop and can also be used for working on other types of equipment

to the bottom of a hole. Plug taps are chamfered up about 3 to 5 threads, which makes them a good all around tap because they're relatively easy to start and will cut nearly to the bottom of a hole. Bottoming taps, as the name implies, have a very short chamfer (1-1/2 to 3 threads) and will cut as close to the bottom of a blind hole as practical. However, to do this, the threads should be started with a plug or taper tap.

Although cheap tap and die sets are available, the quality is usually very low and they can actually do more harm than good when used on threaded holes in aluminum transmissions. The alternative is to buy high-quality taps if and when you need them, even though they aren't cheap, especially if you need to buy two or more thread pitches in a given size. Despite this, it's the best option - you'll probably only need taps on rare occasions, so a full set isn't absolutely necessary.

Taps are normally used by hand (they can be used in machine tools, but not when doing transmission repairs). The square drive end of the tap is held in a tap wrench (an adjustable T-handle). For smaller sizes, a T-handled chuck can be used. The tapping process starts by drilling a hole of the correct diameter. For each tap size, there's a corresponding twist drill that will produce a hole of the correct size. Note how the tapered section progressively decreases across the ridge. Plug taps are normally needed for finishing tapped holes in blind bores.

This is important; too large a hole will leave the finished thread with the tops missing, producing a weak and unreliable grip. Conversely, too small a hole will place excessive loads on the hard and brittle shank of the tap, which can break it off in the hole. Removing a broken off tap from a hole is no fun! The correct tap drill size is normally marked on the tap itself or the container it comes in **(see illustration)**.

Dies

Dies are used to cut, clean or restore external threads. Most dies are made from a hex-shaped or cylindrical piece of hardened steel with a threaded hole in the center. The threaded hole is overlapped by three or four cutouts, which equate to the flutes on taps and allow metal waste to escape during the threading process. Dies are held in a T-handled holder (called a die stock) **(see illustration)**. Some dies are split at one point, allowing them to be adjusted slightly (opened and closed) for fine control of thread clearances.

Dies aren't needed as often as taps, for the simple reason it's normally easier to install a new bolt than to salvage one. However, it's often helpful to be able to extend the threads of a bolt or clean up damaged threads with a die. Hex-shaped dies are particularly useful for mechanic's work, since they can be turned with a wrench **(see illustration)** and are usually less expensive than adjustable ones.

The procedure for cutting threads with a die is broadly similar to that described above for taps. When using an adjustable die, the initial cut is made with the die fully opened, the adjustment screw being used to reduce the diameter of successive cuts until the finished size is reached. As with taps, a cutting lubricant should be used, and the die must be backed off every few turns to clear swarf from the cutouts.

Pullers

You'll need a general-purpose puller for transmission rebuilding. Pullers can removed seized or corroded parts, bad bushings or bearings etc. Universal two- and three-legged pullers are widely available in numerous designs and sizes.

The typical puller consists of a central boss with two or three pivoting arms attached. The outer ends of the arms are hooked jaws which grab the part you want to pull off **(see illustration)**. You can

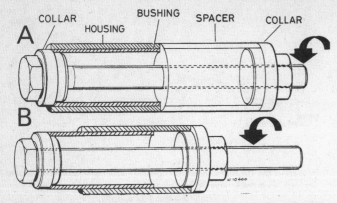

2.41 Typical drawbolt uses - in A, the nut is tightened to pull the collar and bushing into the large spacer; in B, the spacer is left out and the drawbolt is repositioned to install the new bushing

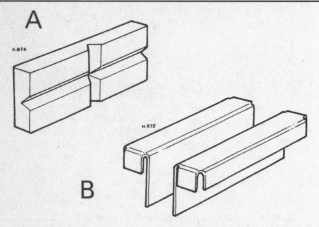

2.43 Sometimes, the parts you have to jig up in the vise are delicate, or made of soft materials - to avoid damaging them, get a pair of fiberglass or plastic "soft jaws" (A) or fabricate your own with 1/8-inch thick aluminum sheet (B)

2.42 A bench vise is one of the most useful pieces of equipment you can have in the shop - bigger is usually better with vises, so get a vise with jaws that open at least four inches

2.44 Although it's not absolutely necessary, an air compressor can make many jobs easier and produce better results, especially when air powered tools are available to use with it

reverse the arms on most pullers to use the puller on internal openings when necessary. The central boss is threaded to accept a puller bolt, which does the work. You can also get hydraulic versions of these tools which are capable of more pressure, but they're expensive.

You can adapt pullers by purchasing, or fabricating, special jaws for specific jobs. If you decide to make your own jaws, keep in mind that the pulling force should be concentrated as close to the center of the component as possible to avoid damaging it.

If all reasonable attempts to remove a part fail, don't be afraid to give up. It's cheaper to quit now than to repair a badly damaged transmission. Either buy or borrow the correct tool, or take the transmission to a dealer or repair shop and ask him to remove the part for you.

Drawbolt extractors

The simple drawbolt extractor is easy to make up and invaluable in every workshop. There are no commercially available tools of this type; you simply make a tool to suit a particular application. You can use a drawbolt extractor to remove bearings and bushings.

To make a drawbolt extractor, you'll need an assortment of threaded rods in various sizes (available at hardware stores), and nuts to fit them. You'll also need assorted washers, spacers and tubing.

Some typical drawbolt uses are shown in the accompanying illustration **(see illustration)**. They also reveal the order of assembly of the various pieces. The same arrangement, minus the tubular spacer section, can usually be used to install a new bushing. Using the tool is quite simple. Just make sure you get the bushing square to the bore when you install it. Lubricate the part being pressed into place, where appropriate.

Bench vise

The bench vise **(see illustration)** is an essential tool in a shop. Buy the best quality vise you can afford. A good vise is expensive, but the quality of its materials and workmanship are worth the extra money. Size is also important - bigger vises are usually more versatile. Make sure the jaws open at least four inches. Get a set of soft jaws to fit the vise as well - you'll need them to grip transmission parts that could be damaged by the hardened vise jaws **(see illustration)**.

Power tools

Really, you don't need any power tools to overhaul an automatic transmission. But if you have an air compressor and electricity, there's a wide range of pneumatic and electric hand tools to make all sorts of jobs easier and faster.

Air compressor

An air compressor **(see illustration)** makes most jobs easier and faster. Drying off parts after cleaning them with solvent, blowing out passages in a case or valve body, running power tools - the list is endless. Once you buy a compressor, you'll wonder how you ever got along without it. Air tools really speed up tedious procedures like removing and installing pan bolts, valve body bolts or case bolts.

2.45 Another indispensable piece of equipment is the bench grinder (with a wire wheel mounted on one arbor) - make sure it's securely bolted down and never use it with the rests or eye shields removed

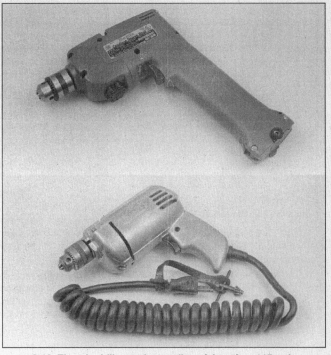

2.46 Electric drills can be cordless (above) or 115-volt, AC-powered (below)

2.47 Get a set of good quality drill bits for drilling holes and wire brushes of various sizes for cleaning up metal parts - make sure the bits are designed for drilling in metal!

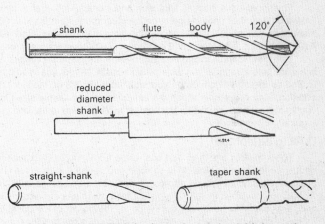

2.48 A typical drill bit (top), a reduced shank bit (center), and a tapered shank bit (bottom right)

Bench-mounted grinder

A bench grinder (see illustration) is also handy. With a wire wheel on one end and a grinding wheel on the other, it's great for cleaning up fasteners, sharpening tools and removing rust. Make sure the grinder is fastened securely to the bench or stand, always wear eye protection when operating it and never grind aluminum parts on the grinding wheel.

Electric drills

Countersinking bolt holes, enlarging oil passages, removing rusted or broken off fasteners, enlarging holes and fabricating small parts - electric drills (see illustration) are indispensable for transmission modification work. A 3/8-inch chuck (drill bit holder) will handle most jobs. Collect several different wire brushes to use in the drill and make sure you have a complete set of sharp metal drill bits (see illustration). Cordless drills are extremely versatile because they don't force you to work near an outlet. They're also handy to have around for a variety of non-mechanical jobs.

Twist drills and drilling equipment

Drilling operations are done with twist drills, either in a hand drill or a drill press. Twist drills (or drill bits, as they're often called) consist of a round shank with spiral flutes formed into the upper two-thirds to clear the waste produced while drilling, keep the drill centered in the hole and finish the sides of the hole.

The lower portion of the shank is left plain and used to hold the drill in the chuck. In this section, we will discuss only normal parallel shank drills (see illustration). There is another type of bit with the plain end formed into a special size taper designed to fit directly into a corresponding socket in a heavy-duty drill press. These drills are known as Morse Taper drills and are used primarily in machine shops.

At the cutting end of the drill, two edges are ground to form a conical point. They're generally angled at about 60-degrees from the drill axis, but they can be reground to other angles for specific applications. For general use the standard angle is correct - this is how the drills are supplied.

When buying drills, purchase a good-quality set (sizes 1/16 to 3/8-inch). Make sure the drills are marked "High Speed Steel" or "HSS." This indicates they're hard enough to withstand continual use in metal; many cheaper, unmarked drills are suitable only for use in wood or other soft materials. Buying a set ensures the right size bit will be available when it's needed.

2.49 Drill bits in the range most commonly used are available in fractional sizes (left) and number sizes (right) so almost any size hole can be drilled

2.50 A good die grinder will deburr, cut, grind, chamfer oil holes and do a lot of other little jobs what would be tedious if done manually

2.51 Buy at least one fire extinguisher before you open shop - make sure it's rated for flammable liquid fires and KNOW HOW TO USE IT!

Twist drill sizes

Twist drills are available in a vast array of sizes, most of which you'll never need. There are three basic drill sizing systems: Fractional, number and letter **(see illustration)** (we won't get involved with the fourth system, which is metric sizes).

Fractional sizes start at 1/64-inch and increase in increments of 1/64-inch. Number drills range in descending order from 80 (0.0135-inch), the smallest, to 1 (0.2280-inch), the largest. Letter sizes start with A (0.234-inch), the smallest, and go through Z (0.413-inch), the largest.

This bewildering range of sizes means it's possible to drill an accurate hole of almost any size within reason. In practice, you'll be limited by the size of chuck on your drill (normally 3/8 or 1/2-inch). In addition, very few stores stock the entire range of possible sizes, so you'll have to shop around for the nearest available size to the one you require.

Drilling equipment

Tools to hold and turn drill bits range from simple, inexpensive hand-operated or electric drills to sophisticated and expensive drill presses. Ideally, all drilling should be done on a drill press with the work-piece clamped solidly in a vise. These machines are expensive and take up a lot of bench or floor space, so they're out of the question for many do-it-yourselfers. An additional problem is the fact that many of the drilling jobs you end up doing will be on the transmission itself or the equipment it's mounted on, in which case the tool has to be taken to the work.

The best tool for the home shop is an electric drill with a 3/8-inch chuck. Both cordless and AC drills (that run off household current) are available. If you're purchasing one for the first time, look for a well-known, reputable brand name and variable speed as minimum requirements. A 1/4-inch chuck, single-speed drill will work, but it's worth paying a little more for the larger, variable speed type.

All drills require a key to lock the bit in the chuck. When removing or installing a bit, make sure the cord is unplugged to avoid accidents. Initially, tighten the chuck by hand, checking to see if the bit is centered correctly. This is especially important when using small drill bits which can get caught between the jaws. Once the chuck is hand tight, use the key to tighten it securely - remember to remove the key afterwards!

High-speed grinders

A good die grinder **(see illustration)** will deburr, cut and grind as well as chamfer oil holes - it will do these jobs ten times faster than you can do them by hand. But be very careful when using a high-speed grinder - they remove allot of material very fast.

Safety items that should be in every shop

Fire extinguishers

You should have at least one fire extinguisher in your shop before doing any maintenance or repair procedures **(see illustration)**. Make sure it's rated for flammable liquid fires. Familiarize yourself with its use as soon as you buy it - don't wait until you need it to figure out how to use it. And be sure to have it checked and recharged at regular intervals. Refer to the safety tips at the end of this chapter for more information about the hazards of gasoline and other flammable liquids.

Gloves

If you're handling hot parts or metal parts with sharp edges, wear a pair of industrial work gloves to protect yourself from burns, cuts and splinters **(see illustration)**. Wear a pair of heavy duty rubber gloves (to protect your hands when you wash parts in solvent.

Safety glasses or goggles

Never work on a bench or high-speed grinder without safety glasses **(see illustration)**. Don't take a chance on getting a metal sliver in your eye. It's also a good idea to wear safety glasses when you're washing parts in solvent.

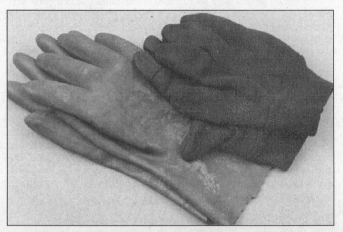

2.52 Get a pair of heavy work gloves for handling hot or sharp-edged objects and a pair of rubber gloves for washing parts with solvent

2.53 One of the most important items you'll need in the shop is a face shield or safety goggles, especially when you're hitting metal parts with a hammer, washing parts in solvent or grinding something on the bench grinder

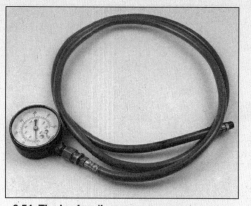

2.54 The hydraulic pressure gauge screws into the test ports on the transmission - it measures the pressure at that port

2.55 The vacuum gauge indicates vacuum, in inches of mercury (in-Hg)

Diagnostic tools

These tools perform special diagnostic tasks. They're indispensable for determining the condition of your transmission. Using these simple tools will help you determine the difference between an engine problem and a transmission problem. You will also be able to test the working components before you disassemble or remove the transmission from the vehicle. There are only a few basic tools you need to use for diagnosis of the transmission.

Hydraulic pressure gauge

The pressure gauge **(see illustration)** is used to perform an oil pressure test (see Chapter 5). The oil pressure test indicates the hydraulic pressure being generated by the oil pump and actually being used in a specific hydraulic circuit. The transmission oil pressure gauge must read up to 300 psi and have long heavy-duty hose with a 1/8-27 NPT (National Pipe Thread) fitting attached to one end.

Vacuum gauge

The vacuum gauge **(see illustration)** indicates the amount of intake manifold vacuum generated by the engine, in inches of mercury (in-Hg). You'll need a vacuum gauge to correctly diagnose the vacuum modulator system found in certain transmissions.

Tachometer

The tachometer is used in conjunction with the oil pressure gauge to perform an oil pressure test. It's also needed to indicate torque converter stall speed and engine rpm at shift points. Basically, the tool indicates the speed at which the engine crankshaft is turning, in revolutions per minute (rpm) **(see illustration)**.

Stethoscope

The stethoscope **(see illustration)** amplifies sounds, allowing you to pinpoint possible sources of pending trouble, such as a bad bearing, pump, or excessive play in the transmission.

Vacuum pump

The hand-operated vacuum pump **(see illustration)** is useful in testing the vacuum modulator and it's circuit.

2.56 The tach/dwell meter combines the functions of a tachometer and dwell meter into one package - for transmission work, you'll be using the tach function, which indicates the speed - in rpm - at which the engine crankshaft is turning. This tool is essential for checking converter stall speed

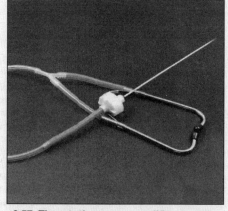

2.57 The stethoscope amplifies sounds, allowing you to pinpoint possible sources of trouble

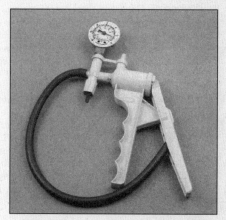

2.58 The vacuum/pressure pump can create a vacuum in a circuit, or pressurize it, to simulate the actual operating conditions

2.59a This low reverse clutch spring compressor for the C6 transmission locks into the case for easy removal of the snap-ring (Hayden tool no. T-0152)

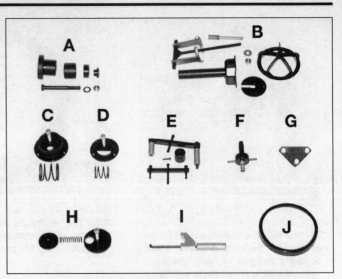

2.59b Special tools required for front wheel drive transaxle overhaul

A   Stator support tool (ATX/FLC)
B   Clutch spring compressor (ATX/FLC and AXOD)
C   Low intermediate servo rod tool (AXOD)
D   Overdrive servo rod tool (AXOD)
E   Servo removal and installation tool (ATX/FLC)
F   Torque converter end play tool (ATX/FLC and AXOD)
G   End play tool (AXOD)
H   Servo piston selection tool (ATX/FLC)
I   Front clutch loading tool (AXOD)
J   Reverse clutch piston lip seal (ATX/FLC)

1175-AC Seal removal tool
T59L-100-B Slide hammer
T58L-101-A Seal removal tool
T57L-77820-A Oil pressure gauge

Special tool list common for all front wheel drive transaxles covered in this manual

T57L-500-B Bench mounted holding fixture
4201-C Dial indicator set
1175-AC Seal removal tool
T81P-7902-B One way clutch torque tool
T81P-7902-C Handles
T65L-77515-A Clutch spring compressor
T81P-78103-A Slide hammer adapter
T81P-78103-B Adapter mounting bolts

Special tool list specific to the C3 transmission

T84P-7341-A Shift linkage grommet removal tool
T84P-7341-B Shift linkage grommet installation tool
T71P-7657-A Extension housing seal removal tool
T77L-7697-E Extension housing bushing removal tool
T77L-7697-F Extension housing bushing installation tool
T780L-7902-A Endplay checking tool
T74P-77028-A Front servo cover compressor
T74P-77052-A Extension housing installation tool
T74P-77103-X Pump alignment tool set
T74P-77190-A Servo rod selecting guide
T74P-77193-A Overrun clutch replacing guide
T74P-77247-A Neutral start switch socket
T74P-77248-A Front pump seal removal tool
T74P-77248-B Front pump seal installation tool
T74P-77404-A Lip seal protector
T74P-77498-A Shift lever seal installation tool
T65L-77515-A Clutch spring compressor
T74P-77548-A Lip seal protector
T74P-77548-B Lip seal protector

Special transmission overhaul tools

Ford Motor Co. requires their dealers to maintain trained personnel and purchase the special tools necessary to repair their transmissions. Since these tools are designed for use in a dealership service department, they are designed to aid the dealer technician in completing the job as quickly as possible in this environment. Many of these tools are not necessary for overhaul - they are simply aids to quicker overhauls. For this reason, we don't recommend you buy all the manufacturer's special tools unless you plan to do frequent overhauls. We have found substitute tools and methods for most of the manufacturer's special tools, and have illustrated this in the overhaul chapters. We realize the special tools are sometimes expensive and the home mechanic doesn't have easy access to the tools, so he generally tries to buy as few special tools as possible.

The special tools illustrated in this section are the most common and necessary tools used to overhaul the transmissions covered in this manual as described in Chapter 8. Although with some extra effort and ingenuity, the resourceful mechanic may be able to perform some of the operations without even those special tools, we highly recommend their use.

Provided in the lists below are all the special tools Ford Motor Co. suggests for overhauling the transmissions covered by this manual **(see illustrations)**. The tools are manufactured by Rotunda Tools for Ford, but unfortunately, are NOT available to the public. They are sometimes available from a dealership on a special order basis, so be prepared for delays. Tools that perform the same function as the factory tools are available from aftermarket tool manufacturers; for their address or phone number see the *Source List* at the end of this manual.

The first two lists are common tools Ford Motor Co. recommends for use on RWD and FWD transmissions. The subsequent lists are tools Ford Motor Co. recommends for each specific transmission. To reiterate: only the tools illustrated in this section and discussed earlier in this Chapter are absolutely required for overhaul. The complete lists are included here as a reference for the advanced transmission specialist.

Ford special tools

Special tool list common for all rear wheel drive transmissions covered in this manual

T57L-500-B Bench mounted holding fixture
4201-C Dial indicator set
T71P-77370-A Band adjustment kit
T50T-100-A Slide hammer

Special tool list specific to the C4 transmission

T66L-7003-B Bushing removal and installation kit
T70P-7D043-A Stator support bushing installation tool
T64P-7B456-A and B Clutch race-to-case bolt socket
T61L-7657-A Extension housing oil seal removal tool
T52L-7000-GAE Extension housing bushing removal tool
T52L-7000-HAE Extension housing bushing installation tool
T56L-77515-A Rear clutch spring compressor
T63L-77837-A Front pump seal installation tool
T73P-77060-A Snap-ring pliers
T78P-77548-A Forward clutch piston seal protector

Special tool list specific to the C5 transmission

T66L-7003-C Bushing removal and installation set
T84P-7341-A Shift linkage grommet removal tool
T84P-7341-B Shift linkage grommet installation tool
T61L-7657-A Extension housing oil seal removal tool
T77L-7697-A Extension housing bushing removal tool
T780L-7902-A Endplay checking tool
T82L-9500-AH Cooler line disconnect tool
T80L-77034-A Extension housing bushing installation tool
T73P-77060-A Snap-ring pliers
T74P-77248-A Front pump seal removal tool
T82P-77404-A Lip seal protector
T74P-77498-A Shift lever seal installation tool
T65L-77515-A Clutch spring compressor
T63L-77837-A Front pump seal installation tool
T64P-7B456-A and B Clutch race-to-case bolt socket

Special tool list specific to the C6 transmission

T66L-7003-C2 Front pump bushing installation tool
T67P-7341-A Shift linkage insulator
T84P-7341-A Shift linkage grommet removal tool
T84P-7341-B Shift linkage grommet installation tool
T61L-7657-A Extension housing seal installation tool
T77L-7697-D Extension housing bushing removal tool
T77L-7697-C Extension housing bushing installation tool
T780L-7902-A Endplay checking tool
T73P-77060-A Snap-ring pliers
TOOL-77288 Manual shaft seal installation tool
T65L-77515-A Clutch spring compressor
T77L-77548-A Lip seal protector
T63L-77837-A Front pump seal installation tool
T83T-7B200-AH VRV gauge block
T69L-7D044-A Clutch housing bushing tool

Special tool list specific to the AOD transmission

T58L-101-A Manual shaft seal removal tool
T73L-6600-A Oil pressure gauge
T61L-7657-A Extension housing seal installation tool
T77L-7697-A Extension housing bushing removal tool
T80-77003-A Endplay gauge bar
T80L-77005-A Intermediate clutch lip seal protector
T80L-77030-A Servo piston selection tool
T80L-77030-B Servo piston removal tool
T80L-77034-A Extension housing bushing installation tool
T80L-77100-A Valve body guide pins
T80L-77103-A Front pump removal adapter
T80L-77110-A Rear case bushing installation tool
T80L-77140-A Forward clutch lip seal protector
T80L-77234-A Direct clutch lip seal protector
T74P-77247-A Neutral start switch socket
T74P-77348-A Extension housing seal removal tool
T80L-77254-A Lip seal protector
T80L-77268-A Front pump bushing installation tool
T80L-77268-B Front pump bushing removal tool
T80L-77403-A Reverse clutch outer seal protector

T80L-77403-B Reverse clutch inner seal protector
T80L-77405-A Reverse clutch spring compressor plate
T74P-77498-A Manual shaft seal removal tool
T65L-77515-A Clutch spring compressor
T80L-77515-A Forward clutch spring compressor adapter
T63L-77837-A Front pump seal installation tool
T76L-7902-C One-way clutch tightening tool
T68P-7D158-A Forward clutch lip seal protector
T82L-9500-AH Cooler line disconnect tool

Special tool list specific to the ATX transaxle

T50T-100-A Slide hammer
T67P-7341-A Shift insulator remover and installer
T77F-1102-A Bearing puller
T80L-77003-A Gauge bar
T80L-77100-A Alignment pins
T80L-77515-A Clutch spring compressor
T81P-177-B Plug
T81P-4026-A Differential rotator
T81P-7902-A Holding wire
T81P-7902-D End play checking tool
T81P-70023-A Servo piston selection tool
T81P-70027-A Servo remover and installer
T81P-70222-A Clutch spring compressor
T81P-70235-A Clutch spring compressor
T81P-70337-A Manual lever seal installer
T81P-70383-A Stator support installation tool
T81P-70363-A6 Stator support guide pins
T81P-70401-A Converter hub seal installer
T81P-70402-A Seal protector
T81P- 77380-A Housing bearing installer
T81P-77389-A End play alignment cup
T82P-7006-B Adapter plate
T82P-7006-C Attaching screws
T84P-7341-A Shift linkage grommet remover
T84P-7341-B Shift linkage grommet installer

Special tool list specific to the AXOD transaxle

D79P-110-A Slide hammer
D80L-515-S Puller
D80L-522-A Gear and pulley support bar
D80L-625-A Shaft protector
D80L-630-3 Step plate adapter
D81P-3504-N Locknut pin remover
T58L-101-A Slide hammer
T59L-100-B Slide hammer
T74P-6700-A Output shaft seal remover
T77L-7902-A Holding wire
T80L-7902-A End play checking tool
T80L-7902-C End play checking tool
T86P-1177-B Output shaft seal installer
T86P-3514-A2 Screw extension
T86P-7902-A Converter guide sleeve tool
T86P-70001-A Lube tube remover
T86P-70023-B Overdrive servo tool
T86P-70023-A Low/intermediate servo rod tool
T86P-70043-A Stator and driven sprocket bearing remover
T86P-70043-B Stator and driven sprocket bearing installer
T86P-70100-A Valve body guide pin set
T86P-70234-A Direct clutch lip seal protector
T86P-70370-A Pump body guide pin
T86P-70373-A Direct and intermediate clutch bushing installer
T86P-70389-A Front clutch loading tool
T86P-70401-A Converter oil seal installer
T86P-70403-A reverse clutch outer lip seal protector
T86P-70422-A Bimetal height gauge
T86P-70423-A Direct clutch bearing installer
T86P-70548 A Forward clutch seal lip protector

2.60 Snap-ring pliers are an essential tool for removal and installation of certain components

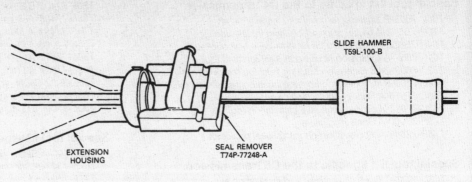

2.61 A typical seal removal tool can be used with a slide hammer to knock the seal free

Special snap-ring pliers

A good pair of snap-ring pliers is essential for overhaul of the transmissions covered by this manual **(see illustration)**. Actually you will need at least two pair, or possibly three. You'll encounter internal and external snap-rings, for which you'll need internal and external snap-ring pliers (or one pair of reversible snap-ring pliers) and larger, stiffer lock-rings; which take a pair of lock-ring pliers with outer gripping jaws to expand the ring.

Seal removal tool

A seal removal tool is not absolutely necessary on every seal , but for certain seal locations it may save time and frustration, not to mention a damaged component. Seal removal tools are available with internal and external locking jaws and are compatible with a slide hammer **(see illustration)**.

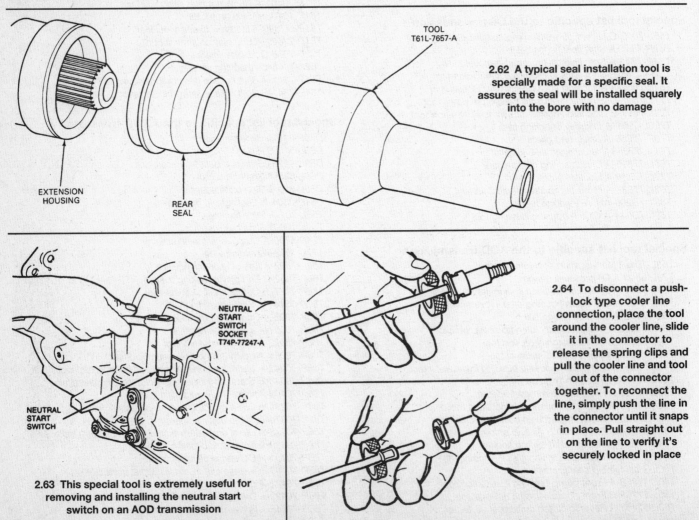

2.62 A typical seal installation tool is specially made for a specific seal. It assures the seal will be installed squarely into the bore with no damage

2.63 This special tool is extremely useful for removing and installing the neutral start switch on an AOD transmission

2.64 To disconnect a push-lock type cooler line connection, place the tool around the cooler line, slide it in the connector to release the spring clips and pull the cooler line and tool out of the connector together. To reconnect the line, simply push the line in the connector until it snaps in place. Pull straight out on the line to verify it's securely locked in place

2.65 Seal protectors are plastic covers or domes that compress and protect piston seals as the clutch piston is installed in the drum

2.66 These two seal protectors (OTC 7110-A and 7110-C) are used to install the reverse clutch piston on an AOD transmission

2.67 This universal clutch spring compressor will work on many different transmissions - we recommend the use of a clutch spring compressor for all the transmissions covered by this manual

Seal installation tool

Again, seal installation tools are not necessary on every seal, but they are sure to drive the seal squarely into the bore without damaging the seal **(see illustration)**. If you want to defiantly eliminate any chance of fluid leakage, use a seal driver whenever possible.

AOD neutral start switch socket

Ford tool no. T74P-77247-A or equivalent, is specially made to fit the AOD neutral start switch **(see illustration)**. It's extremely useful for removal and installation of the switch with the transmission in-vehicle, where the limited access makes using an end wrench impossible.

Cooler line disconnect tool

Ford Tool no.T82L-9500-AH or equivalent, is essential for disconnecting the push-lock transmission cooler line connections found on some late model Ford Motor Co. cars and trucks **(see illustration)**.

Seal protectors

Seal protectors are plastic covers or domes that prevent damage to the piston seal when installing clutch assembly components **(see illustration)**. They are essential for installing certain clutch piston seals that are prone to damage from clutch hub splines and snap-ring grooves.

Universal clutch spring compressor

A clutch spring compressor is essential for removing the clutch piston and seals in most transmissions. You can use the individual Ford special tools or the universal type. The universal type can be used on a wide variety of transmissions for compressing many types of clutch springs. It is available in several different styles from heavy duty full-stand with foot pedal used primarily in professional shops to the bench mount type which can be easily moved and is the most practical for the home mechanic **(see illustrations)**.

Universal bushing removal tool

A universal bushing removal tool makes it easy to remove most of the bushings found in the transmission. The sharp chisel point cuts and lifts the bushing away from the component in the same motion. **(see illustration)**

Bushing driver kit

You can't do without bushing installers when replacing bushings; they are a wise investment. Bushing replacement is an essential part of any overhaul and, without these tools, it is difficult to install a bushing and be sure it won't be damaged or cocked in the bore **(see illustration)**.

2.68 Two C-clamp type clutch spring compressors may also be used to compress a clutch spring. These are much more affordable than the professional type

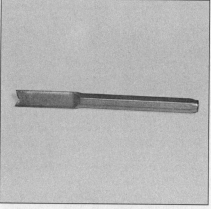

2.69 A general purpose bushing cutter is easy to use and works on most bushings - this one is Hayden tool no. T-0280-C

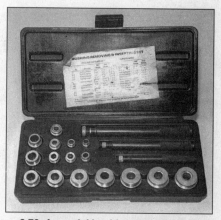

2.70 A special bushing service set is needed to install bushings to the correct depths in their bores

2.71 Check the bushing for alignment and depth before you remove it

2.72 Use a bushing removal tool to drive out the old bushing

How to remove and install bushings

Before you remove a bushing, you need to check the installed depth of the bushing in the component. Measure how far the bushing is recessed in the bore and check to see if there are any oil holes or alignment marks that the new bushing needs to be aligned with **(see illustration)**. It's helpful to mark the location of the original bushing with a permanent marker before you remove the bushing - this provides a reference point for the installation of the new bushing.

Remove the old bushing with a bushing removal tool **(see illustration)**. Using a bushing removal tool prevents the possibility of damage to the bushing bore or surface it rides on by lifting and cutting the old bushing in the same motion. Other styles of chisels or punches can very easily damage the component you're removing the bushing from.

With the old bushing removed, check the bushing seating surface on the component for cracks or marks indicating a bushing that may have spun. Also look for bluing (a sign of overheating) or deep grooves indicating component damage.

After inspecting the component, select a bushing driver head that fits inside the bushing without play **(see illustration)**. Screw the head on the driver handle and place both the bushing and the installer squarely in the bore **(see illustration)**.

2.73 Bushing installers come in various sizes and styles to accommodate most bushings

Strike the driver lightly with a hammer until the bushing is seated properly and to the correct depth. Inspect the bushing to be sure it is installed squarely and not cocked in the bore **(see illustration)**.

2.74 Use the proper-size bushing installer to drive the bushing into the bore

2.75 Check that the bushing is properly seated and not cocked in the bore

Universal seal installation tools

Seal installers are extremely helpful when overhauling an automatic transmission. Close tolerances between pistons and drums with sharp edges can cause seals to be cut or the seal lip will double-over during assembly. Cut (or otherwise damaged) seals are the most common cause of failed overhauls.

Seal installers are hand-held tools that you move around the seal as you install a piston into a clutch housing. The installers come in two basic types: a feeler gauge or "blade" type and a wire loop type. Both types work great for preventing the seals from folding or doubling over (see illustration).

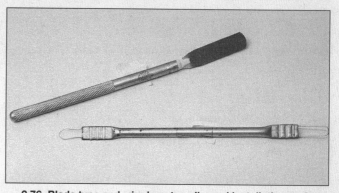

2.76 Blade type and wire loop type lip seal installation tools

How to install a clutch piston seal

Install the seal on the piston and make sure it is properly seated into the piston groove (see illustration). The seal lip always faces the pressure, so make sure the lip faces down into the drum when installed. Properly lubricate the seal with a thin coat of clean automatic transmission fluid (see illustration). Its important that no foreign particles such as hair, lint or dirt get on the seal after you lubricate it. If the piston has an outer seal that could be cut or folded, place a seal protector over it (see illustration).

Some piston/drum combinations have the inner seal on the drum and not on the piston (see illustration). Place the piston

2.77 Install the seal on the piston; make sure the seal is seated in the groove and the lip is facing the proper direction

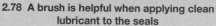

2.78 A brush is helpful when applying clean lubricant to the seals

2.79 Install the seal protector over the piston and seal. Once the outer seal protector is installed, it's impossible to damage the seal

2.80 Install the inner seal protector over the hub (if necessary) - it prevents seal damage from the snap-ring groove or splines

2.81 Install the piston squarely in the drum, push down while turning the piston until it's fully seated

2.82 Pull the seal protectors out when the piston is seated. When the piston is properly installed, you should be able to rotate the piston in the bore

2.83 Carefully slide the seal tool around the piston and work the seal lip into the bore - be very careful and do not cut the seal

with the seal protector in the drum and slowly press down on the piston while twisting to allow the piston to seat **(see illustration)**. Once the piston is fully seated simply pull the protectors out **(see illustration)**.

When installing a piston into a drum and the seal protectors are not available, a seal installation tool is needed. As the piston is being installed, insert the tool between the piston and drum and slowly depress the lip of the seal **(see illustration)**. Move the tool around the seal and slowly push the piston down until it is seated. If you feel the tool bind while you are moving it around the circumference of the piston, it may be necessary to remove the piston and check the seal again. Using the seal installation tool method, it may take several tries to properly seat the piston.

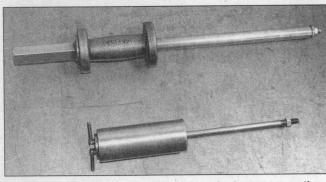

2.84 Slide hammers are used to remove the front pump on the transmissions covered by this manual. Note that the lower slide hammer is a homemade unit

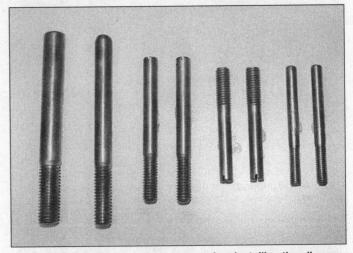

2.86 Alignment studs are necessary when installing the oil pump and valve body. Note that all of these are homemade

Slide hammers

To remove the front pump on the transmissions covered by this manual, a pair of slide hammers are needed. Screw the threaded ends on the slide hammers into the threaded holes on the pump body and tighten securely, then operate the slide hammers in unison **(see illustration)**. Slide hammers are also used with certain types of bushing removal tools.

Pump and valve body alignment stud set

These tools are homemade and simple to make. Basically, they are 2-1/2 to 3-1/2 inch bolts of the correct diameter and thread pitch with the heads cut off and slots cut in the ends so they can be removed and installed with a flat-blade screwdriver. When screwed into the case, these studs help keep gaskets and parts aligned properly as they are installed **(see illustration)**.

2.85 Two of the oil pump bolt holes are threaded so the slide hammers can be installed into the pump body

2.87 The one-inch micrometer is helpful when you need to measure the thickness of selective-fit snap-rings, clutch plates, etc.

2.89 Digital and mechanical readout micrometers are easier to read than conventional micrometers, but they're a bit more expensive

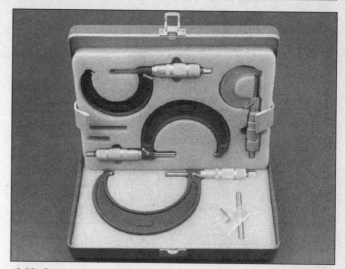

2.88 Get a good-quality micrometer set if you can afford it - this set has four micrometers ranging in size from one to four inches

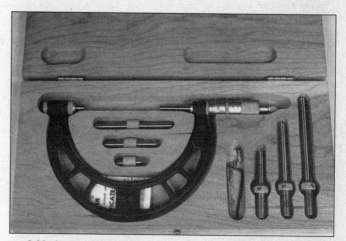

2.90 Avoid micrometer "sets" with interchangeable anvils - they're awkward to use when measuring little parts and changing the anvils is a hassle

Precision measuring tools

Think of the tools in the following list as the final additions to your tool collection. If you're planning to rebuild a transmission, you've probably already accumulated all the screwdrivers, wrenches, sockets, pliers and other everyday hand tools that you need. Now it's time to round up the stuff you'll need to do your own measurements when you rebuild that transmission.

The tool pool strategy

If you're reading this book, you may be a motorhead, but transmission rebuilding isn't your life - it's an avocation. You may just want to save some money, have a little fun and learn something about transmission rebuilding. If that description fits your level of involvement, think about forming a "tool pool" with a friend or neighbor who wants to get into transmission rebuilding, but doesn't want to spend a lot of money. For example, you can buy a set of micrometers and the other guy can buy a dial indicator and a set of pressure gauges.

Start with the basics

It would be great to own every precision measuring tool listed here, but you don't really need a machinist's chest crammed with exotic calipers and micrometers. You can often get by just fine with nothing more than feeler gauges and a dial indicator. Even most professional transmission builders use only three precision measuring tools 95-percent of the time: a one-inch outside micrometer, a dial indicator and a good feeler gauge set. So start your collection with these three items.

Micrometers

When you're rebuilding a transmission , you need to know the exact thickness of a number of pieces. Whether you're measuring the diameter of an apply piston or the thickness of a selective washer or a snap-ring, your tool of choice should be the trusty one-inch outside micrometer **(see illustration)**.

Insist on accuracy to within one ten-thousandths of an inch (0.0001-inch) when you shop for a micrometer. You'll probably never need that kind of precision, but the extra decimal place will help you decide which way to round off a close measurement.

To rebuild most transmissions you only need a 0 to 1-inch micrometer. In very rare cases you could use a 1 to 2-inch micrometer. Eventually you may want to a set that spans four or even five ranges **(see illustration)**.

Digital micrometers and mechanical readout **(see illustration)** are easier to read than conventional micrometers, but they're a bit more expensive. If you're uncomfortable reading a conventional micrometer, then get a digital or mechanical readout type.

Unless you're not going to use them very often, stay away from micrometers with interchangeable anvils **(see illustration)**. In theory, one of these beauties can do the work of five or six single-range micrometers. The trouble is, they're awkward to use when measuring little parts, and changing the anvils is a hassle.

How to read a micrometer

The outside micrometer is without a doubt the most widely used precision measuring tool. It can be used to make a variety of highly accurate measurements without much possibility of error through misreading, a problem associated with other measuring instruments, such as vernier calipers.

Like any slide caliper, the outside micrometer uses the "double contact" of its spindle and anvil (see illustration) touching the object to be measured to determine that object's dimensions. Unlike a caliper, however, the micrometer also features a unique precision screw adjustment which can be read with a great deal more accuracy than calipers.

Why is this screw adjustment so accurate? Because years ago toolmakers discovered that a screw with 40 precision machined threads to the inch will advance one-fortieth (0.025) of an inch with each complete turn. The screw threads on the spindle revolve inside a fixed nut concealed by a sleeve.

On a one-inch micrometer, this sleeve is engraved longitudinally with exactly 40 lines to the inch, to correspond with the number of threads on the spindle. Every fourth line is made longer and is numbered one-tenth inch, two-tenths, etc. The other lines are often staggered to make them easier to read.

The thimble (the barrel which moves up and down the sleeve as it rotates) is divided into 25 divisions around the circumference of its beveled edge and is numbered from zero to 25. Close the micrometer spindle until it touches the anvil: You should see nothing but the zero line on the sleeve next to the beveled edge of the thimble. And the zero line of the thimble should be aligned with the horizontal (or axial) line on the sleeve. Remember: Each full revolution of the spindle from zero to zero advances or retracts the spindle one-fortieth or 0.025-inch. Therefore, if you rotate the thimble from zero on the beveled edge to the first graduation, you will move the spindle 1/25th of 1/40th, or 1/25th of 25/1000ths, which equals 1/1000th, or 0.001-inch.

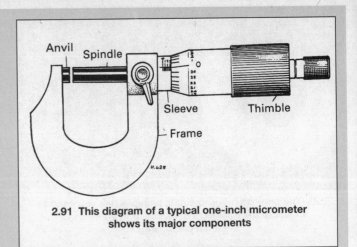

2.91 This diagram of a typical one-inch micrometer shows its major components

Remember: Each numbered graduation on the sleeve represents 0.1-inch, each of the other sleeve graduations represents 0.025-inch and each graduation on the thimble represents 0.001-inch. Remember those three and you're halfway there.

For example: Suppose the 4 line is visible on the sleeve. This represents 0.400-inch. Then suppose there are an additional three lines (the short ones without numbers) showing. These marks are worth 0.025-inch each, or 0.075-inch. Finally, there are also two marks on the beveled edge of the thimble beyond the zero mark, each good for 0.001-inch, or a total of 0.002-inch. Add it all up and you get 0.400 plus 0.075 plus 0.002, which equals 0.477-inch.

Some beginners use a "dollars, quarters and cents" analogy to simplify reading a micrometer. Add up the bucks and change, then put a decimal point instead of a dollar sign in front of the sum!

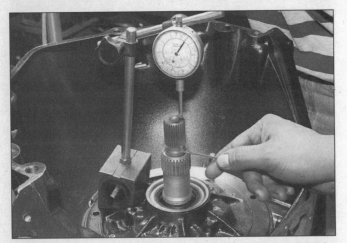

2.92 The dial indicator is indispensable for measuring endplay in a transmission, as well as other critical measurements

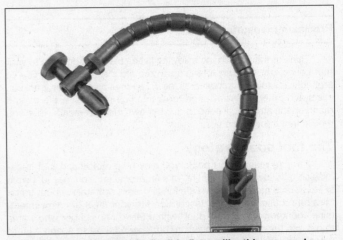

2.93 Get an adjustable, flexible fixture like this one, and a magnetic base, to ensure maximum versatility from your dial indicator

Dial indicators

The dial indicator (see illustration) is another measuring mainstay. It's indispensable for measuring endplay in a transmission and can also be used for engine work. Make sure the dial indicator you buy has a probe with at least one inch of travel, graduated in 0.001-inch increments.

Buy a dial indicator set that includes a flexible fixture and a magnetic stand (see illustration). If the model you buy doesn't have a magnetic base, buy one separately. Make sure the magnet is plenty strong. If a weak magnet comes loose and the dial indicator takes a tumble on a concrete floor, you can kiss it good-bye. Make sure the arm that attaches the dial indicator to the flexible fixture is sturdy and the locking clamps are easy to operate.

Some dial indicators are designed to measure depth or flatness (see illustration). They have a removable base that straddles a hole. To measure the flatness of your valve body halves or the transmission case, you'll also need a U-shaped bridge for your dial indicator.

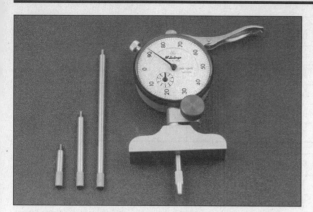

2.94 This dial indicator is designed to measure depth or flatness. It has a removable base that straddles a hole. To measure the flatness of your valve body, pump halves or the transmission case you'll need a U-shaped bridge

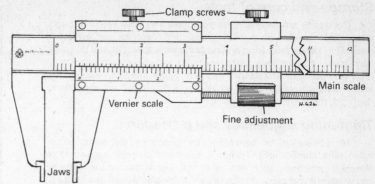

2.95 Vernier calipers aren't quite as accurate as micrometers, but they're handy for quick measurements, are relatively inexpensive, and because they've got jaws that can measure internal and external dimensions, they're versatile

Calipers

Vernier calipers **(see illustration)** aren't quite as accurate as a micrometer, but they're handy for quick measurements and they're relatively inexpensive. Most calipers have inside and outside jaws, so you can measure the inside diameter of a hole, or the outside diameter of a part.

Better-quality calipers have a dust shield over the geared rack that turns the dial to prevent small metal particles from jamming the mechanism. Make sure there's no play in the moveable jaw. To check, put a thin piece of metal between the jaws and measure its thickness with the metal close to the rack, then out near the tips of the jaws. Compare your two measurements. If they vary by more than 0.001-inch, look at another caliper - the jaw mechanism is deflecting.

If your eyes are going bad, or already are bad, vernier calipers can be difficult to read. Dial calipers **(see illustration)** are a better choice. Dial calipers combine the measuring capabilities of micrometers with the convenience of dial indicators. Because they're much easier to read quickly than vernier calipers, they're ideal for taking quick measurements when absolute accuracy isn't necessary. Like conventional vernier calipers, they have both inside and outside jaws which allow you to quickly determine the diameter of a hole or a part. Get a six-inch dial caliper, graduated in 0.001-inch increments.

2.96 Dial calipers are a lot easier to read than conventional vernier calipers, particularly if your eyesight isn't as good as it used to be!

How to read a vernier caliper

On the lower half of the main beam, each inch is divided into ten numbered increments, or tenths (0.100-inch, 0.200-inch, etc.). Each tenth is divided into four increments of 0.025-inch each. The vernier scale has 25 increments, each representing a thousandth (0.001) of an inch.

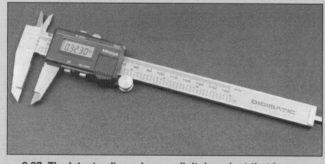

2.97 The latest calipers have a digital readout that is even easier to read than a dial caliper - another advantage of digital calipers is that they have a small microchip that allows them to convert instantaneously from inch to metric dimensions

First read the number of inches, then read the number of tenths. Add to this 0.025-inch; for each additional graduation. Using the English vernier scale, determine which graduation of the vernier lines up exactly with a graduation on the main beam. This vernier graduation is the number of thousandths which are to be added to the previous readings.

For example, let's say:

1) The number of inches is zero, or 0.000-inch;
2) The number of tenths is 4, or 0.400-inch;
3) The number of 0.025's is 2, or 0.050-inch; and
4) The vernier graduation which lines up with a graduation on the main beam is 15, or 0.015-inch.
5) Add them up:
    0.000
    0.400
    0.050
    0.015
6) And you get:
    0.465-inch

That's all there is to it!

The latest calipers **(see illustration)** have a digital LCD display that indicates both inch and metric dimensions. If you can afford one of these, it's the hot setup.

Storage and care of tools

Good tools are expensive, so treat them well. After you're through with your tools, wipe off any dirt, grease or metal chips and put them away. Don't leave tools lying around in the work area. General purpose hand tools - screwdrivers, pliers, wrenches and sockets - can be hung on a wall panel or stored in a tool box. Store precision measuring instruments, gauges, meters, etc. in a tool box to protect them from dust, dirt, metal chips and humidity.

Tightening sequences and procedures

Most threaded fasteners should be tightened to a specific torque value **(see illustration)**. Torque is the twisting force applied to a threaded component such as a nut or bolt. Overtightening the fastener can weaken it and cause it to break, while undertightening can cause it to eventually come loose. Bolts, screws and studs, depending on the material they are made of and their thread diameters, have specific torque values. Be sure to follow the torque recommendations closely. For fasteners not assigned a specific torque, a general torque value chart is presented here as a guide. These torque values are for dry (unlubricated) fasteners threaded into steel or cast iron (not aluminum). As was previously mentioned, the size and grade of a fastener determine the amount of torque that can safely be applied to it. The figures listed here are approximate for Grade 2 and Grade 3 fasteners. Higher grades can tolerate higher torque values.

If fasteners are laid out in a pattern - such as oil pump bolts, oil pan bolts, valve body bolts, etc. - loosen and tighten them in sequence to avoid warping the component. Where it matters, we'll show you this sequence. If a specific pattern isn't that important, the following rule-of-thumb guide will prevent warping.

First, install the bolts or nuts finger-tight. Then tighten them one full turn each, in a criss-cross or diagonal pattern. Then return to the first one and, following the same pattern, tighten them all one-half turn. Finally, tighten each of them one-quarter turn at a time until each fastener has been tightened to the proper torque. To loosen and remove the fasteners, reverse this procedure.

Metric thread sizes	Ft-lbs	Nm
M-6	6 to 9	9 to 12
M-8	14 to 21	19 to 28
M-10	28 to 40	38 to 54
M-12	50 to 71	68 to 96
M-14	80 to 140	109 to 154

Pipe thread sizes		
1/8	5 to 8	7 to 10
1/4	12 to 18	17 to 24
3/8	22 to 33	30 to 44
1/2	25 to 35	34 to 47

U.S. thread sizes		
1/4 – 20	6 to 9	9 to 12
5/16 – 18	12 to 18	17 to 24
5/16 – 24	14 to 20	19 to 27
3/8 – 16	22 to 32	30 to 43
3/8 – 24	27 to 38	37 to 51
7/16 – 14	40 to 55	55 to 74
7/16 – 20	40 to 60	55 to 81
1/2 – 13	55 to 80	75 to 108

2.98 Standard torque values for various bolt sizes

How to remove broken fasteners

Sooner or later, you're going to break off a bolt inside its threaded hole. There are several ways to remove it. Before you buy an expensive extractor set, try some of the following cheaper methods first.

First, regardless of which of the following methods you use, be sure to use penetrating oil. Penetrating oil is a special light oil with excellent penetrating power for freeing dirty and rusty fasteners. But it also works well on tightly torqued broken fasteners.

If enough of the fastener protrudes from its hole and if it isn't torqued down too tightly, you can often remove it with Vise-grips or a small pipe wrench. If that doesn't work, or if the fastener doesn't provide sufficient purchase for pliers or a wrench, try filing it down to take a wrench, or cut a slot in it to accept a screwdriver **(see illustration)**. If you still can't get it off - and you know how to weld - try welding a flat piece of steel, or a nut, to the top of the broken fastener. If the fastener is broken off flush with - or below - the top of its hole, try tapping it out with a small, sharp punch. If that doesn't work, try drilling out the broken fastener with a bit only slightly smaller than the inside diameter of the hole. For example, if the hole is 1/2-inch in diameter, use a 15/32-inch drill bit. This leaves a shell which you can pick out with a sharp chisel.

If THAT doesn't work, you'll have to resort to some form of screw extractor, such as an E-Z-Out **(see illustration)**. Screw extractors are sold in sets which can remove anything from 1/4-inch to 1-inch bolts or studs. Most extractors are fluted and tapered high-grade steel. To use a screw extractor, drill a hole

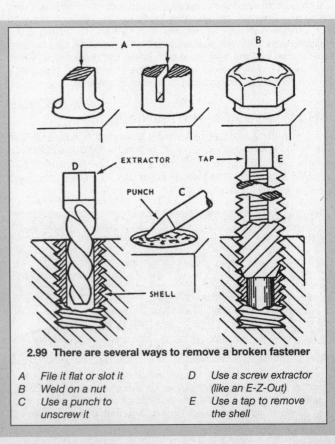

2.99 There are several ways to remove a broken fastener

A	File it flat or slot it	D	Use a screw extractor
B	Weld on a nut		(like an E-Z-Out)
C	Use a punch to	E	Use a tap to remove
	unscrew it		the shell

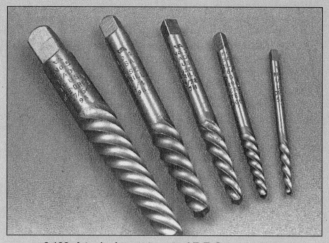

2.100 A typical assortment of E-Z-Out extractors

2.101 When screwing in the E-Z-Out, make sure it's centered properly

slightly smaller than the O.D. of the extractor you're going to use (Extractor sets include the manufacturer's recommendations for what size drill bit to use with each extractor size). Then screw in the extractor **(see illustration)** and back it - and the broken fastener - out. Extractors are reverse-threaded, so they won't unscrew when you back them out.

A word to the wise: Even though an E-Z-Out will usually save your bacon, it can cause even more grief if you're careless or sloppy. Drilling the hole for the extractor off-center, or using too small, or too big, a bit for the size of the fastener you're removing will only make things worse. So be careful!

How to repair broken threads

Sometimes, the internal threads of a nut or bolt hole can become stripped, usually from overtightening. Stripping threads is an all-too-common occurrence, especially when working with aluminum parts, because aluminum is so soft that it easily strips out. Overtightened pan bolts are the most common cause of stripped threads.

Usually, external or internal threads are only partially stripped. After they've been cleaned up with a tap or die, they'll still work. Sometimes, however, threads are badly damaged.

When this happens, you've got three choices:

1) *Drill and tap the hole to the next suitable oversize and install a larger diameter bolt, screw or stud.*
2) *Drill and tap the hole to accept a threaded plug, then drill and tap the plug to the original screw size. You can also buy a plug already threaded to the original size. Then you simply drill a hole to the specified size, then run the threaded plug into the hole with a bolt and jam nut. Once the plug is fully seated, remove the jam nut and bolt.*
3) *The third method uses a patented thread repair kit like Heli-Coil or Slimsert. These easy-to-use kits are designed to repair damaged threads in straight-through holes and blind holes. Both are available as kits which can handle a variety of sizes and thread patterns. Drill the hole, then tap it with the special included tap. Install the Heli-Coil* **(see illustration)** *and the hole is back to its original diameter and thread pitch.*

Regardless of which method you use, be sure to proceed calmly and carefully. A little impatience or carelessness during one of these relatively simple procedures can ruin your whole day's work and cost you a bundle if you wreck an expensive case.

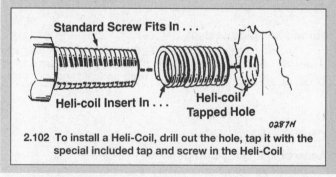

Standard Screw Fits In . . .

Heli-coil Insert In . . .

Heli-coil Tapped Hole

0287H

2.102 To install a Heli-Coil, drill out the hole, tap it with the special included tap and screw in the Heli-Coil

Component disassembly

Disassemble components carefully to help ensure that the parts go back together properly. Note the sequence in which parts are removed. Make note of special characteristics or marks on parts that can be installed more than one way, such as a grooved thrust washer on a shaft. It's a good idea to lay the disassembled parts out on a clean surface in the order in which you removed them. It may also be helpful to make sketches or take instant photos of components before removal.

When you remove fasteners from a component, keep track of their locations. Thread a bolt back into a part, or put the washers and nut back on a stud, to prevent mix-ups later. If that isn't practical, put fasteners in small boxes. A cupcake or muffin tin, or an egg crate, is ideal for this purpose - each cavity can hold the bolts and nuts from a particular area (i.e. oil pan bolts, valve body bolts, transmission mount bolts, etc.). A pan of this type is helpful when working on assemblies with very small parts, such as the valve body or governor. Mark each cavity with paint or tape to identify the contents.

When you unplug the connector(s) between two wire harnesses, or even two wires, it's a good idea to identify the two halves with numbered pieces of masking tape - or a pair of matching pieces of colored electrical tape - so they can be easily reconnected.

Gasket sealing surfaces

Gaskets seal the mating surfaces between two parts to prevent lubricants, fluids, vacuum or pressure from leaking out between them. Age, heat and pressure can cause the two parts to stick together so tightly that they're difficult to separate. Often, you can loosen the assembly by striking it with a soft-face hammer near the mating surfaces. You can use a regular hammer if you place a block of wood between the hammer and the part, but don't hammer on cast or delicate parts that can be easily damaged. When a part refuses to come off, look for a fastener that you forgot to remove.

Don't use a screwdriver or prybar to pry apart an assembly. It can easily damage the gasket sealing surfaces of the parts, which must be smooth to seal properly. If prying is absolutely necessary, use an old broom handle or a section of hard-wood dowel.

Once the parts are separated, carefully scrape off the old gasket and clean the gasket surface. If some gasket material refused to come off, soak it with rust penetrant or treat it with a special chemical to soften it, then scrape it off carefully with a razor blade. The mating surfaces must be clean and smooth when you're done. Never use a gasket sealer when reassembling any internal transmission component.

Automotive chemicals and lubricants

A wide variety of automotive chemicals and lubricants - ranging from cleaning solvents and degreasers to lubricants and protective sprays for rubber, plastic and vinyl - are available.

Cleaners

Brake system cleaner

Brake system cleaner removes brake dust, grease and brake fluid from brake parts like disc brake rotors, where a spotless surface is essential. It leaves no residue and often eliminates brake squeal caused by contaminants. Because it leaves no residue, brake cleaner is often used for cleaning transmission parts as well.

Carburetor and choke cleaner

Carburetor and choke cleaner is a strong solvent for gum, varnish and carbon. Most carburetor cleaners leave a dry-type lubricant film which will not harden or gum up. So don't use carb cleaner on electrical components.

Degreasers

Degreasers are heavy-duty solvents used to remove grease from the outside of the transmission and from chassis components. They're usually sprayed or brushed on. Depending on the type, they're rinsed off either with water or solvent.

Demoisturants

Demoisturants remove water and moisture from electrical components such as alternators, voltage regulators, electrical connectors and fuse blocks. They are non-conductive, non-corrosive and non-flammable.

Electrical cleaner

Electrical cleaner removes oxidation, corrosion and carbon deposits from electrical contacts, restoring full current flow. It can also be used to clean spark plugs, carburetor jets, voltage regulators and other parts where an oil-free surface is necessary.

Lubricants

Moly penetrants

Moly penetrants loosen and lubricate frozen, rusted and corroded fasteners and prevent future rusting or freezing.

Automatic transmission fluid

Automatic transmission fluid is a chemically formulated lubricant that contains additives to make the fluid more slippery under certain operating conditions. It also normally contains a wide variety of additives to prevent corrosion and reduce foaming and wear in automatic transmissions.

Petroleum Jelly

Petroleum jelly is pure, clear petroleum base grease or jelly it is safe and idea for lubricating seals, holding small parts during assembly.

Silicone lubricants

Silicone lubricants are used to protect rubber, plastic, vinyl and nylon parts.

White grease

White grease is a heavy grease for metal-to-metal applications where water is present. It stays soft under both low and high temperatures (usually from -100 to +190-degrees F), and won't wash off or dilute when exposed to water. Another good "glue" for holding parts in place during assembly.

Sealants

Anaerobic sealant

Anaerobic sealant is much like RTV in that it can be used either to seal gaskets or to form gaskets by itself. It remains flexible, is solvent resistant and fills surface imperfections. The difference between an anaerobic sealant and an RTV-type sealant is in the curing. RTV cures when exposed to air, while an anaerobic sealant cures only in the absence of air. This means that an anaerobic sealant cures only after the assembly of parts, sealing them together.

RTV sealant

RTV sealant is one of the most widely used gasket compounds. Made from silicone, RTV is air curing, it seals, bonds, waterproofs, fills surface irregularities, remains flexible, doesn't shrink, is relatively easy to remove, and is used as a supplementary sealer with almost all low and medium temperature gaskets.

Thread and pipe sealant

Thread and pipe sealant is used for sealing hydraulic and pneumatic fittings and vacuum lines. It is usually made from a teflon compound, and comes in a spray, a paint-on liquid and as a wrap-around tape.

Chemicals

Anaerobic locking compounds

Anaerobic locking compounds are used to keep fasteners from vibrating or working loose and cure only after installation, in the absence of air. Medium strength locking compound is used for small nuts, bolts and screws that may be removed later. High-strength locking compound is for large nuts, bolts and studs which aren't removed on a regular basis.

Anti-seize compound

Anti-seize compound prevents seizing, galling, cold welding, rust and corrosion in fasteners. High-temperature anti-seize, usually made with copper and graphite lubricants, is used for exhaust system and exhaust manifold bolts.

Safety first!

Essential DOs and DON'Ts

Regardless of how enthusiastic you may be about getting on with the job at hand, take the time to ensure that your safety is not jeopardized. A moment's lack of attention can result in an accident, as can failure to observe certain simple safety precautions. The possibility of an accident will always exist, and the following points should not be considered a comprehensive list of all dangers. Rather, they are intended to make you aware of the risks and to encourage a safety-conscious approach to all work you carry out on your vehicle.

DON'T rely on a jack when working under the vehicle. Always use approved jackstands to support the weight of the vehicle and place them under the recommended lift or support points.

DON'T attempt to loosen extremely tight fasteners (i.e. wheel lug nuts) while the vehicle is on a jack - it may fall.

DON'T start the engine without first making sure that the transmission is in Neutral (or Park where applicable) and the parking brake is set.

DON'T remove the radiator cap from a hot cooling system - let it cool or cover it with a cloth and release the pressure gradually.

DON'T attempt to drain the transmission oil until you are sure it has cooled to the point that it will not burn you.

DON'T touch any part of the engine or exhaust system until it has cooled sufficiently to avoid burns.

DON'T siphon toxic liquids such as gasoline, antifreeze and brake fluid by mouth, or allow them to remain on your skin.

DON'T inhale brake lining or clutch disc dust - it is potentially hazardous (see Asbestos below)

DON'T allow spilled oil or grease to remain on the floor - wipe it up before someone slips on it.

DON'T use loose-fitting wrenches or other tools which may slip and cause injury.

DON'T push on wrenches when loosening or tightening nuts or bolts. Always try to pull the wrench toward you. If the situation calls for pushing the wrench away, push with an open hand to avoid scraped knuckles if the wrench should slip.

DON'T attempt to lift a heavy component alone - get someone to help you.

DON'T rush or take unsafe shortcuts to finish a job.

DON'T allow children or animals in or around the vehicle while you are working on it.

DO wear eye protection when using power tools such as a drill, sander, bench grinder, etc. and when working under a vehicle.

DO keep loose clothing and long hair well out of the way of moving parts.

DO make sure that any hoist used has a safe working load rating adequate for the job.

DO get someone to check on you periodically when working alone on a vehicle.

DO carry out work in a logical sequence and make sure that everything is correctly assembled and tightened.

DO keep chemicals and fluids tightly capped and out of the reach of children and pets.

DO remember that your vehicle's safety affects that of yourself and others. If in doubt on any point, get professional advice.

Asbestos

Certain friction, insulating, sealing, and other products - such as brake linings, brake bands, clutch linings, torque converters, gaskets, etc. - contain asbestos. Extreme care must be taken to avoid inhalation of dust from such products since it is hazardous to health. If in doubt, assume that they do contain asbestos.

Batteries

Never create a spark or allow a bare light bulb near a battery. They normally give off a certain amount of hydrogen gas, which is highly explosive.

Always disconnect the battery ground (-) cable at the battery before working on the fuel or electrical systems.

If possible, loosen the filler caps or cover when charging the battery from an external source (this does not apply to sealed or maintenance-free batteries). Do not charge at an excessive rate or the battery may burst.

Take care when adding water to a non maintenance-free battery and when carrying a battery. The electrolyte, even when diluted, is very corrosive and should not be allowed to contact clothing or skin.

Always wear eye protection when cleaning the battery to prevent the caustic deposits from entering your eyes.

Fire

We strongly recommend that a fire extinguisher suitable for use on fuel and electrical fires be kept handy in the garage or workshop at all times. Never try to extinguish a fuel or electrical fire with water. Post the phone number for the nearest fire department in a conspicuous location near the phone.

Fumes

Certain fumes are highly toxic and can quickly cause unconsciousness and even death if inhaled to any extent. Gasoline vapor falls into this category, as do the vapors from some cleaning solvents. Any draining or pouring of such volatile fluids should be done in a well ventilated area.

When using cleaning fluids and solvents, read the instructions on the container carefully. Never use materials from unmarked containers.

Never run the engine in an enclosed space, such as a garage. Exhaust fumes contain carbon monoxide, which is extremely poisonous. If you need to run the engine, always do so in the open air, or at least have the rear of the vehicle outside the work area.

Gasoline

Remember at all times that gasoline is highly flammable. Never smoke or have any kind of open flame around when working on a vehicle. But the risk does not end there. A spark caused by an electrical short circuit, by two metal surfaces contacting each other, or even by static electricity built up in your body under certain conditions, can ignite gasoline vapors, which, in a confined space, are highly explosive. Do not, under any circumstances, use gasoline for cleaning parts. Use an approved safety solvent. Also, DO NOT STORE GASOLINE IN A GLASS CONTAINER - use an approved metal or plastic container only!

Always disconnect the battery ground (-) cable at the battery before working on any part of the fuel system or electrical system. Never risk spilling a fuel on a hot engine or exhaust component.

Household current

When using an electric power tool, inspection light, etc., which operates on household current, always make sure that the tool is correctly connected to its plug and that, where necessary, it is properly grounded. Do not use such items in damp conditions and, again, do not create a spark or apply excessive heat in the vicinity of fuel or fuel vapor.

Secondary ignition system voltage

A severe electric shock can result from touching certain parts of the ignition system (such as the spark plug wires) when the engine is running or being cranked, particularly if components are damp or the insulation is defective. In the case of an electronic ignition system, the secondary system voltage is much higher and could prove fatal.

Keep it clean

Get in the habit of taking a regular look around the shop to check for potential dangers. Keep the work area clean and neat. Sweep up all debris and dispose of it as soon as possible. Don't leave tools lying around on the floor.

Be very careful with oily rags. Spontaneous combustion can occur if they're left in a pile, so dispose of them properly in a covered metal container.

Check all equipment and tools for security and safety hazards (like frayed cords). Make necessary repairs as soon as a problem is noticed - don't wait for a shelf unit to collapse before fixing it.

Accidents and emergencies

Shop accidents range from minor cuts and skinned knuckles to serious injuries requiring immediate medical attention. The former are inevitable, while the latter are, hopefully, avoidable or at least uncommon. Think about what you would do in the event of an accident. Get some first aid training and have an adequate first aid kit somewhere within easy reach.

Think about what you would do if you were badly hurt and incapacitated. Is there someone nearby who could be summoned quickly? If possible, never work alone just in case something goes wrong.

If you had to cope with someone else's accident, would you know what to do? Dealing with accidents is a large and complex subject, and it's easy to make matters worse if you have no idea how to respond. Rather than attempt to deal with this subject in a superficial manner, buy a good First Aid book and read it carefully. Better yet, take a course in First Aid at a local junior college.

Environmental safety

At the time this manual was being written, several state and federal regulations governing the storage and disposal of oil and other lubricants, gasoline, solvents and antifreeze were pending (contact the appropriate government agency or your local auto parts store for the latest information). Be absolutely certain that all materials are properly stored, handled and disposed of. Never pour used or leftover oil, solvents or antifreeze down the drain or dump them on the ground. Also, don't allow volatile liquids to evaporate - keep them in sealed containers. Air conditioning refrigerant should never be expelled into the atmosphere. Have a properly equipped shop discharge and recharge the system for you.

Chapter 3
Automatic transmission fundamentals

Simply put, any transmission's function, be it manual or automatic, is to transfer the rotational energy of the engine to the drive wheels of the vehicle so you can move down the road. The most basic example of a transmission is a bicycle chain. Think of your legs as the "engine" and the chain and sprockets as the "transmission."

Gear ratios

Most power sources have an optimum range of rpm (revolutions per minute) when they are most efficient. Using our bicycle example, think about riding up a very steep hill in high gear: your legs will be straining against the pedals, which will be hardly moving - you'll groan and sweat, but make little progress. Likewise, if you're riding downhill in low gear, you'll be moving your legs so fast that it will be difficult to apply any force with your legs during the short time that each pedal is moving down.

In this example, your legs during bicycle riding are like an automobile engine. Like your legs, engines have a certain range of rpm during which they'll operate efficiently without strain, generally between about 2,000 and 4,000 rpm. In order to move a vehicle both quickly down the freeway and slowly down a residential street while maintaining rpm within this range, varying gear ratios are necessary.

If you can remember your first drive in a vehicle with a manual transmission, you'll probably remember alternately bogging the engine by selecting too high a gear and winding out the engine by selecting too low a gear. Automatic transmissions use a torque converter to maintain a continuous fluid coupling between the engine and drive wheels, a set of controls (the hydraulic system) to sense when it's the correct time for a gearchange and a planetary geartrain that can shift gears without disengaging the engine from the transmission **(see illustration)**.

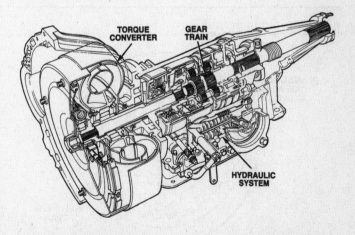

3.1 The automatic transmission uses a torque converter instead of a clutch, a planetary geartrain that can shift gears while power is still applied to the drive wheels and a sophisticated hydraulic system that controls shifting

PLANETARY GEARSET

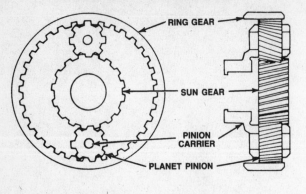

3.2 A front and side view of a planetary gearset

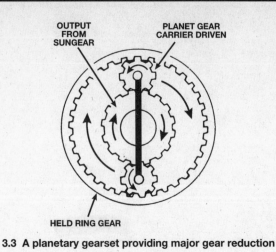

3.3 A planetary gearset providing major gear reduction

Planetary gearsets

Planetary gearsets allow gearchanges without disconnecting the engine from the drive wheels with a clutch, as with a manual transmission. These gearsets are so named because of the way they operate - planet gears within a ring gear rotate around a sun gear **(see illustration)**. Gear changes with planetary gearsets are made by holding one member of the set (the planet carrier, ring gear or sun gear) and driving another. Any member of a planetary gearset can play any part in transmitting power by being held or driven. The planet gears are held in a *planet carrier*, which keeps the planet gears evenly spaced between the ring and sun gears.

Operation of a simple planetary gearset

Let's look at the way a simple planetary gearset operates. If the ring gear is held and the sun gear is rotated, the planet gears will "walk" around the sun gear and rotate the planet carrier in the same direction as the sun gear, but at a much slower speed than the sun gear (major gear reduction) **(see illustration)**. If the sun gear is held and the ring gear is rotated, the planet gears will walk around the sun gear at a somewhat slower speed than the ring gear (minor gear reduction) **(see illustration)**. By holding the planet carrier and driving the sun gear, the ring gear is turned in the opposite direction (reverse

and gear reduction) **(see illustration)**. Direct drive can be achieved by locking any two elements of the planetary gearset together.

The compound planetary gearset

Some planetary gearsets are *compound*, meaning more than one set of planetary gears share a single sun gear. The most common compound gearset is the Simpson planetary gearset, which is used in C3, C4, C5 and C6 transmissions. This gearset uses two planetary assemblies on a single sun gear, which is attached to the transmission output shaft. This arrangement of gears allows for more possible gear ranges than the simple planetary gearset described above.

The AOD transmission uses another kind of compound planetary gearset: the Ravigneaux gearset. The Ravigneaux gearset uses two sets of planetary gears and two sun gears, all of which share a common ring gear.

Apply devices

To make an automatic transmission work, methods must be provided to hold members of the planetary gearsets and provide the shifts into different gear ranges. We call these components *apply devices* because they apply the various gear ranges. There are three apply devices: Clutches, bands and one-way clutches.

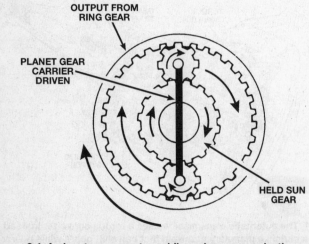

3.4 A planetary gearset providing minor gear reduction

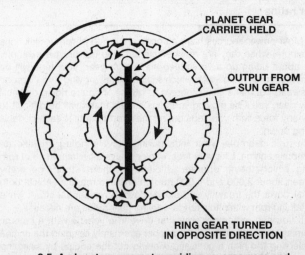

3.5 A planetary gearset providing reverse gear and gear reduction

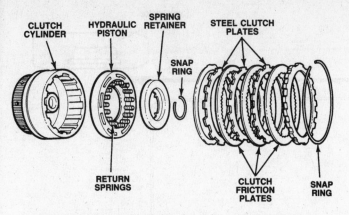

3.6 A typical clutch pack and actuating piston assembly - exploded view

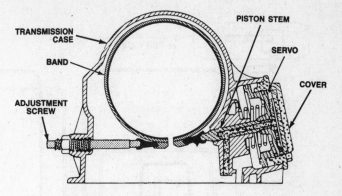

3.7 A typical band and servo assembly - cutaway view

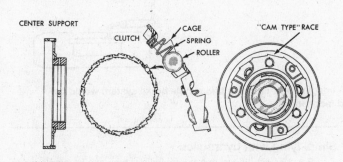

3.8 A typical roller clutch assembly - when the outer race is rotating clockwise in relation to the inner race, the rollers are in the notched area of the cam-type race and the two races rotate independently; however, when the outer race is rotating counter-clockwise in relation to the inner race, the rollers move up their ramps, locking the inner and outer races together

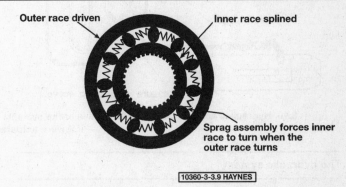

3.9 Sprag-type clutches are a little different from roller clutches - the dog-bone shaped sprags allow the inner race to turn independently when it is rotating clockwise in relation to the outer race but lock the races together when the inner race is rotating counter-clockwise in relation to the outer race

Clutches

Well, you caught us. There really *are* clutches in automatic transmissions. However, the clutches are of much smaller diameter than the big clutch plate in a manual-transmission vehicle, and the clutches in automatic transmissions consist of multiple friction plates. They are often referred to as "clutch packs." These clutches are very similar to motorcycle multiple-plate clutches, having a set of friction plates sandwiched together with a set of plain steel plates. The friction plates are made of an asbestos-type friction material. The friction plates are attached to one driving member while the steel plates are attached to another. When the clutch piston applies force to squeeze the sandwich of plates together, the clutch applies and the two members are locked together. When the piston releases force, the clutch return springs force the piston up, allowing the plates to freely rotate, releasing the two members from each other **(see illustration)**.

Like other components in automatic transmissions, the clutch packs operate in an environment of transmission fluid, which prevents excessive wear to the friction plates, rinses away worn clutch material and cools the clutch assembly so it does not overheat and become less effective.

Bands

Bands, like clutches, use a friction surface of an asbestos-type material that's attached to the inside surface of a thin, flexible steel shell. As its name implies, the band encircles the drum of a planetary drive assembly. When a servo piston applies force to one of the ends of the band (the other end is held stationary), the drum is clamped securely by the band and held stationary **(see illustration)**. When the piston force is released, the band expands and the drum is allowed to rotate freely.

One-way clutches

As alternatives to bands or disc-type clutches, one-way clutches are used in automatic transmissions to provide a simpler method of applying and releasing a particular gear range. These devices do not use hydraulic pressure, but instead use a simple mechanism that allows rotation in one direction only. Not only are these apply/release devices simpler, they are actually preferred in some situations, since they are faster in their apply/release cycles than are hydraulic-type devices, since hydraulic devices must build up and release fluid pressure, causing a brief delay.

Two types of clutches are used in the vehicles covered by this manual. The roller-type clutch **(see illustration)** is the most common and is used in all the transmissions covered by this manual. This type of clutch uses roller-type bearings that are held into pockets when the inner or outer drum is rotating in one direction, but, when the drum is turned the other direction, the rollers move up ramps, locking the rollers against the other drum. Sprag-type clutches **(see illustration)** use the same principle as roller-type clutches, but use *sprags* (dog-bone shaped locking devices) instead of rollers. Since the sprags are taller when rotated in one direction than when they are rotated in the other direction, they allow freewheeling in one direction and lock-up in the other direction.

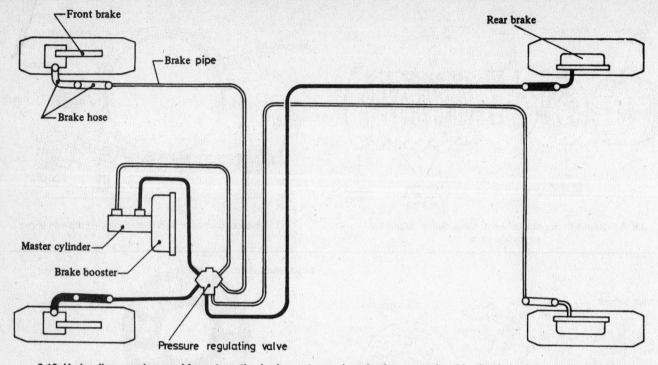

3.10 Hydraulics are also used for automotive brake systems - imagine how complex this simple brake system would be if it were actuated mechanically

The hydraulic system

Hydraulic basics

Shifting in an automatic transmission is controlled through hydraulics. Hydraulics rely on the *non-compressibility* of liquids to transmit power. Unlike air or other gasses, which can be compacted in devices like an air compressor or automotive engine to store energy in the form of pressure, liquids can only *transmit* forces that try to compress them. An example of this property of liquids has been observed by many mechanics when a blown head gasket or other malfunction causes a cylinder of an automotive engine to fill with a liquid (like oil or coolant) when it's towards the bottom of its compression stroke. When the driver attempts to start the engine, the engine immediately stops when the piston tries to compress the liquid against the top of the combustion chamber. Depending on the force generated by the starter, the steel connecting rod will often bend, but under no circumstances will the liquid compress! While this phenomenon, generally referred to as *hydrostatic lock* can cause serious damage in this situation, it can be very beneficial when harnessed in an automatic transmission.

Shift parameters

If you've driven cars with manual transmissions you know that you don't always shift at the same road speed and engine rpm. If you're climbing a hill, you'll "hold out" a shift, bringing the vehicle to a higher rpm and road speed before shifting, then, if the hill gets steeper and the engine starts "bogging," you downshift to a lower gear to allow the engine to operate at a more efficient rpm range. If you're trying to accelerate quickly, you'll allow the engine to rev higher and develop more horsepower before you shift. Automatic transmissions consider these operating conditions automatically and make shifting decisions for you, so many individual actions must happen to make sure each shift takes place at the correct rpm, at the correct road speed and with force sufficient to match the amount of load on the engine.

Needless to say, the shifting decisions made by an automatic transmission are complex. Carrying out an automatic transmission's duties requires a versatile method of transmitting force.

Simplifying with hydraulics

Because liquids are non-compressible, they can be employed to transmit force in situations where levers and cables would be awkward or wouldn't work at all. Automotive brake systems **(see illustration)** use hydraulics to transmit the force of your foot on the brake pedal to all four wheels, proportion the force so there's the correct front-to-rear balance and multiply the brake-pedal-force many times to permit moderate foot pressure to stop a two-ton vehicle. Without hydraulics, a complex system of cables and levers would be required, employing cams and/or bellcranks to proportion force from front to rear, and gearing would be necessary to multiply force. Such a system would be very heavy and so complex as to be unsafe. Since the operations of an automatic transmission are much more complex than this brake-system example, you can see why hydraulics are so necessary.

A basic transmission hydraulic system

To develop an understanding of basic transmission functions, we'll look at the most basic type of transmission possible - one planetary gearset and one band. The hydraulic circuit to actuate the band consists of transmission fluid, a pump to generate pressure from the fluid, a pressure regulator valve to keep pressure constant in the circuit, a shift valve and a shift servo **(see illustration)**.

The pump

Pumps in automatic transmission hydraulic systems are generally *positive displacement* pumps driven by the engine. A positive displacement pump is one which has the same output per revolution regardless of pump speed or pressure already developed in the system. Positive-displacement pumps include piston, gear and rotor-type pumps **(see illustrations)**. Because of their size, piston-type pumps are not used in automatic transmissions, but gear- and rotor-type pumps are common. Gear- and rotor-type pumps are also used as oil pumps in engine lubrication systems (another type of hydraulic system), so if you understand the workings of a lubricating oil pump, you're well on your way to understanding automatic transmission pumps.

Vane-type pumps are also used in automatic transmissions **(see**

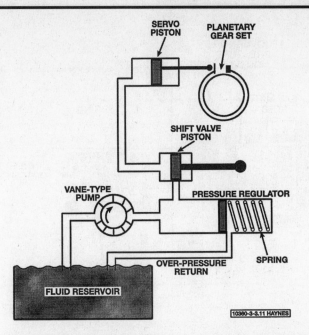

3.11 This simple hydraulic system provides two gear ranges - neutral and drive. By manually moving the shift valve piston to the right, fluid pressure generated by the pump will move the servo piston to the right, tightening the band on the planetary gearset. When the pump generates excessive pressure, the pressure regulator spring is compressed and excess pressure is returned to the fluid reservoir

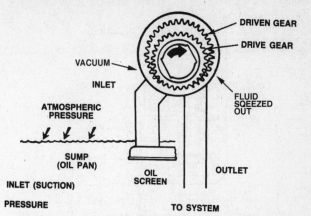

3.12a The most common type of pump in an automatic transmission is the gear-type pump. When the gears rotate, vacuum is created at the inlet and fluid is squeezed out at the outlet

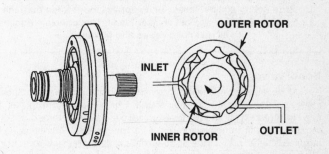

3.12b Rotor-type pumps work by the same principle as gear-type pumps - the only difference is the shapes of the components

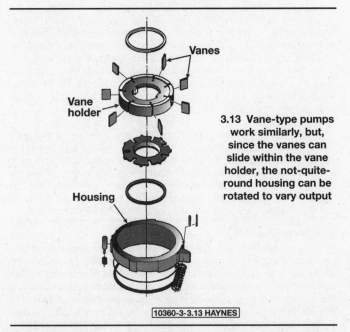

3.13 Vane-type pumps work similarly, but, since the vanes can slide within the vane holder, the not-quite-round housing can be rotated to vary output

illustration). Vane-type pumps use sliding vanes in place of gears or rotors, but operate by a similar principle. The vane holder rotates while the housing remains stationary, and the fluid between the vanes is forced through the pump to the outlet. The vanes are free to slide in and out of the vane housing in their slots and are held against the housing in operation by centrifugal force. A primary advantage of the vane-type pump is that, when the not-quite-circular housing is rotated, output per revolution can be varied.

The pressure regulator

Since most pumps generate the same output-per-revolution regardless of speed or pressure already in the hydraulic circuit, it is necessary to regulate the pressure so it does not get too high and damage components **(see illustration 3.11)**. A basic pressure regulator employs a piston and a spring that compresses at a specific pressure to allow some oil to flow back to the reservoir, bypassing the hydraulic circuit and thus reducing pressure. By using a pressure regulator with a spring calibrated to a pressure much lower than the pump's output, constant pressure can be maintained in the system. When the engine is at low speed, the pressure regulator will be nearly closed, while at high engine speed the pressure regulator will be nearly open. But high speed or low speed, a constant pressure is maintained in the hydraulic system.

The shift valve

Although more complex in a real automatic transmission (actual operation will be discussed in detail later), the shift valve in our example is simply a piston that can be moved to uncover a passage leading to the shift servo **(see illustration 3.11)**.

The servo

The pressure applied to the servo piston when the shift valve is opened moves the servo piston against the band, which in turn immobilizes the drum of the planetary gearset and provides output **(see illustration 3.11)**.

Components for automatic operation

The basic hydraulic circuit just described helped us understand the operation of a simple transmission, but this transmission is so basic that it requires the shift valve to be moved manually, and the shift firmness could not be controlled. The information that follows discusses the hydraulic components necessary to provide fully automatic operation in a modern automatic transmission.

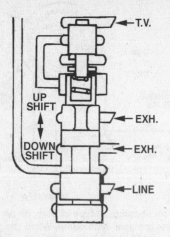

3.14 This converter clutch shift valve illustrates a typical spool valve - note how the lower lands are larger in diameter. Fluid pressure acting against larger lands applies more force than the same pressure acting against smaller lands. This principle applies to all hydraulic valves and pistons

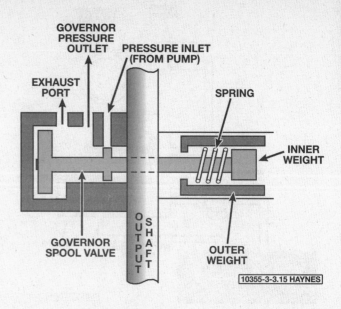

3.15 The governor, which is attached to the transmission output shaft, varies pressure to the shift valves and apply devices as vehicle road speed increases or decreases

Spool valves

Most valves in an automatic transmission are spool valves. Spool valves get their name from their shape, which is similar to that of a sewing-thread-type spool. However, unlike a sewing-thread spool, most automatic transmission spool valves have several *lands* (the larger-diameter part of the spool) to allow fluid pressure to act on several different parts of the valve. Many spool valves have different-sized lands to allow fluid pressure to act differently upon different parts of the valve **(see illustration)**. Since a large-diameter land has more surface area on its face than a smaller-diameter land, fluid pressure applied to the face of the larger-diameter land will have more force on the spool valve than an equal fluid pressure applied to the face of the smaller-diameter land.

Spool-type valves are used for the governor, throttle valve, vacuum modulator valve, manual valve and automatic shift valves.

The governor

The governor's purpose is to vary transmission fluid pressure based on output shaft rotational speed (road speed). The governor's output pressure is then delivered to one side of the automatic shift valve to affect the point at which a shift takes place. The higher the governor's rotational speed, the higher the pressure delivered to the automatic shift valve so, as vehicle speed increases, a shift into the next higher gear becomes more likely.

The governors on all the transmissions covered by this manual are shaft-mounted governors that use centrifugal force acting on weights to vary outlet pressure **(see illustration)**. Two sets of weights and springs are installed on one side of the transmission output shaft, while a spool valve, connected to the weights, is on the other side of the shaft.

When the vehicle is not moving, but in gear with the engine running, the spool valve closes the port that would normally allow pressurized fluid from the pump into the valve. Any small amount of fluid that does get through the valve inlet will flow out the exhaust port, which is fully open at this time. At this point, there is no pressure delivered to the outlet port.

As the vehicle begins to move and the output shaft turns, centrifugal force begins to act upon the weights, causing them to move away from the output shaft. This in turn pulls the spool valve, moving it closer to the output shaft. As this happens, the pressure inlet port begins to open and the exhaust port begins to close. This causes pressure to begin building between the lands of the spool valve, where

the governor pressure outlet is located, and pressurized fluid begins to flow through the outlet. As output shaft speed increases, the weights are thrown farther away from the shaft by centrifugal force, pulling the spool valve closer to the shaft. This causes the inlet to be opened more and the exhaust port to close more, thus increasing pressure delivered to the outlet. As output shaft speed continues to increase, the weights continue to pull the spool valve toward the shaft until the inlet is fully open and the exhaust port is fully closed, at which point governor output pressure is the same as pump outlet pressure. When output shaft speed decreases, spring pressure causes the weights to move toward the output shaft. The spool valve begins closing the inlet and opening the exhaust port, thus lowering governor outlet pressure.

Two centrifugal weights are used in the governor to precisely control outlet pressure. The large weight allows quick response at low speeds. This weight begins moving at very low output shaft speeds to move the spool valve and also to compress the spring. When the spring is compressed, the small weight begins moving at the same speed as the large weight, increasing the centrifugal force that moves the spool valve, thus causing the spool valve to move at a faster rate.

The throttle valve

When climbing a hill, a driver finds he has press down the accelerator farther to maintain the same road speed. Also, when the driver needs to accelerate quickly, she will press the accelerator down farther. Both of these actions require a downshift, but the operation of the transmission, as discussed up to now, will not provide it. The throttle valve provides this function by monitoring engine throttle position and allowing lower-speed shifts when the vehicle speed is relatively low compared with the engine throttle opening.

The throttle valve in the transmission provides a fluid pressure that also acts against the shift valves, but in opposition to it. To understand operation of the throttle valve, we'll first examine the most simple type of throttle valve: the mechanical valve. Basically, the mechanical valve in the transmission is operated through a cable that attaches to the throttle linkage on the engine's carburetor or throttle body. The valve itself is a spool-type valve that uses a spring and plunger to oppose mainline pressure acting through its inlet port. When the engine throttle valve is opened, the cable pulls the lever arm and compresses the spring, applying pressure to the throttle valve in the

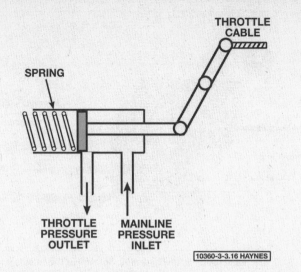

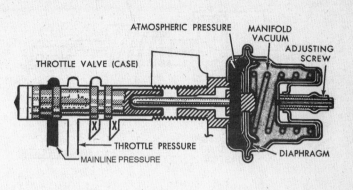

3.16 The throttle valve varies fluid pressure in the transmission based on the position of the throttle in the carburetor or throttle body.

3.17 Vacuum modulators provide the same function as throttle valves, except engine manifold vacuum is used instead of throttle position to determine the load on the engine

transmission. This causes the valve to move to the left and open the outlet port **(see illustration)**. The throttle pressure outlet port is connected to many parts of the transmission. Some of the fluid pressure is sent to the other side of the throttle valve to act against the opening pressure, preventing the valve from opening all at once and also permitting the valve to stabilize at various positions between fully open and fully closed, depending on position of the engine throttle valve.

Fluid pressure from the throttle valve outlet is also routed to the opposite side of the shift valves to balance governor pressure against throttle position and allow shifts to occur at the correct time (this will be discussed further under the heading "The automatic shift valve"). Throttle pressure is also routed to the apply devices that are in operation (bands, accumulators and/or pistons) to supplement apply pressure, thus preventing slippage, since the transmission is under much higher load during hill climbing and acceleration than it is during normal cruising.

The vacuum modulator

The vacuum modulator that is used on some transmissions has the same function and operates very similarly to the throttle valve. The difference is that the modulator operates using engine vacuum rather than a mechanical linkage **(see illustration)**.

When the engine is operating normally (such as when idling or cruising), the vacuum in the engine's intake manifold is very high. When the engine is under load (such as during acceleration or hill climbing), the vacuum is lower. A tube connects the intake manifold to one side of a rubber diaphragm in the vacuum modulator on the transmission. Atmospheric pressure operates on the other side of the diaphragm. The diaphragm is connected to the throttle spool valve in the transmission. When engine vacuum is high (engine load low), the diaphragm moves to the right and closes the inlet and outlet ports of the throttle valve. When engine vacuum is low (engine load high), the diaphragm moves to the left and opens the inlet and outlet ports, increasing transmission throttle pressure.

The manual valve

Simply put, the manual valve in an automatic transmission is a spool valve connected by linkage or a cable to the shift lever inside the passenger compartment. The manual valve, which is connected to the manual lever on the side of the transmission **(see illustration)**, directs fluid flow within the transmission to provide the correct type of operation for the selected range. For example, when Neutral or Park

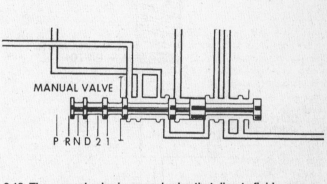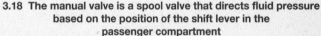

3.18 The manual valve is a spool valve that directs fluid pressure based on the position of the shift lever in the passenger compartment

are selected, fluid is directed to an exhaust port that sends pressure back to the transmission pan so no apply devices are engaged. When Drive is selected, fluid is directed to the Low gear clutch piston and to the 1-2 shift valve.

The automatic shift valve

Earlier, when discussing operation of a basic transmission hydraulic system, the shift valve had to be moved manually to select a gear. Automatic transmissions perform this operation by sensing vehicle speed and throttle position to determine the correct shift point. Basically, an automatic shift valve is a simple spool valve that balances pressure from the governor output against spring pressure and fluid pressure from the throttle valve (or vacuum modulator) output **(see illustration)**. When governor pressure overcomes spring and throttle pressure, the shift takes place.

The valve body

The valve body is the hydraulic "brain" of the automatic transmission **(see illustration)**. The valve body houses most of the hydraulic valves - the shift valves, manual valve, throttle valve, converter lock-up valve, etc. - used in the transmission. Additionally, the valve body has many passages that connect together the drilled galleries within the transmission.

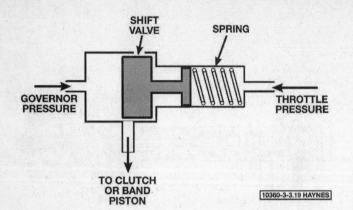

3.19 Automatic shift valves balance governor fluid pressure against throttle fluid pressure and spring pressure. When governor pressure overcomes the opposing force, the shift takes place

3.20 The valve body is the hydraulic "brain" of the automatic transmission - it contains the shift valves, manual valve and throttle valve

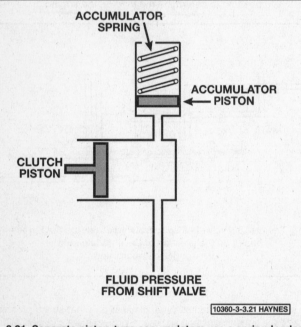

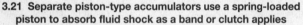

3.21 Separate piston-type accumulators use a spring-loaded piston to absorb fluid shock as a band or clutch applies

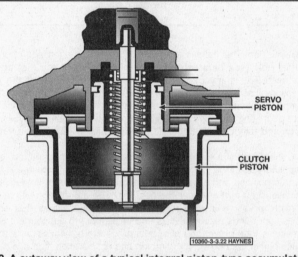

3.22 A cutaway view of a typical integral piston-type accumulator

The accumulator

In a transmission hydraulic system, when fluid under pressure is sent to a servo piston, it arrives with great force. If allowed to act directly against the servo piston, a phenomenon known as *fluid shock* would occur. Fluid shock is the same phenomenon sometimes found in household plumbing systems that causes pipes to rattle when a valve is opened. Since liquid is not compressible, the entire force of the pressurized liquid hits the pipes (or, in a transmission, the servo piston) all at once. In a household plumbing system, this force causes the pipes to rattle. In an automatic transmission, it causes vibration and harsh shifting. To prevent this from happening, accumulators are used. In automatic transmissions, accumulators are either separate or integral piston types.

The operation of a separate piston-type accumulator is relatively self-evident **(see illustration)**. When fluid pressure is applied to the circuit, much of the force is absorbed by the accumulator piston. The accumulator piston spring will absorb force until the spring behind it is fully compressed, when full pressure will act against the servo piston.

By the time the spring is compressed, there will be no engagement shock. In some applications, fluid shock can be further reduced by applying a lower auxiliary pressure to the spring side of the servo to help supplement spring pressure.

The integral piston-type accumulator operates similarly to the separate piston-type, except that both the accumulator piston and the servo piston occupy the same cylinder bore in the transmission **(see illustration)**. These types of accumulator systems are usually arranged so that the accumulator piston is part of the apply-pressure circuit for a different servo. In the illustration, you can see that the accumulator piston for the 1-2 clutch is installed in the same bore as the low-reverse servo piston. When the low-reverse band and the 1-2 clutch are both released, accumulator pressure is applied to the spring side of the accumulator piston, which forces the accumulator piston against the servo piston and holds the servo in the released position. When the 1-2 clutch is applied, part of the fluid from that circuit is routed into the accumulator through internal passages in the accumulator piston. The fluid enters the area between the accumulator and servo pistons and forces the accumulator piston up, to the top of its travel, against accumulator and spring pressure. This cushions the pressure increase when the 1-2 clutch is applied, much the same as with an independent accumulator. During accumulator operation, 1-2 clutch pressure works against the spring side of the low-reverse servo piston. This pressure holds the servo in the released position.

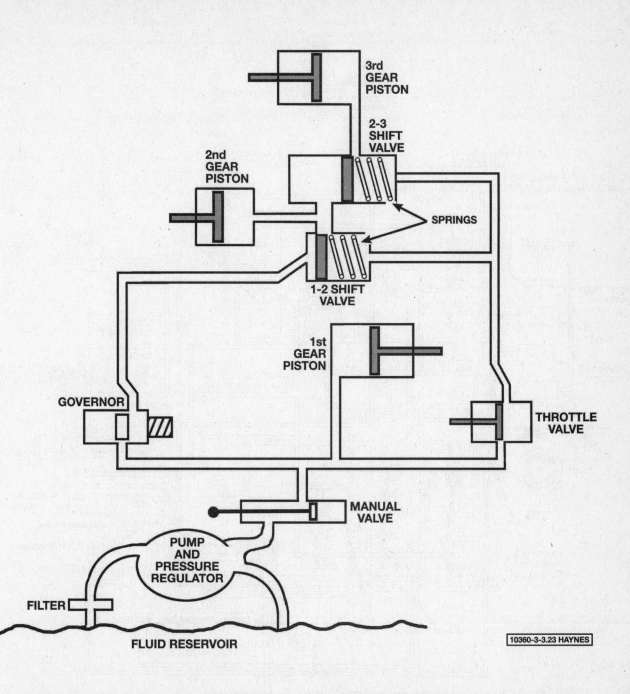

3.23 This schematic of an automatic transmission hydraulic system is overly simplified to show basic functions

Working examples of hydraulic systems

In operation, there is a great deal of interaction among the components in a hydraulic system. The shift valves, by balancing governor and throttle pressures not only assure a shift occurs at the right speed, but also that the shift will have the correct amount of firmness. For example, in looking at the first, simplified example **(see illustration)**, you'll see that pressing the accelerator to the floor will not only cause a shift to occur at a higher speed, but also assure it is firmer. This is because pressing the throttle to the floor will make the throttle valve apply greater fluid pressure to the right side of the shift valve. This will mean it will take greater governor pressure against the

left side of the shift valve to make the shift take place. This means a higher road speed for the shift, but it also means higher pressure will act against the piston when the shift does take place, limiting slippage during high power output by the engine. Conversely, light throttle pressure will allow shifts at lower speeds, but will also apply less pressure to the piston, allowing a less harsh shift for smooth transition in normal driving.

The next example **(see illustration)** is an actual transmission hydraulic system. It is included here as a learning aid to help you understand the intricacies of a modern hydraulic system. While fairly complex, a little time studying the interaction of components will give you a broader understanding of hydraulic systems.

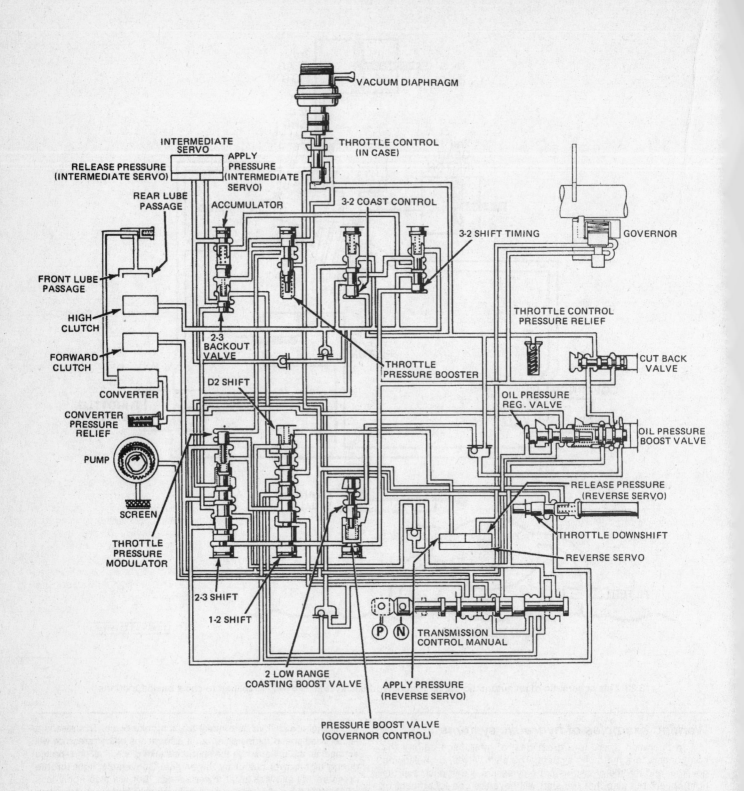

3.24 Spend some time studying this typical hydraulic system schematic. It will help you better understand the functioning of an automatic transmission

3.25 The torque converter is a fluid coupler that replaces the clutch in a manual transmission

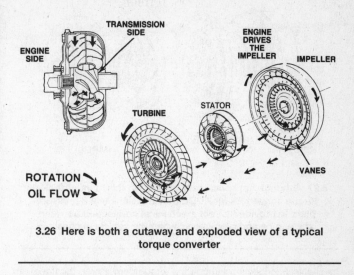

3.26 Here is both a cutaway and exploded view of a typical torque converter

The torque converter

The torque converter **(see illustration)** replaces the clutch used in manual transmissions. Since planetary gearsets are meshed at all times and can be "shifted" without interrupting power delivery to the rear wheels, a disengaging-type clutch is not necessary. However, a means of allowing the engine to idle in gear with the vehicle motionless must be provided. Also, to help provide for smooth gear shifts at low-speed, part-throttle driving and to reduce wear on clutches and bands during these driving conditions, some *slippage* (when the engine is momentarily allowed to operate at a slightly higher speed without affecting road speed) must also be provided. The torque converter is a very flexible power transmitter that provides all these functions and more.

The basic principle of torque converter operation can be observed by placing the blades of two electric fans opposite each other and turning on one of the fans. If one of the fans is turned on, the force of the air column produced will act upon the motionless blades of the other fan. The blades of the fan that is turned off will begin turning and will accelerate and finally reach a speed approaching the speed of the fan that's powered.

To put this principle into automotive terms, imagine the blades of one fan are attached to the rear of the engine's crankshaft and the blades of the other fan are attached to the driveshaft, which is connected to the rear wheels. Start the engine and we're ready to drive down the road, right? Not quite. Remember that, since air is compressible, it is not efficient at transmitting power. This is why the blades of an automotive torque converter are sealed in a case that's filled with transmission fluid, which is non-compressible. The fluid is capable of transmitting driving force efficiently enough to provide power to the rear wheels and move the vehicle.

However, there's a big difference between just *moving* a vehicle and moving it *efficiently*, achieving good fuel economy and low-speed torque. To achieve this efficiency, torque converters use some unique design features. First, the inside of a torque converter does not look like two sets of fan blades facing each other **(see illustration)**. The *impeller* (the part attached to the engine crankshaft, which is sometimes called a *pump*) and the *turbine* (the part attached to the transmission) look more like two bundt-cake pans facing each other. Inside both are dividers that create individual cavities shaped like slices of bundt cake that are cut at angles. The purpose of these shapes is to allow the transmission fluid to circulate, in a circular motion, between the turbine and impeller. The angled cavities in the impeller force fluid out of the impeller when the engine rotates it, like a fan, but, unlike our fan example, the angled cavities in the turbine redirect the remaining fluid force back to the impeller. Greater

efficiency is achieved by this circular motion of fluid since it takes full advantage of the force generated by the impeller. Force is not lost like in the fan example, where the airflow not used to rotate the idle fan is lost.

The stator

When the vehicle is cruising down the road and the impeller and turbine are rotating at approximately the same speed, this fluid coupling works well. But, think hard about the motion of the fluid in this arrangement of parts when the vehicle is accelerating, particularly when it's accelerating from a stop. Since the fluid returning from the turbine, after acting upon it, will be redirected against the impeller, which is turning at a higher speed than the turbine, the redirected fluid flow will actually be counterproductive, interfering with turbine fluid flow and reducing the efficiency of the fluid coupling.

To solve this problem, a third member, called the *stator*, is necessary. The stator has blades angled to reverse the direction of fluid flow as it leaves the turbine so that it will again act against the impeller, in the direction of rotation, and therefore assist the engine in turning the impeller. To further aid in redirecting fluid flow, the stator rotates on a one-way roller clutch so that it's free to rotate in the direction of engine rotation but not in the opposite direction. This allows the stator to remain efficient when the turbine is turning, and not just when it's standing still. The re-direction of fluid flow results in an actual multiplication of the torque developed by the engine during acceleration, particularly from a stop. Torque converters are so efficient that, during acceleration from a stop, the torque delivered to the transmission is frequently *twice* the torque developed by the engine.

The lock-up converter

AOD and C5 transmissions are equipped with mechanisms to lock up their torque converters under certain operating conditions. The purpose of the lock-up converter is to provide for direct drive when the vehicle is cruising at higher speeds. Since there is always some slippage in the viscous coupling of a torque converter, some power is lost and fuel economy suffers. By providing a direct mechanical coupling through the transmission during cruising, the lock-up converter helps improve fuel economy during cruising.

C5 transmissions use a centrifugal mechanism at the torque converter that is engaged in any gear at higher (cruising and above) engine speeds. This mechanism provides a mechanical link through the torque converter.

AOD transmissions use a direct driveshaft that is connected to the front of the torque converter through a damper assembly. The driveshaft is connected to the direct clutch and provides a partial

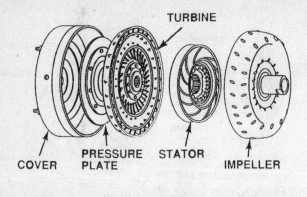

3.27 Although not specifically covered in this manual, lock-up torque converters for AODE transmissions use a pressure plate to provide a direct mechanical connection between the engine and rear wheels when the vehicle is cruising

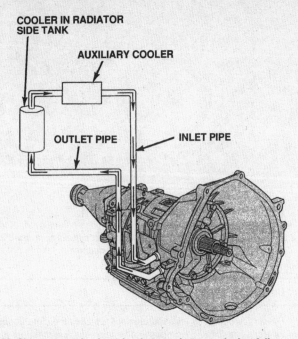

3.28 Since excessive heat leads to early transmission failure, an auxiliary cooler can greatly extend transmission life, particularly if you haul heavy loads or tow

mechanical connection through the torque converter in third gear. In fourth (overdrive) gear, a totally mechanical connection through the torque converter is provided by the damper and driveshaft assembly.

Although not specifically covered in this manual, the latest variation of the AOD transmission, called the AODE (the "E" is for electronic), uses a more modern system of converter lock-up that is also used in virtually all transmissions being produced for automobiles today: the electronic/hydraulic converter clutch system. This system uses a pressure plate within the converter housing, just in front of the impeller/turbine assembly (see illustration). The pressure plate has friction material on its front. When the vehicle is cruising and lock-up is desired, an electric solenoid is energized which opens the converter clutch valve in the valve body. This allows fluid pressure to act upon the rear of the pressure plate. The pressure plate is then forced against a machined surface on the converter cover and, like on a manual-transmission-type clutch, the pressure plate and converter cover become as one assembly. Since the pressure plate is splined to the transmission input shaft, a direct mechanical link through the torque converter is established. When lock-up is no longer required, a port opens that allows the pressurized fluid to exhaust. Fluid then flows out from in front of the pressure plate through centrifugal force and the pressure plate moves away from the converter housing, re-establishing the fluid coupling. Lock-up in electronic converter clutch systems is controlled by the vehicle's Powertrain Control Module (PCM). When this computer senses the engine is warm, the vehicle is traveling over about 40 miles per hour in high gear and at a steady speed, lock-up is initiated. When speed falls below about 40 miles per hour, the brakes are applied, a lower gear is selected or the vehicle is accelerated quickly, fluid is exhausted to end lock-up. The inputs to the computer that control lock-up are: the coolant temperature sensor, the vehicle speed sensor, the throttle position sensor and a brake-off switch (that tells the computer when the brakes are applied).

The fluid cooler

Slippage within an automatic transmission generates heat, and heat is the greatest enemy of any automatic transmission. Heat causes fluid to break down, losing its lubricating and heat-transfer properties, and heat also causes clutch friction material to varnish, causing still more slippage. Since transmission fluid is in contact with virtually all components within an automatic transmission, cooling the fluid will ultimately cool the transmission. Fluid coolers circulate pressurized fluid through lines (usually steel tubes) to the radiator. A separate transmission fluid chamber within the radiator bottom or side tank is in constant contact with engine coolant. Since normal engine coolant temperature is lower than normal transmission fluid temperature, the

transmission fluid chamber transfers heat to the engine coolant, cooling the transmission fluid.

This "heat exchanger" works well under normal conditions, but if the engine overheats, the transmission will likewise overheat. Also, if the transmission is slipping excessively and building up excessive heat, the engine will also overheat. To overcome these problems and extend transmission life by reducing operating temperature, it is wise to install an auxiliary transmission cooler in your vehicle, especially if the vehicle is used for towing or moving heavy loads (see illustration). Installation of an auxiliary transmission cooler is covered in Chapter 9.

The parking pawl

When PARK is selected, an actuating rod within the transmission actuates a pawl that moves into contact with teeth on the outside of the direct-clutch drum. This mechanically locks the output shaft so the vehicle cannot move.

The final drive

On RWD vehicles, the final drive is more commonly known as the differential and is mounted in the rear axle housing. Final drive/differential set-ups on RWD vehicles typically consist of a ring and pinion gear which are known as hypoid type gears. Hypoid type gears are used when the power from the motor must be transmitted to the driveaxles at a 90 degree angle, such is the case on most RWD vehicles and some FWD vehicles that have the engine mounted longitudinally in the vehicle. Regardless of the type of vehicle, the final drive/differential is always the last set of gears that power from the engine is transferred through on its way to the driveaxles. The majority of FWD vehicles today have transversely mounted engines, therefore power from the engine is transmitted parallel with the driveaxles, which allows the manufacturers to employ simple helical type gears mounted in the transaxle as the final drive to apply power to the driveaxles.

Chapter 4
Transmission identification

Transmissions covered by this manual

This manual covers the C3, C4, C5, C6 and AOD automatic transmissions used in rear-wheel drive cars and light trucks and the ATX/FLC and AXOD transaxles used in front wheel drive cars produced by Ford, Lincoln and Mercury.

Rear wheel drive
C3, C4 and C5 transmissions

The C3, C4 and C5 transmissions are all three-speed automatic gearboxes sharing the same basic design.

The C4 transmission is the earliest-design transmission covered by this manual. It was originally designed for small and intermediate cars and light trucks equipped with six-cylinder and small V8 engines. The C4 was introduced in 1964 and continued to be produced through 1982, when it was superseded by the C5 transmission.

The C3 transmission is essentially a light-duty version of the C4 transmission. It was used from 1974 through 1986 on smaller cars with four-cylinder, V6 and small V8 engines.

The C5 transmission began production in 1981 and superseded the C4 in 1982. The C5 is fundamentally a modernized version of the C4 with a torque converter clutch to provide converter lock-up during cruising. The C5 transmission stopped production in 1986, when it was replaced by the AOD transmission.

C6 transmission

The C6 is Ford's heavy-duty three-speed automatic transmission, used with large V8 engines, primarily in full-size cars, pick-ups and vans. The C6 was introduced in 1966 and, at the time this manual was written, was still being produced for heavy-duty pick-up trucks and vans.

AOD transmission

The AOD is a four-speed automatic overdrive transmission used in larger cars and light trucks. The AOD was designed as a replacement for the C4/C5 and was used from 1980 through 1994, when it was replaced by a fully electronic version.

Front wheel drive
ATX transaxle

The ATX is a front wheel drive version of a three speed automatic transmission that was produced from 1984 through 1994. It was primarily designed for light duty use on four cylinder engines, although in 1992 it was adapted to the V6 engine in the Tempo/Topaz line of vehicles. During the span of coverage on the ATX transaxle it has been used in Escort/Lynx/EXP/Tempo/Topaz/Taurus and Sable vehicles. Aside from the different types of torque converters implemented on different vehicles through the model years all ATX transaxles are typically the same in design. Please note that on 1987 and later Tempo/Topaz models and 1988 and later Taurus/Sable models, the ATX transaxle is equipped with a fluidically linked torque converter, which is commonly referred to as the FLC transmission.

AXOD transmission

The AXOD transaxle is a four speed automatic front wheel drive transaxle. It was produced from 1986 through 1990 when it was superseded by the fully electronic version AXOD-E. It was primarily designed for medium duty use on V6 engines in the Taurus and Sable line of vehicles.

Visual identification

The quickest and easiest way to identify the type of transmission you have is to climb under the vehicle (make sure it's safely supported!) and look at the shape of the transmission pan bolted to the bottom of the transmission. The accompanying drawings show the shapes of Ford rear-wheel drive and front wheel drive transmission pans **(see illustrations)**. Note that C4 and C5 transmissions share the

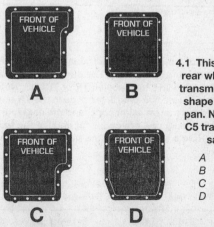

4.1 This chart identifies Ford rear wheel drive automatic transmissions based on the shape of the transmission pan. Note that the C4 and C5 transmission have the same pan shape

A   C3
B   C4 and C5
C   C6
D   AOD

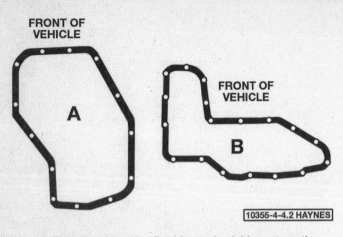

FRONT OF VEHICLE

FRONT OF VEHICLE

A

B

10355-4-4.2 HAYNES

4.2 This chart identifies Ford front wheel drive automatic transaxles based on the shape of fluid pan. Note that the ATX/FLC transaxles have the same pan shape

A   ATX/FLC   B   AXOD

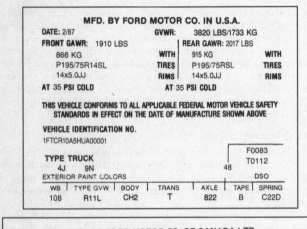

MFD. BY FORD MOTOR CO. IN U.S.A.

DATE: 2/87		GVWR:	3820 LBS/1733 KG	
FRONT GAWR: 1910 LBS		**REAR GAWR:** 2017 LBS		
866 KG	**WITH**	915 KG		**WITH**
P195/75R14SL	**TIRES**	P195/75RSL		**TIRES**
14x5.0JJ	**RIMS**	14x5.0JJ		**RIMS**
AT 35 PSI COLD		AT 35 PSI COLD		

THIS VEHICLE CONFORMS TO ALL APPLICABLE FEDERAL MOTOR VEHICLE SAFETY STANDARDS IN EFFECT ON THE DATE OF MANUFACTURE SHOWN ABOVE

VEHICLE IDENTIFICATION NO.

1FTCR10A5HUA00001

TYPE TRUCK				F0083	
4J	9N		48	T0112	
EXTERIOR PAINT COLORS					DSO
WB	TYPE GVW	BODY	TRANS	AXLE	TAPE	SPRING
108	R11L	CH2	T	822	B	C22D

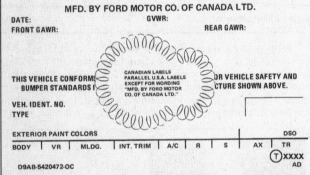

MFD. BY FORD MOTOR CO. OF CANADA LTD.

DATE: GVWR:
FRONT GAWR: REAR GAWR:

CANADIAN LABELS PARALLEL U.S.A. LABELS EXCEPT FOR WORDING "MFD. BY FORD MOTOR CO. OF CANADA LTD."

THIS VEHICLE CONFORMS ... OR VEHICLE SAFETY AND BUMPER STANDARDS I ... CTURE SHOWN ABOVE.

VEH. IDENT. NO.
TYPE

EXTERIOR PAINT COLORS   DSO

BODY	VR	MLDG.	INT. TRIM	A/C	R	S	AX	TR
								(T)XXXX
								AD

D9AB-5420472-OC

4.3 Here are examples of typical Vehicle Certification Labels (the label is located in the driver's door jamb). The transmission code is at the bottom of the label, in a box labeled TR or TRANS. Note that many later models have a five-character code in the TR box.
The first character is the transmission code, and the next four characters, which you can ignore, are codes for each of the four suspension springs. Here's what the transmission codes mean:

B	ATX/FLC	U	C6
C	C5	V	C3
T	AOD (rear wheel drive)	W	C4
T	AXOD (front wheel drive)	Z	C6 (Police)

same shape. As a general rule, if you have a 1964 through 1980 vehicle with the C4/C5 transmission pan shape, it is a C4. 1983 and later vehicles with this transmission pan shape will be a C5. If you have a 1981 or 1982 vehicle with the C4/C5 pan shape, it could be either a C4 or C5, since both were in production during these years. See "Identifying by transmission code" for an easy way to tell whether you have a C4 or a C5. The ATX/FLC transaxles also share the same fluid pan shape, since they are the same transaxles with the exception of the torque converter design.

Identifying by transmission code

All Ford-built vehicles come from the factory with a Vehicle Certification Label at the rear of the driver's door **(see illustration)**. A letter code on this label can be used to accurately identify the transmission installed in the vehicle at the factory. Note that the "T" code is used by Ford to identify all four-speed automatic transmissions on later models, such as the A4LD, which is not covered by this manual. To be sure the "T" code on your vehicle is identifying an AOD or and AXOD, check the shape of the transmission pan.

Identifying by transmission ID tag

All transmissions covered by this manual have a stamped-steel identification tag attached to the outside of the transmission housing **(see illustration)**. This tag provides specific information on the model of the transmission, identifies when it was built and often includes a serial number. Parts suppliers frequently request information from this tag to be sure they supply you with the correct parts, so always bring this tag with you when you're ordering parts. On C3 and AOD transmissions, the tag is attached to the lower rear extension housing bolt, on the left side of the transmission. On C4, C5 and C6 transmissions, the tag is attached to an intermediate servo cover bolt. On ATX/FLC transaxles the tag is attached to the valve body cover at the top of the transaxle. On AXOD transaxles there is a sticker affixed to the top of the bellhousing.

4.4 The transmission tag is bolted to the transmission case - when a dealer or parts supplier deciphers it, it provides information concerning assembly line modifications which could affect parts interchangeability. Always take this tag with you when ordering parts

Chapter 5
Troubleshooting

Introduction

The purpose of this chapter is to help you determine, first of all, if your transmission actually needs an overhaul, or if it can be repaired in the vehicle. If an overhaul is unavoidable, it's best to identify the possible problem area, or areas, before you begin teardown so you can inspect the problem area thoroughly. You should have a basic understanding of your transmission's basic operating fundamentals, and how the components interact to achieve shifting, to totally benefit from the symptom-based troubleshooting sections we give you in this Chapter (see Chapter 3 for more information, if necessary).

Always start by checking the following items before you begin any in-depth troubleshooting (all items do not apply to all transmissions):

a) Check the transmission fluid for proper level and color.
b) Check to see if the manual linkage is properly installed and adjusted (see Chapter 6).
c) Check the throttle valve cable for proper installation and adjustment (see Chapter 6).
d) Check the vacuum modulator vacuum hose for proper installation. Make sure the hose is not cracked or broken and vacuum is reaching the modulator.
e) Check the engine timing and idle speed is set correctly.
f) Check to make sure there are no engine vacuum leaks.

After you have completed all the above checks, perform a thorough road test.

Fluid examination

General information

Ford automatic transmissions are designed to operate with the fluid level between the marks on the dipstick indicator, with the fluid at normal operating temperature (see illustration). The normal operating temperature is attained by driving the car for 8 to 15 miles or running the engine approximately 10 minutes, while shifting through the gears several times during this period. The fluid temperature should reach 150 to 200-degrees F when normal operating temperature is reached. **Note:** *If the car has been driven for a long period of time or the fluid temperature is over 200-degrees F, you must wait for the fluid to cool down before you can accurately check the fluid level.*

Examining the fluid color and odor

The normal color of automatic transmission fluid (ATF) is deep red or orange red and should not be black, brown or pink. The best way to check the color of the ATF is to use white paper. Remove the dipstick and wipe the fluid off of the dipstick onto the white paper; this will allow you to see the true color of the fluid as it is absorbed into the paper. Inspect the paper for the proper color and for black, brown or metal specks.

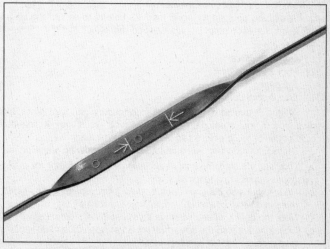

5.1 Automatic transmission fluid should be maintained between the two marks on the dipstick with the fluid at operating temperature

If the color of the ATF is a green/brown shade and does not have a burned odor, this indicates that regular maintenance is need to prevent possible transmission damage.

If the color of the ATF is a black or brown shade and has a burned odor, this indicates that the transmission has been overheated or possibly burned. With this type of fluid condition the transmission has probably been damaged and servicing of the fluid and filter at this point may not help.

If the color of the ATF has a pink shade or milky feel to it, the transmission oil cooler in the radiator is leaking water or coolant into the transmission through the oil cooler lines. Repair or replacement of the transmission cooler is necessary before servicing the transmission. After the leak has been repaired, the transmission will require servicing and flushing. Unfortunately this does not mean the problem has been solved. Damaged may have occurred and flushing might only be successful if only water has contaminated the transmission. If coolant has contaminated the system, flushing and servicing will not cure the problem. The ethylene glycol in the antifreeze breaks down the bonding material in the bands and clutch discs, causing the friction material to tear apart. This will cause severe transmission damage and failure.

If the ATF is red but has bubbles or is foamy the fluid level is too high and the internal parts of the transmission are not being properly lubricated. To remedy this problem drain the excess transmission fluid from the pan or use a suction gun and hose to remove fluid through the fill tube.

If the transmission is operating properly, but there are tiny particles in the fluid, this is considered normal. If large amounts of particles are found, they're most likely from worn bushings, bands, clutches and/or friction material. If excessive material is found remove the pan and filter, inspect for aluminum, brass or bronze flakes or friction material, this indicates extreme wear and internal damage **(see illustration)**.

If the ATF has a burned or bad odor, regardless of color, this indicates the fluid has overheated and possible clutch or band failure may have occurred. To test for burned fluid, put a small amount of fluid from the dipstick on your fingers and rub it together. If it smells like burned oil, the fluid has been overheated. Typically, burned fluid will be dark brown or black.

Road test

General information

After you have performed the preliminary inspection outlined in the Introduction, the road test is next. A properly conducted road test is a valuable tool in diagnosing the transmission. Again, you must have a basic understanding of how the transmission operates to totally benefit from the road test (see Chapter 3).

When you perform the road test, it's helpful to record the actual shift points for each gear. During the road test check for:

a) Vibrations
b) Unusual noises
c) Poor shift quality
d) Slippage
e) Erratic shift pattern

A lightly traveled road is ideal for conducting the road test. Take advantage of your areas natural features, such as curves and hills that could enhance the problem and make it easier to diagnose.

During the road test you should check the following major points:

a) Operate the transmission in all gear ranges to check for differences in shifting and for slippage.
b) Check that you have all upshift, downshift, coasting downshift, manual downshift and engine braking capabilities.
c) Note the quality of each shift. Is it firm, soft, harsh or mushy?
d) Check and record the speeds at which all upshifts and downshifts take place.
e) Watch the engine speed for sudden engine speed increase indicating slippage. If this occurs in a gear it usually indicates a clutch, band or one-way clutch has a problem.

5.2 If material is found on the dipstick remove the oil pan and filter and look for large particles in the pan

Note: *If there is a delay on initial engagement when the transmission is placed into gear, the check valve in the oil pump is probably stuck or sticking and has allowed the fluid to drain from the converter into the transmission oil pan.*

How to conduct a road test

Begin the road test from a stop with the gear selector in the Drive, or Overdrive position if equipped. Be sure that the engine and transmission are both at normal operating temperature. Accelerate the car moderately. Record all the upshift points. The 1-2, 2-3 and 3-4 (on the AOD transmission) shifts should occur while you are accelerating , but shift points should vary depending on how quickly you are accelerating.

To test for part throttle downshift accelerate the vehicle to approximately 45-mph in high gear, then quickly depress the accelerator half way (you only want to open the throttle half way). The transmission should downshift one gear. Repeat the procedure, opening throttle fully, to test the full throttle downshift. Depending on the speed and transmission model, the transmission may downshift one or two gears. Test for a coasting downshift by decelerating from cruising speed to a complete stop. You should feel the transmission downshift from 4-3 (AOD only), 3-2 and finally 2-1. Make a note of the downshift speeds.

To check the operation of manual second or manual low, accelerate from a standing start with the gear selector in the range you wish to check. For manual second, there should be a 1-2 upshift (some models will take off in second gear in manual second). The transmission should stay in second gear after the 1-2 upshift regardless of the vehicle speed, and provide engine braking on deceleration. No 2-3 upshift should occur. When manual low is selected the transmission will remain in the low gear and provide engine braking on deceleration. No 1-2 upshift should occur.

Check the manual 3-2 downshift quality by moving the selector lever from Drive to manual second at a moderate speed. Observe the shift quality and check for engine braking.

The last two operations to check are Neutral and Reverse. Stop the car and place the selector lever into the Neutral position and listen for noise. Feel for vehicle movement; there should be no engagement of the transmission in Neutral or the Park position. Finally, place the gear selector lever in Reverse. Check the transmission operation in Reverse, both at idle and part throttle.

Take the information you have gathered on the road test and compare it to the applicable chart listed below. Use the chart to narrow the problem down to a specific component or apply device in the transmission by noting the components that are applied in the particular problem range. For example, if your transmission has no second gear, but low and high gear are OK, a problem with the intermediate band is indicated (except AOD).

Rear wheel drive Road Test Application Chart

C3, C4 and C5

Range	Band Applied	Clutch Applied
Park/Neutral	No band applied	No clutch applied
Drive range 1st gear	No band applied	Forward clutch applied, one-way clutch holding
Drive range 2nd gear	Intermediate band applied	Forward clutch applied
Drive range 3rd gear	No band applied	Forward clutch applied and high-reverse clutch applied
Drive range Overdrive	No band applied	Direct clutch applied, forward clutch applied and fourth clutch applied
Manual Low	Low-reverse band applied	Forward clutch applied
Manual Second	Intermediate band applied	Forward clutch applied
Reverse	Low-reverse band applied	High-reverse clutch applied

C6

Range	Band Applied	Clutch Applied
Neutral	No band applied	No Clutch Applied
Drive range 1st gear	No band applied	Forward clutch applied, one-way clutch holding
Drive range 2nd gear	Intermediate band applied	Forward clutch applied
Drive range 3rd gear	No band applied	Forward clutch applied, high-reverse clutch applied
Manual Low	No band applied	Forward clutch applied and low-reverse clutch applied
Manual Second	Intermediate band applied	Forward clutch applied
Reverse	No band applied	High-reverse clutch applied and low-reverse clutch applied

AOD

Range	Band Applied	Clutch Applied
Park/Neutral	No band applied	No clutch applied
Drive range 1st gear	No band applied	Forward clutch applied and low one-way clutch holding
Drive range 2nd gear	No band applied	Forward clutch applied, intermediate clutch applied intermediate one-way clutch holding
Drive range 3rd gear	No band applied	Forward clutch applied and direct clutch applied
Drive range Overdrive	Overdrive band applied	Direct clutch applied
Manual Low	Low-reverse band applied	Forward clutch applied
Reverse	Low-reverse band applied	Reverse clutch applied

Front wheel drive Road Test Application Chart

ATX/FLC

Range	Band Applied	Clutch Applied
Neutral	No band applied	No Clutch Applied
Drive range 1st gear	Low intermediate band applied	One way clutch applied,
Drive range 2nd gear	Low intermediate band applied	High intermediate clutch applied
Drive range 3rd gear	No band applied	Direct clutch applied and high intermediate clutch applied
Manual Low	Low intermediate band applied	Direct clutch applied
Manual Second	Low intermediate band applied	High intermediate clutch applied
Reverse	No band applied	Reverse clutch applied and direct clutch applied

AXOD

Range	Band Applied	Clutch Applied
Park/Neutral	No band applied	No clutch applied
Drive range 1st gear	No band applied	Forward clutch applied and low one-way clutch holding
Drive range 2nd gear	No band applied	Forward clutch applied, intermediate clutch applied intermediate one-way clutch holding
Drive range 3rd gear	No band applied	Forward clutch applied and direct clutch applied
Drive range Overdrive	Overdrive band applied	Direct clutch applied
Manual Low	Low-reverse band applied	Forward clutch applied
Reverse	Low-reverse band applied	Reverse clutch applied

Oil pressure test

General information

An automatic transmission is a hydraulically operated device, therefore adequate oil pressure must be maintained for correct operation of all the internal components. The oil pump creates oil pressure and supplies transmission fluid to the components through the oil circuits of the transmission. The pressure is regulated by a pressure regulator device in the oil pump body.

A hydraulic pressure test is an accurate way to pinpoint the specific causes of transmission pressure related problems. As with the road test, having some idea of the possible causes of a problem before you remove the transmission might save you from unnecessary work.

There are many oil circuits in the transmission, and several subsystems such as the throttle pressure system and the governor system. They all have one thing in common; they are supplied by main line oil pressure (or simply "line pressure") by the oil pump. When an oil pressure test is performed, typically it's the line pressure that's checked. Line pressure is also known as control pressure and is used to activate and hold the clutches and bands and provide the pressure to move the control valves. Throttle pressure is line pressure directed and controlled at and by the throttle valve. The throttle valve is connected to the engine by mechanical linkage, a cable or a vacuum modulator. Throttle pressure increases with the engine load and throttle opening. It interacts with the governor pressure to control shift points. Governor pressure is line pressure that is increased in relation to vehicle road speed and regulated by the governor valve. The governor valve is a centrifugal operated valve driven off of the output shaft and works in conduction with throttle pressure to control shift points. If the line pressure is high or low, it can affect the entire transmission because it supplies the pressure to regulate shifting.

How to perform an oil pressure test

To perform an oil pressure test you'll need an oil pressure gauge and a tachometer (see illustration). The gauge must be capable of reading up to 300 psi and equipped with a heavy duty hose with a 1/8-inch NPT fitting. The hose must be at least 10 feet long if you're planning to read the gauge from inside the vehicle.

Locate the test port plug on the side of the transmission and remove the plug (see illustrations). If necessary raise the vehicle and support it securely on jackstands to access the transmission test port from under the vehicle. Install the oil pressure gauge into the line pressure test port and tighten the fitting securely. Start the engine and

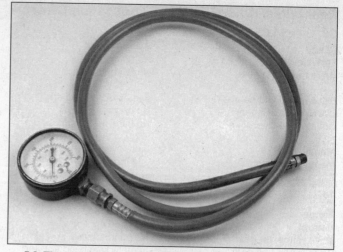

5.3 The oil pressure test gauge hose fitting threads into the transmission test port, the dial on the gauge should read up to 300 psi

allow the engine and transmission to reach normal operating temperature. Firmly apply the brake, shift the transmission into gear and record the test pressure. Shift the transmission to the next range and perform the test in each of the indicated ranges. Do not take more than 20 seconds to record the pressure in any one range and do not exceed two minutes total test time. Compare your readings with the normal oil pressure from the applicable chart below.

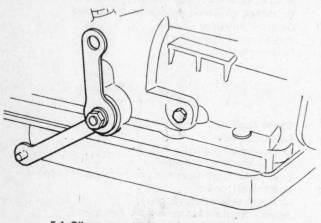

5.4 Oil pressure test port location for the C3

5.5 Oil pressure test port location for the C4, C5 and C6

Rear wheel drive Oil Pressure Test Chart

C3

Range			Normal oil pressure
Neutral	Engine idling	Brakes applied	50 to 75 psi
Drive, 2 or 1	Engine idling	Brakes applied	50 to 75 psi
Reverse	Engine idling	Brakes applied	65 to 110 psi

C4 and C5

Range			Normal oil pressure
Neutral	Engine idling	Brakes applied	50 to 90 psi
Drive	Engine idling	Brakes applied	60 to 90 psi
2 or 1	Engine idling	Brakes applied	90 to 110 psi
Reverse	Engine idling	Brakes applied	150 to 180 psi (C4); 60 to 90 psi (C5)

Rear wheel drive Oil Pressure Test Chart (continued)

C6

Range			Normal oil pressure
Neutral	Engine idling	Brakes applied	50 to 80 psi
Drive, 2 or 1	Engine idling	Brakes applied	50 to 95 psi
Reverse	Engine idling	Brakes applied	60 to 150 psi

AOD

Range			Normal oil pressure
Neutral	Engine idling	Brakes applied	55 to 65 psi
Overdrive, Drive or 1	Engine idling	Brakes applied	55 to 65 psi
Reverse	Engine idling	Brakes applied	75 to 90 psi

Caution: *Do not exceed 2 minutes running time.*

Front wheel drive Oil Pressure Test Chart

ATX/FLC

Range			Normal oil pressure
Neutral	Engine idling	Brakes applied	80 to 95 psi
Drive	Engine idling	Brakes applied	80 to 95 psi
1st gear	Engine idling	Brakes applied	112 to 169 psi
Reverse	Engine idling	Brakes applied	93 to 152 psi

AXOD

Range			Normal oil pressure
Neutral	Engine idling	Brakes applied	80 to 95 psi
Overdrive or Drive	Engine idling	Brakes applied	80 to 95 psi
1st gear	Engine idling	Brakes applied	112 to 169 psi
Reverse	Engine idling	Brakes applied	93 to 152 psi

Caution: *Do not exceed 2 minutes running time.*

Typical diagnosis of high or low oil pressure

Note: *Not all conditions apply to all transmissions.*

Oil pressure low in all ranges

1   Check for a poor idle condition.
2   Check the transmission fluid level and condition.
3   Check the oil filter for blockage or a restriction.
4   Check for loose oil tubes.
5   Check for excessive leakage in the oil pump, case or valve body.
6   Check the TV exhaust ball for sticking or damage.
7   Check the pressure regulator valve for sticking.

Oil pressure high in all ranges

1   Check the line to the vacuum modulator for proper manifold vacuum.

2   Check the vacuum modulator for defects or a sticking control rod.
3   Check the throttle valve for sticking or improper adjustment.
4   Check the regulator boost valve for sticking.

Oil pressure low in Neutral only

1   Check for a leak in the valve body.

Oil pressure low in Drive, 2 or 1 only

1   Check for a leak in the forward/direct clutch, intermediate clutch or servo, or the reverse clutch or servo.

Oil pressure low in Reverse only

1   Check for a leak in the high/direct clutch, or the reverse clutch or servo.

5.6 Oil pressure test port location for the AOD

5.7 Oil pressure test port location - ATX/FLC

5.8 Oil pressure test port location - AXOD

Symptom-based troubleshooting

You can make an accurate diagnosis of a transmission problem from the symptom-based troubleshooting information listed below. This section list common symptoms along with their possible causes and items to check. Remember that many common transmission problems can be caused a variety of different components or systems. The troubleshooting information listed in this section can be helpful in inspecting the transmission components during an overhaul to determine the exact cause of the failure.

The information listed is general for all transmission types covered by this manual. Not all items apply to all transmission types, you must be familiar with your particular transmission components to make the correct diagnosis. For example; a defective modulator will not apply to an AOD because it's not equipped with a vacuum modulator system. Use the information from this section along with your road test results and oil pressure readings together to make a competent diagnosis.

Oil leaks

1   Check the oil pan for loose or missing bolts, a damaged or incorrectly installed gasket or a bent or warped sealing flange.
2   Check the oil filler pipe for a damaged or missing seal.
3   Check the throttle valve cable for an improperly installed or damaged seal.
4   Check the rear seal assembly for an improperly installed or damaged seal.
5   Check the drive shaft yoke for scoring or grooves.
6   Check the speedometer driven gear for a damaged shaft seal or O-ring seal.
7   Check the manual shaft for a damaged or incorrectly installed seal.
8   Check the case for a loose or missing line pressure tap plug.
9   Check the case for cracks or porosity.
10   Check the oil pump for loose or missing attaching bolts or a damaged front pump seal or housing O-ring.
11   Check the servo cover for a damaged gasket or seal.
12   Check the vacuum modulator for a damaged O-ring seal.

No movement in Drive range

1   Check the fluid for proper level, color and condition.
2   Check the manual linkage for proper adjustment.
3   Check the oil filter for a plugged or restricted screen.
4   Check the oil pump for a stuck pressure regulator or a damaged pump drive gear.
5   Check for proper oil control pressure.
6   Check for loose valve body.
7   Check the valve body for damaged or sticking valves.
8   Check for proper clutch and band application (see Road Test Application Charts).
9   Check the forward clutch for:
   a) *Worn or burned clutch plates.*
   b) *Damaged piston or seals.*
   c) *Forward clutch housing retainer and check ball not sealing or damaged.*
   d) *Forward clutch feed passage plugged or restricted.*
10   Check the low intermediate band for burned or broken ends.
11   Check the low intermediate servo for damage or loose oil tubes.

High or low shift points

1   Check the fluid for proper level, color and condition.
2   Check the engine for proper operation, especially the EGR system.
3   Check the TV cable for proper adjustment, binding or a broken cable.

4   Check the modulator vacuum line for damage, restrictions or leaks.
5   Check the vacuum modulator for defects or a sticking control rod.
6   Check the governor assembly for damage or a sticking governor valve.
7   Check for proper clutch and band application (see Road Test Application Charts).
8   Check the valve body assembly for dirty or sticking valves.
9   Check the speedometer gear for correct application.

Will not shift out of 1st gear

1   Check the fluid for proper level, color and condition.
2   Check the manual linkage for damage or misadjustment.
3   Check the TV cable or control rod for proper adjustment, binding or a broken cable/linkage.
4   Check the vacuum modulator vacuum line for leaks.
5   Check the vacuum modulator for defects or sticking.
6   Check the governor assembly for damage or a sticking governor valve.
7   Check the valve body for dirty or sticking valves.
8   Check the intermediate band assembly for a damaged or worn band or servo; or a band not adjusted properly.
9   Check the intermediate clutch for worn clutch plates or leaking piston seals.

Slips in 1st gear or during 1-2 shift

1   Check the fluid for proper level, color and condition.
2   Check the engine for proper performance.
3   Check the TV cable for proper adjustment, binding or a broken cable.
4   Check the intermediate band for proper adjustment, wear or damage. Check for a damaged servo.
5   Check the intermediate clutch for damaged piston seals or burned clutch plates.
6   Check the oil pump for proper control pressure (see oil pressure test).
7   Check the valve body for dirty or sticking valves.
8   Check the governor for damage or a sticking governor valve.

Rough, harsh, early or late 1-2 shift

1   Check the fluid for proper level, color and condition.
2   Check the engine for proper performance.
3   Check for proper oil control pressure.
4   Check the vacuum lines and make sure they're connected to the vacuum modulator and the proper engine source.
5   Check the vacuum modulator for defects or a sticking control rod.
6   Check the TV cable for proper adjustment, binding or a broken cable/linkage.
7   Check the governor assembly for damage or a sticking governor valve.
8   Check the valve body for dirty or sticking valves.
9   Check the intermediate band for proper adjustment.
10   Check the intermediate servo for damage.
11   Check the 1-2 accumulator for sticking regulator valve or broken spring.
12   Check the 1-2 accumulator for sticking modulator valve or broken spring.

No 2-3 shift

1   Check the fluid for proper level, color and condition.
2   Check the TV cable for proper adjustment, binding or a broken cable.
3   Check the direct clutch or reverse-high clutch for damaged piston seals or burned clutch plates.
4   Check the valve body for dirty or sticking valves.

5   Check the torque converter for internal damage.
6   Check the low intermediate servo for:

a) *Incorrect apply rod (too short)*
b) *Damaged piston or seals.*
c) *Damaged oil tubes*
d) *Damaged case bores*
e) *Broken or damaged return spring or retaining clip*

7   Check the direct one way clutch damaged or missing rollers.

Slipping, rough, early or late 2-3 shift

1   Check the engine for proper performance.
2   Check the vacuum lines and make sure they're connected to the vacuum modulator and the proper engine source.
3   Check for proper oil control pressure.
4   Check the vacuum modulator for defects or a sticking control rod.
5   Check the TV cable for proper adjustment, binding or a broken cable/linkage.
6   Check the valve body for dirty or sticking valves.
7   Check the 2-3 accumulator for:

a) *Damage.*
b) *Plugged or restricted apply passage.*
c) *Leaking or damaged seals.*

8   Check the intermediate servo for damage.
9   Check the high clutch piston check ball for sticking.
10   Check the direct clutch or reverse-high clutch for damaged piston seals or burned clutch plates.
11   Check the backout valve for damage.

No 3-4 shift

1   Check the fluid for proper level, color and condition.
2   Check the governor for:

a) *Governor valve sticking.*
b) *Damaged seal rings on the output shaft.*
c) *Deep scoring of the seal ring bore at the rear of the case.*
d) *Loose governor-to-output shaft retaining ring.*
e) *Loose governor counterweight on the output shaft.*
f) *Governor weights binding.*

3   Check the valve body for:

a) *Incorrectly adjusted or missing throttle valve cable/linkage.*
b) *Sticking or binding overdrive servo regulator valve, 3-4 shift valve, 3-4 TV modulator valve or orifice control valve.*
c) *Warped valve body or case sealing surface.*
d) *Bolts tightened to proper torque specifications.*
e) *Damaged, missing or incorrectly installed spacer plate or gaskets.*

4   Check the direct clutch for:

a) *Burned clutch plates.*
b) *Damaged or leaking piston seals.*
c) *Leaking piston check ball.*

5   Check the direct clutch-to-output shaft seal rings for damage or leakage.
6   Check the output shaft oil feed passages and cup plug for leakage.
7   Check the overdrive band for damage.

Harsh or delayed 3-4 shift; or slipping in 4th gear

1   Check the TV cable for proper adjustment, binding or a broken cable/linkage.
2   Check the valve body for dirty or sticking valves.
3   Check the valve body bolts for proper torque.
4   Check the 3-4 accumulator piston seals for wear or damage. Check the piston for a blocked drain passage.

5   Check the overdrive band for:

a) *Wear, damage or overheating.*
b) *Mislocated apply pin.*
c) *Not seated on anchor pin.*

6   Check the overdrive servo for:

a) *Leaking seals or O-rings.*
b) *Cracked or porous servo cover.*
c) *Servo apply passage blocked or restricted.*

7   Check the torque converter for internal damage.

No movement in reverse or slips in reverse

1   Check the fluid for proper level, color and condition.
2   Check the manual linkage for damage, misadjustment or proper installation.
3   Check for a plugged or restricted oil filter screen.
4   Check the oil pump assembly for worn or damaged gears.
5   Check the valve body assembly for dirty or sticking valves.
6   Check the valve body bolts for proper torque.
7   Check the high-reverse clutch or reverse clutch stator support seal rings for leaking or damage.
8   Check the reverse clutch assembly for:

a) *Worn or damaged clutch plates.*
b) *Leaking piston seals or piston check ball.*

9   Check the intermediate servo piston seals for leaking or damage.
10   Check the low-reverse servo piston seals for leaking or damage.
11   Check the low one-way clutch for damage.
12   Check the reverse band for misadjustment or damage.
13   Check for a leaking reverse apply tube.

No (or delayed) downshifts

1   Check the kickdown linkage or TV cable/linkage and bracket assembly for misadjustment, damage or correct installation.
2   Check the governor assembly for a stuck governor valve.
4   Check the valve body assembly for dirty or sticking valves.
5   Check the vacuum modulator system for proper operation.
6   Torque converter clutch does not disengage properly.

No engine braking in manual low or second

1   Check the manual linkage for proper adjustment.
2   Check the intermediate band for proper adjustment.
3   Check the intermediate servo for leaking seals.
4   Check the intermediate one-way clutch for damage.
5   Check the low-reverse band for proper adjustment.
6   Check the low-reverse servo for leaking seals.
7   Check for a glazed band or drum.

Drive range in neutral

1   Check the manual linkage and valve link for proper installation or link disconnected.
2   Check the case for cracks or machined surfaces warped.

Takes off in 2nd or 3rd gear

1   Check the governor assembly for damage or a stuck valve.
2   Check the valve body for dirty or sticking valves.
3   Check the valve body bolts for proper torque.
4   Check for cross leaks between the valve body or case oil passages.
5   Check the intermediate clutch pack for improper clearance.

Engine stalls when coming to a stop

1   Check the engine for proper performance.
2   Torque converter clutch not disengage properly.

Does not lock in Park

1　Check the parking linkage for proper adjustment.
2　Check for damaged park mechanism.

Transmission overheats

1　Check the fluid for proper level, color and condition.
2　Check the engine for proper performance.
3　Check for a restriction in the cooler or lines.
4　Check the valve body for dirty or sticking valves.
5　Check the torque converter for internal damage.
6　Check for improper clutch or band application (see Road Test Application Charts).

Transmission noisy

1　Check the fluid for proper level, color and condition.
2　Check the manual linkage for proper adjustment.
3　Check the driveplate-to-torque converter bolts for looseness.
4　Check the oil pump for internal leakage or damaged gears.
5　Check the valve body for dirty or sticking valves.
6　Check for damaged bushings, planetary gear set or one-way clutch.
7　Check for a damaged speedometer gear.
8　Check for cooler lines grounding on frame.

Chapter 6   Maintenance, adjustments and in-vehicle repairs

Fluid type recommendations

Rear wheel drive
  C3 and C4

Fluid and filter change

1   Changing the transmission fluid and filter is the single most important thing you can do to prolong the life of your transmission. Check your owner's manual for the manufacturer's recommended service intervals. Although factory recommendations are often less frequent, we recommend you change fluid and filter at least every 30,000 miles. Service the transmission sooner (every 15,000 miles) if the fluid shows signs of overheating (dark color, burnt smell), if the vehicle is operated in extreme heat conditions, used for towing or operated in continuous stop-and-go driving situations.

2   Before beginning, make sure you have all the necessary tools and supplies to complete the job. You'll need a large drain pan, the proper pan gasket and filter and enough of the correct fluid type. Approximate drain and refill capacities are as follows:

Rear wheel drive

C3 transmission	8 qts
C4 transmission	10 qts
C5 transmission	11 qts
C6 transmission	14 qts
AOD transmission	13 qts

Front wheel drive

ATX/FLC transaxle	8.3 qts (does not include all wheel drive)
AXOD transaxle	12.8 qts

3   The transmission fluid should be warm when drained, but not so hot as to burn you, so, when the vehicle is cold, drive the vehicle a few miles to warm up the fluid. Park the vehicle on a level cement or asphalt surface, raise the vehicle and support it securely on jackstands.

4   Place the drain pan under the transmission and loosen all the bolts 2 to 3 turns. Fluid should begin draining from around the pan; if not, tap the sides of the pan gently with a rubber mallet to break the gasket seal. Begin removing the bolts from the front of the pan, then work down the sides to the rear. The idea here is to allow the pan to hinge down from the rear, draining the fluid from the front edge **(see illustration)**. After most of the fluid has drained, remove the rear bolts, carefully remove the pan and drain the remaining fluid from the pan.

6.1   Pry the pan free of the gasket and allow the fluid to drain

5   On C4 and C6 transmissions, remove the screws from around the perimeter of the filter **(see illustration)**; C4s have 9 screws, while C6s have 11 screws. On C3 and AOD transmissions, remove the three screws retaining the filter to the valve body **(see illustration)**. On C5 transmissions, only one screw attaches the filter to the valve body. On ATX/FLC transaxles there are three bolts securing the filter to the bottom of the transmission **(see illustration)**. On AXOD transaxle there is simply a clip which must be pulled down to release the filter from the bottom of the transaxle **(see illustration)**.

6   Detach the filter and remove the filter grommet, O-ring or gasket from the transmission **(see illustration)**. **Note:** *In some instances the filter grommet, O-ring or gasket may be removed with the filter as the filter is removed, but typically tend to remain on the transmission. In either case, make sure the grommet, O-ring or gasket from the old filter does not remain attached to the transmission or the new filter grommet/gasket will not seal properly.*

7   On rear wheel drive transmissions, remove the torque converter cover (see Chapter 7, if necessary) and rotate the torque converter until the torque converter drain plug is at the bottom **(see illustration)**. Unscrew the drain plug and allow the fluid to drain out of the torque converter. **Note:** *Front wheel drive transaxles do not have a drain plug on the torque converter.*

8   Inspect the inside of the pan for pieces of metal or friction material that may indicate a problem. A small amount of clutch material is normal, but pieces of metal or piles of clutch material generally mean the transmission is close to failing. Remove all traces of gasket material from the transmission and oil pan sealing surfaces **(see illustration)** and clean the inside of the pan thoroughly with solvent. Wipe the transmission and pan sealing surfaces with lacquer thinner or acetone

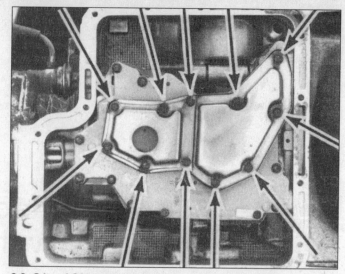

6.2 C4 and C6 transmissions have screws around the edge of the filter - C4s have 9 screws, while C6s (shown) have 11

and allow them to air-dry.

9   Inspect the oil pan for damage. Hammer out any dents and straighten the sealing flange, if necessary. Tap the bolt holes with the rounded end of a ball-peen hammer to eliminate any indentations caused by previous overtightening of the bolts.

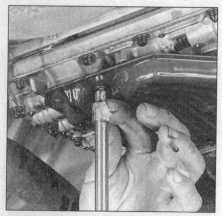

6.3 C3 and AOD transmissions have three screws securing the filter (AOD shown)

6.4 On some transaxles, the filter is held in place by bolts (arrows) . . .

6.5 . . . while others have a clip (arrow) which is pulled down to release the filter

6.6 If the old filter grommet or gasket remains attached the transmission, be sure to remove it before installing the new filter

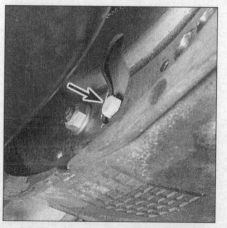

6.7 The torque converter drain plug (arrow) must be at the bottom prior to removal - rear wheel drive vehicles only

6.8 Be sure to clean all traces of old gasket material from the pan before installing a new gasket

6.9a Install the gasket, grommet . . .

6.9b . . . or O-ring on the filter, making sure it stays in place as the filter is installed

6.9c Note that AXOD transaxles use two O-rings on the filter tube

10   Install a new gasket or seal on the filter (see illustrations) and install the filter, tightening the screws securely - note that the filter can only be installed one way and some filters are marked "front."

Note: *AOD transmissions use a rubber seal and a cork gasket to seal the filter to the valve body. All other transmissions only have one or the other (a seal or a gasket).*

11   Install a new gasket on the oil pan. Gasket sealant is not recommended (especially since the pan will need to be removed frequently), although RTV sealant may be used between the gasket and oil pan, if desired. Install the oil pan and tighten the bolts to 10 ft-lbs. **Caution:** *Do not overtighten the oil pan bolts or leaks may develop.*

12   Fill the transmission with the recommended fluid. Add four quarts of fluid to the transmission at first, then start the engine and immediately add three more quarts of fluid (this is to replace some of the fluid that will now be in the torque converter). Holding your foot firmly on the brake, slowly shift the transmission through all the gear ranges, ending again in Park. Now check the fluid level, which will be low. Add fluid until the level is at the bottom of the operating range on the dipstick. C3 transmissions will usually take one more quart; C4 transmissions will usually take 2.6 to 3 more quarts; C5 transmissions will usually take four more quarts; C6 transmissions will usually take 4.7 to 6.5 more quarts; AOD transmissions will usually take 5.3 more quarts. If you have a deep pan, still more fluid may be required.

13   Test drive the vehicle, noting transmission operation and check the fluid level once more. Monitor the fluid level closely the next few trips.

Shift linkage adjustment

Note: *The transmission shift lever is controlled by shifting rod(s) or by a control cable. Typically most early model Ford vehicles are equipped with shifting rods and later model vehicles are equipped with a shift control cable. The procedure for adjusting either type of shift linkage is similar, although they physically appear different.*

1   Set the parking brake securely and block the wheels, since the vehicle's Park mechanism will be disengaged during this procedure.

2   Move the shift lever in the passenger compartment tightly against the stop in the Drive (on three speed transmissions), or in Overdrive position (on four speed transmissions). To ensure the shift lever stays against the stop during linkage adjustment, hang a weight from the shift lever (eight pounds on 1990 and earlier models; three pounds on 1991 and later models) or have an assistant apply a small amount of pressure to the lever.

3   Raise the vehicle and support it securely on jackstands.

4   Loosen the shift rod or cable adjusting nut (see illustrations). On some models equipped with a cable, it will be necessary to disengage the cable from the manual lever stud by prying it off.

5   On AOD transmissions, pull down the cable freeplay locking tab on the lower cable body end.

6   Shift the manual lever at the transmission into the Drive (three speed transmissions) or Overdrive (four speed transmissions) position by rotating the lever all the way to the rear, then forward 2 detents to

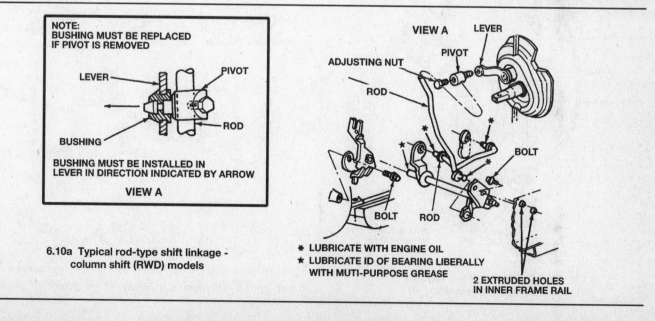

NOTE:
BUSHING MUST BE REPLACED IF PIVOT IS REMOVED

LEVER

PIVOT

BUSHING

ROD

BUSHING MUST BE INSTALLED IN LEVER IN DIRECTION INDICATED BY ARROW

VIEW A

6.10a Typical rod-type shift linkage - column shift (RWD) models

VIEW A

LEVER

PIVOT

ADJUSTING NUT

ROD

BOLT

BOLT

ROD

★ LUBRICATE WITH ENGINE OIL
★ LUBRICATE ID OF BEARING LIBERALLY WITH MUTI-PURPOSE GREASE

2 EXTRUDED HOLES IN INNER FRAME RAIL

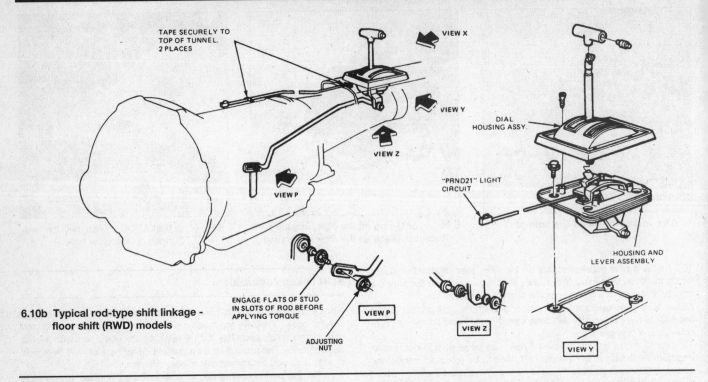

6.10b Typical rod-type shift linkage - floor shift (RWD) models

Drive or Overdrive. **Note:** *On AXOD transaxles the full rearward position for the manual lever is towards the driver side of the vehicle.*

7   On all transmissions except AOD using pry-off cable ends, tighten the adjusting nut or bolt securely with the selector lever and transmission manual lever both in Drive (on three speed transmissions) or Overdrive position (on four speed transmissions), Use care to prevent movement between the stud and the rod.

8   On AOD transmissions using pry-off cable ends, with the selector lever and transmission manual lever both in the Overdrive position, snap the shift cable onto the transmission lever ballstud and re-lock the cable freeplay locking tab by pushing the tab back into the cable body.

9   Release pressure from the shift lever in the passenger compart-ment or remove the weight. Check the operation of the shift lever in all positions to make sure the manual lever at the transmission is in full detent in all gear ranges. Readjust the linkage as required.

Kickdown linkage (C-series transmissions) - adjustment

Kickdown rod (early models)

1   Raise the vehicle and support it securely on jackstands.

2   Have an assistant hold the TV lever in the Wide Open Throttle (WOT) position (as far to the rear as possible). An alternative method is to hang approximately six pounds of weight onto the transmission

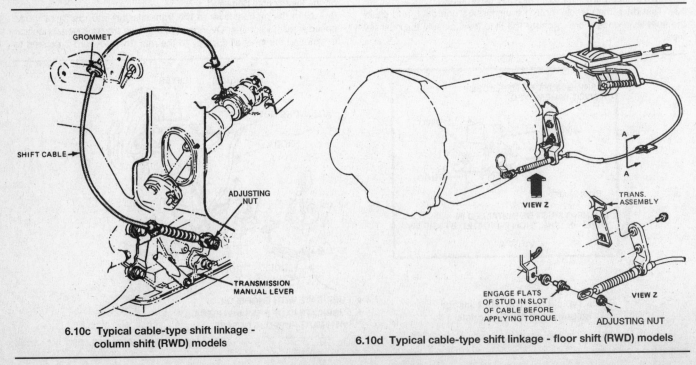

6.10c Typical cable-type shift linkage - column shift (RWD) models

6.10d Typical cable-type shift linkage - floor shift (RWD) models

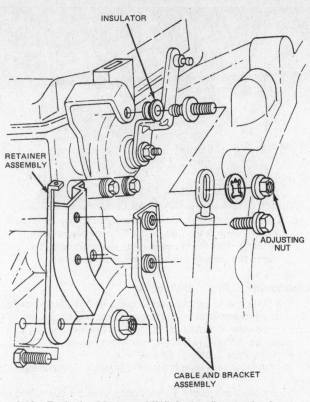

6.10e Typical cable-type shift linkage - floor and column shift (FWD) models

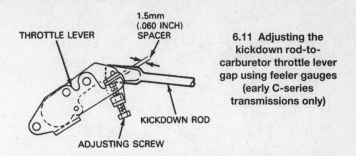

6.11 Adjusting the kickdown rod-to-carburetor throttle lever gap using feeler gauges (early C-series transmissions only)

tion). The feeler gauge should slide between the pieces with light resistance.

4   If necessary, adjust the screw until the proper feeler gauge resistance is obtained.

5   If used, remove the weight at the transmission kickdown lever.

6   Remove the jackstands and lower the vehicle. Test drive the vehicle to check for proper shift points and/or kickdown operation.

Kickdown cable (later models)

7   Ratchet the cable self-adjusting mechanism to obtain maximum outer conduit length **(see illustration)**.

8   Insert a 0.060-inch feeler gauge between the upper cable conduit body and the cable bracket on the conduit side of the bracket.

9   Set the cable length by opening the throttle to the wide open position. The self-adjuster should ratchet as the cable outer conduit shortens in length.

Throttle Valve (TV) linkage (AOD transmission) - adjustment

Note: *The AOD transmission does not have a vacuum modulator: shift points, shift firmness and downshift are all controlled by the TV linkage. Never operate a vehicle with an AOD transmission if the TV linkage is out of adjustment, since serious damage to the transmission can result.*

kickdown lever to hold it against the WOT stop.

3   Working in the engine compartment, hold the throttle lever in the wide open position and insert a 0.060-inch feeler gauge between the throttle lever and adjusting screw and check for proper fit **(see illustra-**

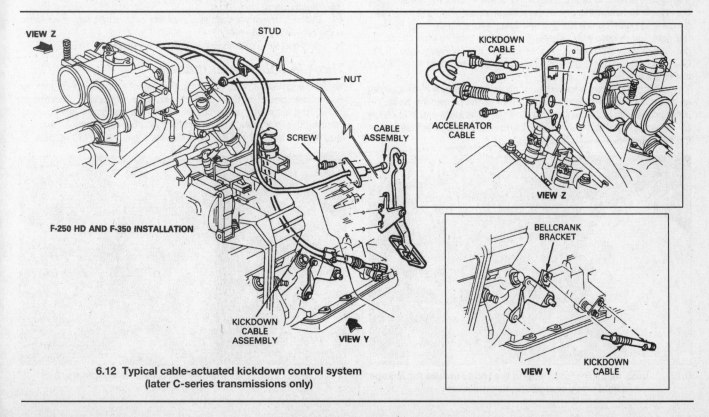

6.12 Typical cable-actuated kickdown control system (later C-series transmissions only)

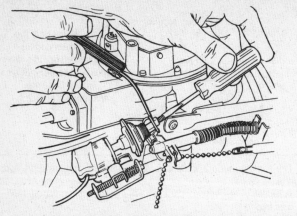

6.13 Adjusting the TV control rod at the carburetor or throttle body using a feeler gauge (early AOD only)

6.14 To adjust the TV rod at the transmission on early AOD models, loosen the bolt on the TV control rod sliding trunnion block and remove any dirt and corrosion from the control rod so the block slides freely . . .

Throttle rod (early models)

Adjustment at the carburetor or throttle body

1   If the throttle rod has not been removed and the lower rod-to-transmission lever relationship has not been disturbed, a minor adjustment at the carburetor/throttle body TV rod adjustment screw should be attempted prior to trying adjustment at the transmission.

2   Check that the engine idle speed has been properly set. **Note:** *Idle speed adjustments of 50 rpm or greater (either higher or lower) subsequent to TV adjustment require that the rod adjustment be checked and readjusted, if required.*

3   With the engine at normal operating temperature, verify the choke plate (carbureted models) is open and the throttle lever is resting on its idle stop.

4   Place the transmission in N (neutral) and set the parking brake.

5   Back out the throttle linkage TV adjusting screw until it's flush with the outside face of the lever.

6   Insert a 0.006-inch feeler gauge between the adjusting screw and the throttle lever and turn the adjusting screw in until the feeler gauge fits snugly between the pieces **(see illustration)**. Remove the feeler gauge and push the adjusting screw linkage forward (tending to close the gap) and release it to remove any residual friction, then check the gap again. **Note:** *When checking the gap, do not apply any load on the levers, as this will give a false gap measurement.* Re-adjust if necessary to get the proper gap.

7   After the gap has been set, turn the adjusting screw in (clockwise) an additional four complete turns to complete the procedure. **Note:** *If it is not possible to obtain at least two turns or if the initial gap is too wide for the adjustment screw to bridge, perform the linkage adjustment at the transmission.*

Adjustment at the transmission

8   The linkage lever adjusting screw has a limited adjustment range. If the above procedure fails to provide adequate adjustment, the length of the TV rod assembly must be adjusted, as follows:

9   Raise the vehicle and place it securely on jackstands.

10   Perform Steps 2 through 4 above.

11   Set the TV linkage lever adjustment screw at approximately midpoint.

12   Locate the transmission TV lever and loosen the control rod trunnion block set bolt to free the rod **(see illustration)**. Remove any corrosion or dirt that might prevent free movement of the block along the rod.

13   Push up on the control rod to seat the upper lever adjusting screw against the throttle lever, then release it **(see illustration)**.

14   Push the transmission's TV lever and trunnion block up until the transmission lever firmly bottoms against its internal stops. Hold the lever in this position and tighten the trunnion block set screw securely **(see illustration)**.

15   Perform adjustment at the carburetor or throttle body, as detailed in the previous procedure.

16   Remove the jackstands and lower the vehicle.

Throttle cable (later models)

17   On engines without Electronic Fuel Injection (EFI), check that the engine idle speed has been properly set. **Note:** *Idle speed adjustments of 150 rpm or greater (either higher or lower) subsequent to TV adjustment require that the cable adjustment be checked and readjusted, if required. Do not attempt to adjust the idle set screw on EFI models.*

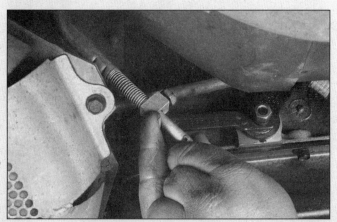

6.15 . . . push up on the lower end of the rod to ensure the linkage is held firmly against the throttle lever . . .

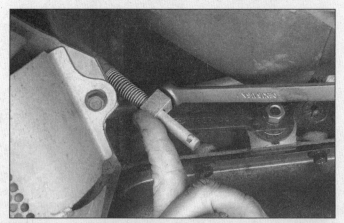

6.16 . . . and, while maintaining pressure, tighten the bolt

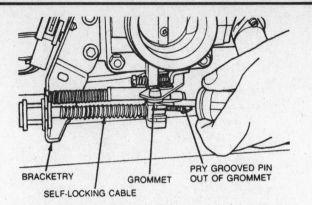

BRACKETRY   GROMMET   PRY GROOVED PIN
                                    OUT OF GROMMET
     SELF-LOCKING CABLE

**6.17 If you have this TV cable design, pry the TV cable pin
out with a screwdriver . . .**

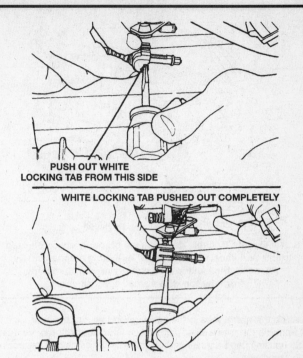

PUSH OUT WHITE
LOCKING TAB FROM THIS SIDE

WHITE LOCKING TAB PUSHED OUT COMPLETELY

6.18 . . . push out the white locking tab with a screwdriver . . .

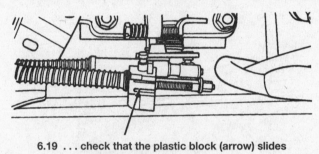

**6.19 . . . check that the plastic block (arrow) slides
freely on the notched rod . . .**

18   Verify the cable routing is free of sharp bends and that the cable operates freely.
19   On non-EFI engines equipped with idle positioning solenoids, make sure the solenoids are in the retracted (anti-diesel) position.
20   On carbureted engines (except 7200 Variable Venturi carburetors), if the engine is cold, decam the fast idle cam by first wedging the choke plate fully open, then open the throttle all the way and let it return to the idle stop. Verify the carburetor throttle lever is resting on its normal idle stop.
21   On 7200 Variable Venturi carburetors, if the engine is cold, decam the fast idle cam by retracting the choke control diaphragm linkage against choke spring tension and open the throttle to allow the cam to rotate to its normal idle position. Release the throttle and verify the throttle is resting on its normal idle stop.

Passenger cars

22   The engine should not be running and the throttle lever must be at its minimum idle stop during this adjustment.

23   Remove the air cleaner cover, inlet tube and any other components necessary to provide access to the TV cable at the carburetor or throttle body.
24   Pry the grooved pin on the cable assembly out of the grommet on the throttle body lever with a wide-bladed screwdriver **(see illustration)**.
25   Push the white locking tab out with a small screwdriver **(see illustration)**.
26   Make sure the plastic block with the pin and tab slides freely on the notched rod **(see illustration)**. If it doesn't, the white tab may not be pushed out far enough.
27   Hold the throttle lever firmly against the idle stop and push the grooved pin into the grommet on the throttle lever as far as it will go **(see illustration)**. Be sure not to move the throttle lever away from the idle stop during this procedure.
28   Install the air cleaner assembly.

Light trucks and vans

29   Place the transmission in N (neutral) and set the parking brake.
30   At the carburetor or throttle body, unlock the TV control cable self-adjusting lock mechanism at the end of the cable housing body by

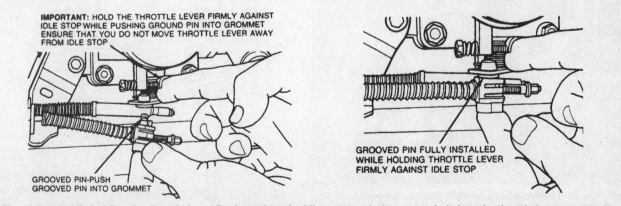

IMPORTANT: HOLD THE THROTTLE LEVER FIRMLY AGAINST
IDLE STOP WHILE PUSHING GROUND PIN INTO GROMMET
ENSURE THAT YOU DO NOT MOVE THROTTLE LEVER AWAY
FROM IDLE STOP

GROOVED PIN-PUSH
GROOVED PIN INTO GROMMET

GROOVED PIN FULLY INSTALLED
WHILE HOLDING THROTTLE LEVER
FIRMLY AGAINST IDLE STOP

6.20 . . . then, while holding the throttle lever firmly against the idle stop, push the grooved pin into the throttle lever grommet

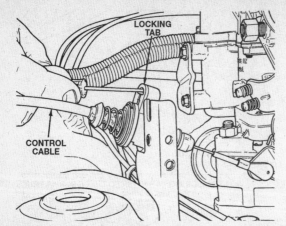

6.21a On this TV cable design, used primarily on carbureted trucks and vans, unlock the self-adjusting mechanism by releasing the locking tabs and prying the clamp out from the top with a small screwdriver

releasing the clamp tabs in the housing window and prying the clamp out from the top with a small screwdriver **(see illustrations)**. Verify the cable housing can be pushed freely towards the cable bracket against spring tension.

31   From under the vehicle, have an assistant hold the transmission TV lever against its idle position stop (as far to the rear as possible). The cable slack take-up spring will then set the proper cable length automatically. An alternative method is to install a suitable spring (or springs) to hold the lever rearward with about 10 pounds of force **(see illustration)**.

32   While still holding the transmission lever against the idle stop, lock the upper cable clamp in place by pushing the clamp back into the cable body until it's flush. **Note:** *Prior to re-locking the cable, verify the throttle lever is resting on its normal idle stop.*

33   If used, remove the transmission lever retention springs.

34   Remove the jackstands and lower the vehicle.

Throttle valve (TV) linkage (AXOD and ATX/FLC transaxles) - adjustment

AXOD transaxle

1   The AXOD TV cable should only require adjustment if the cable, the bracket, the transaxle, the main control assembly or the throttle control assembly have been disconnected or replaced.

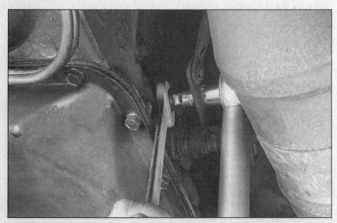

6.23 The front (intermediate) band is located at the left front of the transmission - when tightening, hold the adjustment screw so it can't move, then tighten the nut

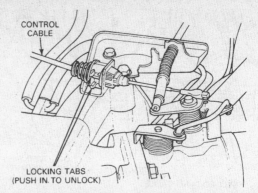

6.21b This TV cable design is primarily used on fuel-injected trucks and vans - push the locking tabs in to unlock them

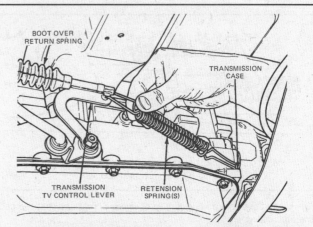

6.22 On later AOD-equipped trucks and vans with TV cables, springs are helpful when adjusting the cable - the springs should hold the transmission TV control lever to the rear with about 10 pounds of force

2   The TV cable eye must be connected to the throttle control lever link and the cable boot attached to the chain cover.

3   Make sure the threaded shank is retracted all the way with the cable mounted in the engine bracket. To retract it, hold the spring rest and wiggle the top of the threaded shank while pressing the shank

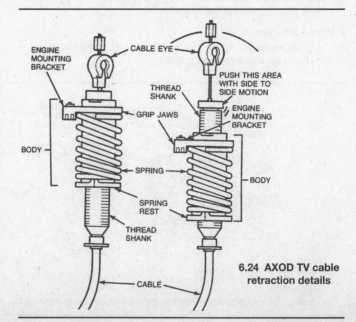

6.24 AXOD TV cable retraction details

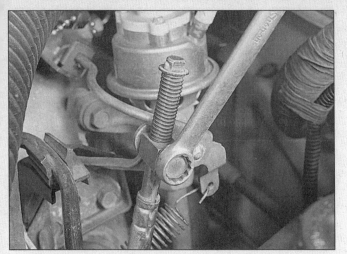

6.25 To adjust the ATX/FLC transaxles TV control linkage, loosen the bolt on the sliding trunnion block at least one turn . . .

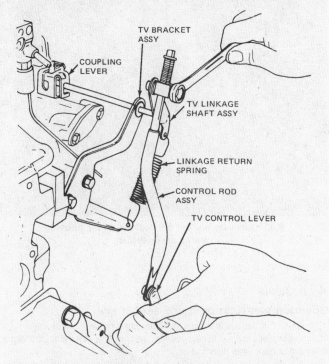

6.26 . . . then, using one finger, rotate the TV control lever at the transaxle up against the internal idle stop and tighten the bolt on the trunnion block

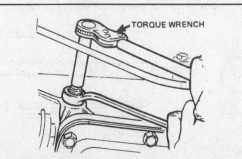

6.27 On C4 and C5 transmissions, you must also adjust the Low-and-Reverse band, which is located at the right rear of the transmission

through the spring **(see illustration)**.
4   Connect the end of the TV cable to the throttle body.
5   Rotate the throttle lever to the wide open throttle position and then release it. The threaded shank must move or "ratchet" out of the grip jaws. If it does not, check for broken or disconnected components and repeat the procedure.

ATX/FLC transaxles

6   Symptoms of the need for TV linkage adjustment on these models are early or erratic shifts and/or lack of downshifting.
7   With the engine idling at normal operating temperature, loosen the bolt on the sliding trunnion block of the TV control rod assembly at least one turn **(see illustration)**.
8   Remove any corrosion from the control rod and free up the trunnion block so it slides freely.
9   Rotate the TV control lever up, using one finger and light force to make sure the TV control lever is against the internal idle stop **(see illustration)**. Without relaxing the force on the TV control lever, tighten the bolt on the trunnion block securely.

Band adjustment (C-series transmissions)

Note: *No other transmissions covered by this manual require band adjustments.*
1   Because of normal band wear, bands require adjustment at approximately 15,000 mile intervals. Bands should also be adjusted whenever performance-related symptoms are noted. Normal wear can cause sluggish shifts, delayed shifts, slipping and, in extreme cases, a loss of drive.
2   Raise the vehicle and support it securely on jackstands.

Intermediate (front) band (C3, C4, C5 and C6)

3   The intermediate or front band is used to hold the sun gear stationary to produce Second gear. If it is not correctly adjusted, there will be noticeable slip during the First-to-Second gear shift or on the downshift from the Third-to-Second gear. The first symptoms of these problems will be very sluggish shifts.
4   To adjust the intermediate band, loosen, remove and discard the locknut on the band adjustment screw (located on the left-hand side of the case). Tighten the adjusting screw to 120 in-lbs (10 ft-lbs), then loosen it exactly 1-1/2 turns (1980 and earlier C3), 2 turns (1981 and later C3), 1-3/4 turns (C4), 4-1/4 turns (C5) or 1-1/2 turns (C6) **(see illustration)**. Install a new locknut and tighten it to 40 ft-lbs while holding the adjustment screw to keep it from turning.

Low and Reverse band (C4 and C5)

5   The Low and Reverse band is operational when the selector lever is placed in the Low or Reverse positions. If it is not correctly adjusted, there will be no drive with the selector lever in Reverse (also associated with no engine braking with the selector lever in Low).
6   To adjust this band, remove the adjusting screw locknut from the screw (located on the right-hand side of the case, at the rear) and discard it. Tighten the adjusting screw to 120 in-lbs (10 ft-lbs), then loosen it exactly three turns **(see illustration)**. Install a new locknut and tighten it securely while holding the adjusting screw to keep it from turning.

Seal replacement

Rear wheel drive

Extension housing (rear) seal

1   Raise the vehicle and support it securely on jackstands.
2   Remove the driveshaft (see Chapter 7).
3   Pry out the seal with a seal removal tool or use a large screwdriver and hammer to tap around the circumference of the seal, bending it in

6.28a Use a large screwdriver or prybar to pry the seal out of the transmission extension housing . . .

6.28b . . . or, if prying is difficult, carefully tap around the flange of the seal with a hammer and chisel until the seal can be pried off

6.29 A hammer and a large socket can be used to drive the new seal evenly into the bore

until it can be pried out with a screwdriver (see illustrations).

4   Lubricate the seal lip with ATF. Using a seal driver, a large socket or a section of pipe the exact diameter of the outer metal portion of the seal, drive the seal squarely into the bore with a hammer until it's flush with the end of the extension housing (see illustration).

5   Install the driveshaft and lower the vehicle.

Front wheel drive

Driveaxle seals

Caution: *Whenever both the right and left driveaxles are removed at the sane time on ATX/FLC transaxles, the differential side gears must be supported so they don't fall into the case (except on 4-speed automatic transaxles). A wooden dowel, approximately 15/16-inch in diameter, inserted into each side gear will work. If this precaution is not heeded and the side gears do drop, the differential will have to be removed from the transaxle to realign the gears (which will necessitate towing the vehicle to a Ford dealer service department or a repair shop).*

6   Refer to your Haynes auto repair manual and remove the driveaxle.

7   Pry the seal from the transaxle case with a large screwdriver or pry bar (see illustration). Be careful not to damage the case.

8   Coat the outer edge of the new seal with oil or grease, then position it in the bore and carefully drive it in with a hammer and large socket (if a socket isn't available, a section of pipe will also work) (see illustration).

9   Lubricate the seal lip with moly-base grease, then install the

6.30 Carefully pry the old seal out of the housing with a screwdriver

driveaxle.

All models

Speedometer gear or speed sensor seal

10   Raise the vehicle and support it securely on jackstands.

11   On models with a speed sensor, unplug the electrical connector from the sensor (see illustration).

6.31 Drive the new seal into the transmission case with a large socket (arrow) or piece of pipe - be careful not to cock the seal in the bore

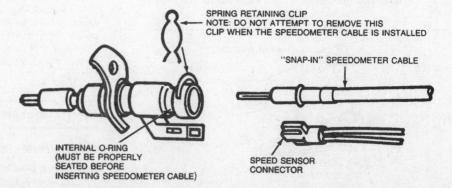

SPRING RETAINING CLIP
NOTE: DO NOT ATTEMPT TO REMOVE THIS
CLIP WHEN THE SPEEDOMETER CABLE IS INSTALLED

"SNAP-IN" SPEEDOMETER CABLE

INTERNAL O-RING
(MUST BE PROPERLY
SEATED BEFORE
INSERTING SPEEDOMETER CABLE)

SPEED SENSOR
CONNECTOR

6.32 Details of the speedometer driven gear housing

6.33 To replace the outer O-ring on the housing, pull it off with a hooked removal tool, as shown here

6.34 To get to the manual shaft seal, remove this nut (arrow) and detach the linkage

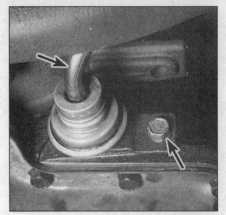

6.35 To remove the vacuum modulator, detach the vacuum line (arrow) and remove the hold-down bolt (arrow)

12 Remove the retaining bolt and clip.

13 Twist the housing back-and-forth to free the seal and pull it straight out of the case.

14 Inspect the speedometer gear for nicks, damaged teeth or a worn shaft and replace it if necessary. Be sure you replace it with the exact replacement gear or your speedometer calibration will be affected.

15 Using a small hooked tool, remove the O-ring from the housing **(see illustration)**. The internal O-ring can also be removed after removing the clip and cable.

16 Installation is the reverse of removal. Test drive the vehicle and check for leaks.

Filler tube seal

Note: *On some early C4 transmissions, the filler tube threads into the right side of the pan. On this filler tube design, there is no seal to replace - just make sure the filler tube is threaded tightly into the fitting on the pan.*

17 On all except early C4 transmissions, remove the dipstick from the tube. Raise the vehicle and support it securely on jackstands.

18 Remove the filler tube retaining bolt. On rear wheel drive vehicles this bolt is typically one of the bellhousing bolts. On front wheel drive AXOD transaxles it's located on the rear side of the transaxle case. On ATX/FLC transaxles it's located on the front side of the transaxle case.

19 Pull the tube straight out of the transmission case. Some filler tubes are in two sections, so remove the upper section first, then the lower section.

20 Remove the seal and install a new seal. **Note:** *On ATX/FLC transaxles the seal will remain in the transaxle case, remove the seal from case and install a new one.*

21 Lubricate the seal with ATF and press the tube into the case until it's fully seated.

22 Replace and tighten the filler tube retaining bolt, lower the vehicle and check the transmission fluid level.

Manual shaft seal

Note: *This procedure is for replacing the outer seal on all transmissions, except ATX/FLC transaxles. An inner O-ring type seal is also used on all transmissions, but replacement requires removal of the valve body and the manual shaft. Replacement of the inner seal and the outer manual shaft seal on ATX/FLC transaxles is covered as a part of overhaul.*

23 Raise the vehicle and support it securely on jackstands.

24 Disconnect the shift linkage and TV cable/linkage or the kickdown linkage at the transmission levers. Remove the nut retaining the manual lever and remove the lever from the manual shaft **(see illustration)**.

25 On C4, C5, C6 and AXOD transmissions, remove the neutral start switch.

26 Using a hooked tool, pry the seal from the transmission case, being careful not gouge the seal bore or the manual shaft.

27 Lubricate the new seal with ATF, then position it in the bore and carefully tap it in with a hammer and the appropriate sized socket (if a socket isn't available, a section of pipe will also work).

28 On C4, C5, C6 and AXOD transmissions, install the neutral start switch and the lever on the manual shaft, then adjust the neutral start switch as outlined in the following Section.

29 On C3 and AOD transmissions, simply install the manual lever and tighten the retaining nut.

30 Connect and adjust the shift linkage and the TV cable/linkage as described in the previous Sections, then lower the vehicle.

Vacuum modulator (rear wheel drive only) - replacement

1 Raise the vehicle and support it securely on jackstands.

2 Disconnect the vacuum line at the modulator. Inspect the rubber section of hose for cracks or deterioration and replace the hose, if necessary.

3 Remove the modulator bolt and clamp and remove the modulator **(see illustration)**.

4 If you'll be reinstalling the same modulator, remove the modulator O-ring and replace it with a new one **(see illustration)**. Lubricate the O-ring and replace the modulator.

5 Attach the vacuum line, lower the vehicle and check the vacuum line at the intake manifold. Replace the rubber section if it is cracked or deteriorated.

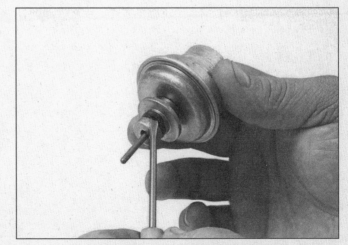

6.36 Remove the old modulator O-ring seal with a small screwdriver

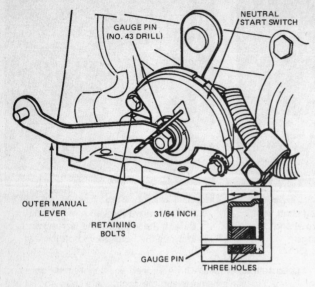

6.37 Neutral start switch adjustment details
(C4, C5 and C6 models)

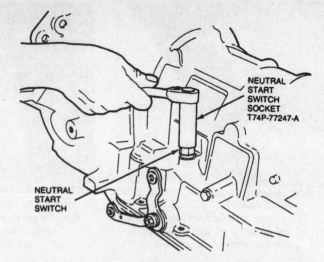

6.38 On C3 and AOD transmissions, the neutral start switch is not
adjustable. Since the switch is very fragile, use the special Ford
socket (part number TZ4P-77247-A), or equivalent, when
removing or installing the switch

Neutral start switch - adjustment and replacement

C4, C5, C6, AXOD and ATX/FLC transmissions

Adjustment

1   With the shift linkage properly adjusted (see the Section earlier in
this Chapter), loosen the two Neutral start switch retaining bolts **(see
illustration)**.

2   Place the shift lever in Neutral.

3   Rotate the switch and insert a No. 43 drill bit (shank end) into the
gauge pin holes of the switch. **Note:** *The drill shank must be inserted
through all three holes of the switch and that drill cannot be inserted as
far into the adjustment hole in any other gear as it can in Neutral.*

4   Tighten the switch retaining bolts securely, then remove the drill
bit from the switch.

5   Check the operation of the switch. The back-up lights should
come on only when the transmission is in Reverse and the engine
should start only with the transmission lever in Park or Neutral.

Replacement

6   Remove the retaining bolts described in Step 1.

7   Remove the nut at the center of the switch and disconnect the
manual lever from its shaft.

8   Disconnect the neutral start switch electrical connector and carefully pull the switch off the manual shaft.

9   Installation is the reverse of removal. Be sure to adjust the new
switch after installation.

C3 and AOD transmissions

Adjustment

10   There is no adjustment possible on this switch design. If the
switch does not function to allow starting in Park or Neutral only,
replace the switch.

Replacement

11   A special tool is required to replace this switch design, since the
housing of the switch is very fragile. Disconnect the electrical connector, attach the special tool to a ratchet and carefully unscrew the
switch from the housing **(see illustration)**. When installing the new
switch, use a new O-ring and tighten it to approximately 10 ft-lbs.

Chapter 7
Transmission removal and installation

This is the dirtiest part of the overhaul (don't wear clothes you care about!) and the part that will require the most planning - read through this entire Chapter before beginning work, since you'll need some special tools and equipment. The most important piece of equipment is a transmission jack, which can usually be rented from an equipment rental yard. During removal and installation, the higher you can safely raise the vehicle, the easier and cleaner the job will be.

Removal

Rear wheel drive

1   Disconnect the negative cable from the battery, then remove the transmission fluid dipstick. Place the gear selector lever in Neutral. On early four-wheel drive models (NP208, BW13-56 and BW13-45 transfer cases), get inside the vehicle and remove the shifter floor pan cover, then unbolt and remove the upper transfer case shift lever.
2   Raise the vehicle and support it securely on jackstands. Since the transmission will need to be slid out from under the vehicle, support both the front and rear of the vehicle with four sturdy jackstands. Raise the vehicle as high as safely possible.
3   Before removing the transmission, check the transmission mount to see if it will need replacement. To check the mount, insert a large screwdriver or pry bar into the space between the transmission and the crossmember and try to pry the transmission up slightly **(see illustration)**. The transmission should not move away from the insulator much. If the mount moves appreciably or there is any separation of the rubber, the mount is worn out; remove the mount from the transmission in Step 26 and replace it on installation. **Note:** *Transmission mounts are subjected to considerable stress and transmission fluid leaks cause them to deteriorate rapidly. It's wise to replace the mount routinely at overhaul time.*
4   Drain the transmission fluid and reinstall the pan. On four-wheel drive models, also drain the transfer case lubricant.
5   Disconnect the TV and shift linkage from the arms on the transmission. Most connections use a nylon retainer and are easily disconnected by prying the rod off the arm on the transmission with a screwdriver **(see illustration)**. Other connections may use retainer clips or

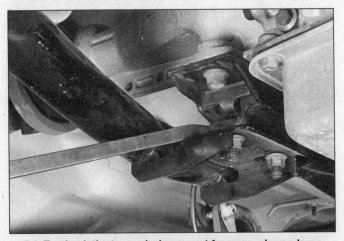

7.1 To check the transmission mount for wear, place a large screwdriver or pry bar between the crossmember and the mount and try to pry up on the transmission - it shouldn't move much. Excessive movement means the transmission mount needs replacement

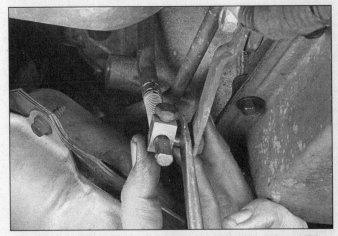

7.2 When nylon retainers are used to retain the shift and TV linkage, you can use a large screwdriver to pry the linkage from the arms on the transmission. Some models use clips or pins, which can be removed with pliers

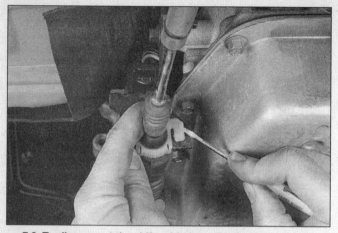

7.3 To disconnect the shift cable from this bracket, pop the retainer clip positioning pin loose with a small screwdriver, then pry off the retainer clip

7.4 To remove the torque converter cover, remove the bolts (arrows)

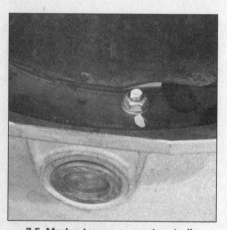

7.5 Mark a torque converter stud's relationship to the driveplate to ensure that they're still in dynamic balance when reassembled

7.6 With the engine locked from turning, use a socket and extension to remove the torque converter nuts

7.7a The starter wire(s) are connected with nuts to the terminals at the top of the starter

pins. If nylon retainers are used, it's best to use new retainers on reassembly. On some models, the shift cable housing will also need to be disconnected from the transmission **(see illustration)**.

6   Remove the torque converter cover **(see illustration)**.

7   Mark the torque converter stud and the driveplate with a scribe or chalk so they can be installed in the same position **(see illustration)**.

8   Remove the driveplate-to-torque converter nuts - there are usually four **(see illustration)**. Turn the crankshaft (in a clockwise direction only, viewed from the front) for access to each bolt.

9   Disconnect the wires from the electrical terminals on the starter motor, then remove it **(see illustrations)**.

10   Remove the driveshaft **(see illustrations)**. If the vehicle is equipped with four-wheel drive, remove the front driveshaft also.

11   If the vehicle has a speedometer cable, disconnect it **(see illustration)**. If it has a vehicle speed sensor, unplug the electrical connector.

12   Unplug the neutral start switch electrical connector and any remaining wire harness connectors from the transmission.

13   On all except the AOD transmission, disconnect the vacuum hose from the vacuum modulator on the side of the case, toward the rear of the transmission.

14   If there's a steel vacuum tube for the vacuum modulator on the side of the transmission, disconnect it from the clip(s) on the transmission and position the tube to the side, out of the way.

15   Look at the exhaust system to see if it will interfere with transmission removal. Often you can remove the transmission without disturb-

ing the exhaust system, but sometimes you'll have to disconnect the pipe(s) from the exhaust manifold(s) **(see illustration)**. If clearance still looks tight, disconnect the exhaust system hangers and remove the exhaust system from the vehicle.

Four-wheel drive models only

Note: *We recommend removing the transfer case before removing the transmission, as described here, since the transmission/transfer case assembly can be very cumbersome to remove together as a unit.*

16   Remove the skid plate under the transfer case, if equipped. Also unbolt and remove the transfer case-to-engine support strut(s).

17   If not already done, disconnect the shift linkage from the transfer case. On some models, the shift rod snaps into place on the transfer case lever and can be disconnected by prying it loose with a screwdriver. On other models you'll have to remove a clip or a nut. On models where a rubber boot covers the lower shift lever, move the boot out of the way and unbolt the lever from the case.

18   Support the transfer case with a jack, preferably a jack designed for this purpose. Use safety chains to secure the transfer case to the jack.

19   Remove the bolts and/or nuts securing the transfer case to the transmission **(see illustration)**.

20   Make a final check that all cables, wires and shift linkage are disconnected from the transfer case, then move the jack to the rear until the transfer case input shaft is clear of the transmission. Lower the transfer case and remove it from under the vehicle.

7.7b The starter is attached to the transmission bellhousing with two or three bolts (arrows)

7.8a Mark the relationship of the driveshaft to the differential companion flange to ensure that the driveshaft retains its dynamic balance after reinstalling it

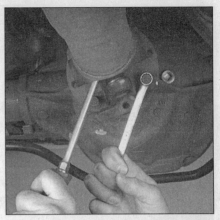

7.8b To remove the bolts that attach the driveshaft to the differential companion flange, insert a small prybar or large screwdriver through the rear U-joint and hold the driveshaft while you break loose the four bolts or nuts

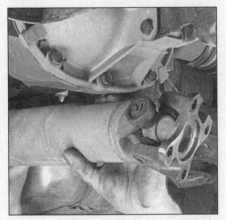

7.8c Lower the driveshaft and pull it to the rear

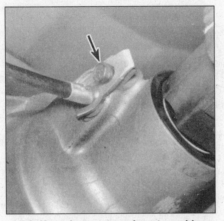

7.9 If you have a speedometer cable, remove the bolt and retainer (arrow) and pull the cable and driven gear out of the transmission case. If you have a speed sensor, simply disconnect the electrical connector

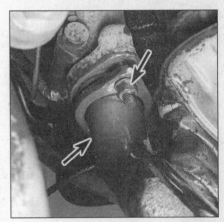

7.10 Remove the nuts (arrows) that hold the exhaust pipe flange to the exhaust manifold

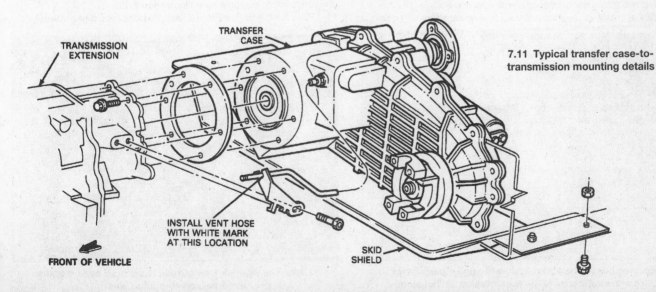

7.11 Typical transfer case-to-transmission mounting details

TRANSMISSION EXTENSION

TRANSFER CASE

INSTALL VENT HOSE WITH WHITE MARK AT THIS LOCATION

FRONT OF VEHICLE

SKID SHIELD

7.12 A special transmission jack, like the one shown here, is the only safe way to remove an automatic transmission

7.13 Remove the two nuts (lower arrows) that attach the transmission mount to the crossmember; if you'll be replacing the mount, remove the bolts (upper arrows) and remove the mount

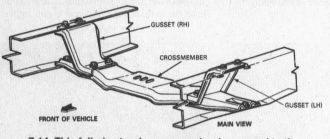

7.14 This full-size truck crossmember is secured to the frame rails by six bolts and nuts . . .

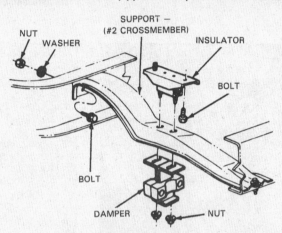

7.15 . . . while this crossmember is secured by only three bolts and nuts

All rear wheel drive models

21   Support the engine with a jack. Use a block of wood under the oil pan to spread the load. Keep the engine supported during the entire time the transmission is out of the vehicle so you don't strain the engine mounts.

22   Support the transmission with a jack - preferably a jack made for this purpose **(see illustration)**. Safety chains will help steady the transmission on the jack.

23   If equipped, unbolt any support struts attached to the transmission.

24   Remove the rear transmission mount-to-crossmember nuts **(see illustration)**.

25   Remove the crossmember-to-frame nuts and bolts. Some models may have as many as six bolts and nuts **(see illustration)** that must be removed to disconnect the crossmember from the frame rails, while some may have only three bolts **(see illustration)** or two long through-bolts, one on each side.

26   Raise the transmission with the jack enough to allow removal of the crossmember. If you'll be replacing the transmission mount, unbolt and remove it at this time **(see illustration 7.13)**.

27   Remove the transmission-to-engine bolts **(see illustrations)**.

7.16a Remove all the transmission-to-engine bolts (arrows) from the perimeter of the transmission bellhousing

7.16b The dipstick tube (arrow) is secured by one of the transmission-to-engine bolts

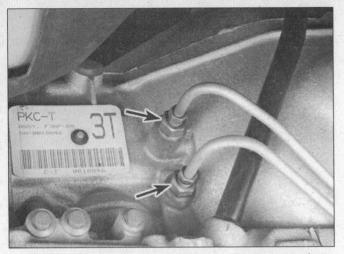

7.17 After lowering the transmission, use a flare-nut wrench to disconnect the cooler lines (arrows) and plug them to prevent fluid loss. It may be necessary to use a back-up wrench on the transmission-side fittings to prevent twisting the lines

7.18 A combination wrench bolted to one of the mounting bolt holes will secure the torque converter during removal

28   Lower the transmission slightly and, using a flare-nut wrench, unscrew the flare-nuts on the transmission fluid cooler lines from the fittings on the transmission case **(see illustration)**. Use a back-up wrench to hold the fittings threaded into the transmission case steady while you unscrew the flare-nuts on the lines. After disconnecting the lines, plug the cooler lines to prevent fluid leakage. An easy way to plug the lines is to connect a short piece of 3/8-inch diameter fuel hose between the two disconnected lines.

29   Remove the transmission dipstick tube by pulling it straight up, out of the transmission housing.

30   Move the transmission to the rear to disengage it from the engine block dowel pins and make sure the torque converter is detached from the driveplate. Secure the torque converter to the transmission so it won't fall out during removal. One way to secure the torque converter is to clamp a pair of Vise Grips onto the transmission housing, just in front of the torque converter. Another way is to bolt a long 15 mm or 9/16-inch combination wrench onto the front of the transmission, using one of the lower transmission-to-engine bolt holes **(see illustration)**. Use a large washer on the bolt and put it through the box end of the wrench, with the angle on the wrench pointing toward the rear of the vehicle. Place the open end of the wrench near the center of the torque converter. When you put the bolt into the transmission bolt hole, put a nut on the other end and tighten it, the wrench will press against the converter, holding it securely in the transmission.

Front wheel drive

Note 1: *The engine on front wheel drive vehicles must be supported from above when the transaxle is removed. This is done with a bar-type fixture that rests on the fender flanges. The engine is suspended from the fixture with brackets or chains so the transaxle can be removed. In addition, automatic transaxles are heavy and awkward to handle and a transmission jack should be used to remove and install the unit because the transaxle will not balance on a regular floor jack. Both the engine support fixture and a transmission jack can be rented from some auto parts stores and most equipment rental companies.*

Note 2: *On 1984 and 1985 Tempo/Topaz models equipped with an ATX transaxle and a 2.3L HSC engine, the engine and transaxle must be removed as an assembly. If any attempt is made to remove either component separately, damage to the transaxle or to the lower engine compartment structure may result. Refer to your Haynes automotive repair manual for this procedure.*

Warning: *Do not work or place any part of your body under the car when it is supported only by a jack. Jack failure could result in severe injury or death.*

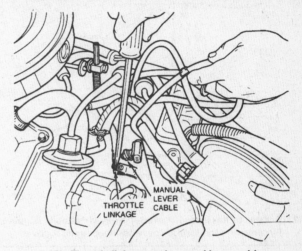

7.19a Throttle linkage and manual lever cables (ATX/FLC transaxles)

7.19b On AXOD transaxles, disconnect the TV cable from the throttle lever by lifting it off the lever flange . . .

31   Disconnect the negative battery cable from the battery.

32   Remove the air cleaner if necessary to provide access for transmission removal.

33   Disconnect the throttle valve linkage. Also remove the shift cable and bracket from the transaxle **(see illustrations)**.

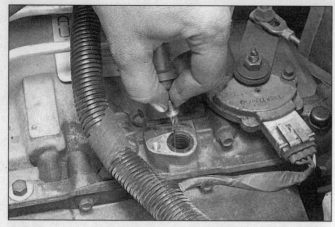

7.19c . . . then at the other end, remove the bolt, pull up and disengage the hooked end

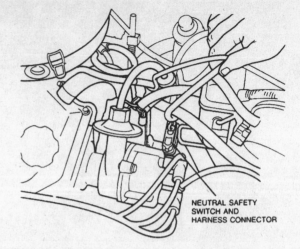

NEUTRAL SAFETY
SWITCH AND
HARNESS CONNECTOR

7.20 Unplug the electrical connector for the neutral safety switch (ATX/FLC transaxle shown)

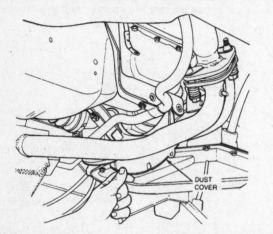

DUST
COVER

7.21 Access to the torque converter-to-flywheel bolts is gained by removing the torque converter housing dust cover

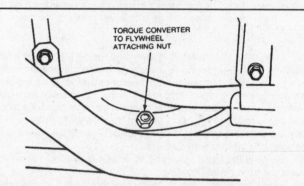

TORQUE CONVERTER
TO FLYWHEEL
ATTACHING NUT

7.22 Turn the crankshaft pulley with a wrench on the pulley bolt to bring each of the torque converter-to-flywheel bolts to an accessible position - if you remove the spark plugs it will let the engine rotate easier

34   Loosen the front wheel nuts. Raise the vehicle and position it securely on jackstands. DO NOT get under a vehicle that is supported only by a jack! Remove the front wheels and drain the transmission fluid.
35   Disconnect the electrical connector from the neutral safety switch **(see illustration)**. On AXOD transaxles also disconnect the electrical connectors at the rear of the transaxle.
36   Remove the steering gear tie-rod nuts and detach the tie rods from the steering knuckles.
37   Remove and discard the balljoint clamp bolt on each side of the vehicle, then disengage the lower suspension arms from the steering knuckles.
38   Remove the stabilizer bar.
39   Pry the right-hand driveaxle from the transaxle and support it with wire. Do not allow it to hang by its own weight. **Note:** *On some models, it will also be necessary to remove the bolts and detach the intermediate shaft from the right side of the transaxle.*
40   Remove the left driveaxle. Support the driveaxle with wire; do not allow it to hang by its own weight. **Note:** *On ATX/FLC transaxles, use a long narrow punch or screwdriver inserted through the right hand differential side gear to drive the left driveaxle stub shaft outward just far enough to unseat the driveaxle circlip from the transaxle side gear (be careful not to damage the pinion gear shaft). Then install the seal plug (Ford tool T81P-1177-B or equivalent) into the right driveaxle hole. Remove the left driveaxle and insert another seal plug or wooden dowel into the left driveaxle hole. If the plugs are not available, install 15/16-inch wood dowels. Plugs or dowels must be installed or the differential side gears could drop displacing the side gears and the side gear shims.*
41   Remove the starter.

42   Remove the torque converter housing dust cover **(see illustration)**.
43   Turn the crankshaft with a socket on the pulley bolt to bring each of the torque converter-to-flywheel nuts into view **(see illustration)**. Remove the nuts.
44   Support the engine from above with a three bar support fixture **(see illustrations)**.

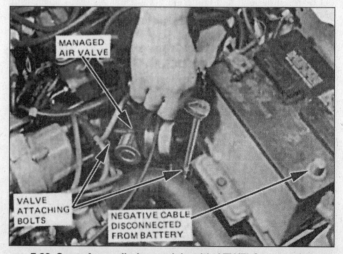

MANAGED
AIR VALVE

VALVE
ATTACHING
BOLTS

NEGATIVE CABLE
DISCONNECTED
FROM BATTERY

7.23 Some four cylinder models with ATX/FLC transaxles are equipped with a managed air valve - unbolt it from the top of the transaxle

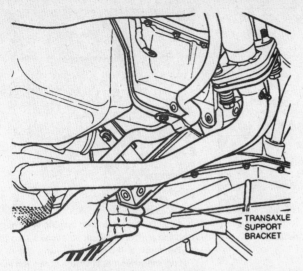

7.24 On Tempo/Topaz/Escort/Lynx and EXP models, remove the transaxle support bracket . . .

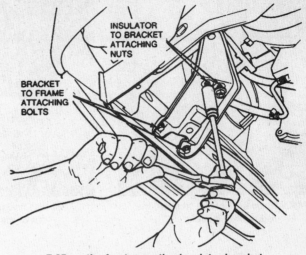

7.25 . . .the front mounting insulator bracket . . .

Tempo/Topaz/Escort/Lynx and EXP models

45   If the vehicle has a managed air thermactor valve attached to the transaxle top cover, unbolt it **(see illustration)**. Remove the thermactor hose retaining bolts as needed and position the hoses out of the way.

46   Remove the ground strap above the upper engine mount (if equipped).

47   Remove the ignition coil and bracket (if applicable).

48   Unbolt the brake hose clip from the suspension strut on each side of the vehicle.

49   Unbolt and remove the transaxle support bracket **(see illustration)**.

50   Place a transmission jack beneath the transaxle. Make sure the transaxle is securely supported, then remove the attaching nuts and bolts and take out the left front mounting insulator bracket **(see illustration)**.

51   Remove the rear support bracket nuts **(see illustration)**.

Taurus and Sable models

52   On ATX transaxles (four-cylinder models), remove the timing window plug and rotate the crankshaft until the timing marker on the flywheel lines up with the timing pointer. Mark the crankshaft at the 12 o'clock (TDC) position and then rotate the crankshaft pulley mark 180 degrees to the 6 o'clock (BDC) position. This step is taken as a precautionary measure to avoid damaging the timing pointer at the rear of the engine as the transaxle is removed.

53   Remove the power steering hose retaining bracket.

54   Remove the transaxle dipstick.

55   Remove the left side inner front fender liner.

56   On ATX transaxles (four cylinder models), remove the exhaust air hose assembly.

57   Remove the front exhaust pipe.

58   Detach the bolts securing the steering gear to the engine sub-frame leaving the steering gear attached to the steering column. Position the steering gear aside and hang it up with a piece of wire.

59   Unbolt the engine and transaxle mounts from the engine sub-frame. Place a floor jack beneath the sub-frame, making sure the sub-frame is securely supported, then remove the sub-frame retaining bolts and lower the sub-frame to the ground.

All front wheel drive models

60   Unbolt the shifter cable bracket from the transaxle case **(see illustration)**.

61   Disconnect the fluid cooler lines at the transaxle. On most models, a special tool (available at auto parts stores) is required to disconnect the lines; don't try to unscrew quick connect type fittings. Insert

7.26 . . . and the rear mounting insulator bracket with the engine supported securely from above

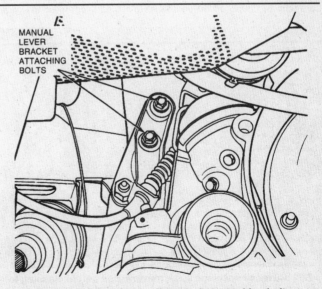

7.27 Remove the shifter cable bracket attaching bolts

7.28a Push the special tool into the fitting until it clicks . . .

7.28b . . . and pull the tool and line out of the transmission

7.29 Transmission-to engine retaining bolts are often difficult to access - so take your time and be patient! - the use of a long extension and a swivel are usually necessary when removing these bolts

the tool into the fitting until a click (indicating the internal retainer has disengaged) is felt and pull the tool and fitting out **(see illustrations)**.

62   Support the transaxle with a jack - preferably a jack made for this purpose **(see illustration 7.12)**. Safety chains will help steady the transaxle on the jack.

63   Remove the transaxle-to-engine bolts **(see illustration)**.

64   Carefully insert a screwdriver between the driveplate and torque converter and pry the engine and transaxle apart until the torque converter studs clear the driveplate.

65   Lower the transaxle 2 to 3 inches and disconnect the speedometer cable or the vehicle speed sensor.

66   Check to be sure all hoses and wires are disconnected, then lower the transaxle out of the vehicle.

Cleaning

The transmission you've just removed has undoubtedly accumulated a lot of grease and grime. To make the overhaul a cleaner experience for you and to prevent any of this crud from winding up inside the transmission, it's essential to clean the transmission now.

Steam cleaning is the best method, but this expensive equipment is not normally available to the do-it-yourselfer. Aerosol cleaning solvents are readily available from auto parts stores. These solvents that spray on and hose off do an adequate job and represent the most

cost-effective alternative to steam cleaning.

Before cleaning, seal up all openings in the transmission - at the input shaft, output shaft, cooler line connections, etc. - so no solvent or water winds up inside the transmission **(see illustration)**. Then follow the solvent manufacturer's label instructions. Generally, you'll spray on the solvent, allow it to soak in for about ten minutes, then scrub the surfaces with a stiff brush (be sure to wear gloves!). When all grime has been loosened, spray off the solvent with a garden hose and allow the transmission to air-dry.

Flushing the transmission cooler

The transmission cooler in your radiator, as well as the lines leading to and from it, now contain burned transmission fluid and debris such as clutch material and metal particles that were deposited by your failing transmission. If you don't flush out this gunk, it will wind up inside your newly rebuilt transmission and possibly damage it - flushing the cooler is essential at overhaul time.

The best way to flush the cooler is with a special tank-type flushing machine. Transmission shops have these machines, but it's generally not practical to tow your vehicle into a shop just to have the cooler and lines flushed.

The best at-home method we found is to use an electric drill-pow-

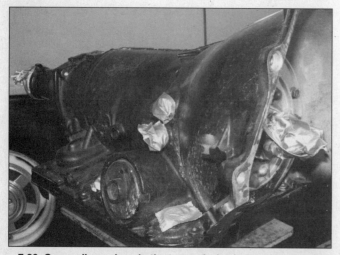

7.30 Cover all openings in the transmission before cleaning to prevent entry of water and dirt

7.31 Drill-operated pumps work well for flushing coolers - set up like this, the pump will circulate solvent from the container, through the cooler and back to another container

7.32 Support the converter with both hands and slide it straight out of the transmission. Some fluid may drain out during removal, so be prepared to tilt the converter rear-side-up as soon as it clears the input shaft

ered fluid pump. These pumps are commonly available from hardware stores at a reasonable price. Fill up a bucket or similar container with solvent and connect the suction side of the pump to a short hose, placing the other end of the hose in the bucket. Connect another short hose between the pump outlet and one of the cooler lines, then connect a hose from the other cooler line, placing the other end of the hose in the bucket **(see illustration)**. Run the pump until the solvent coming out of the return line comes out clean. Then disconnect the pump and blow compressed air through the cooler line until no more solvent comes out the other line. If solvent does not flow through to the return line, the cooler is plugged, and you'll need to either replace the radiator or take the cooler to a transmission shop to have it unplugged.

After flushing the cooler with solvent and blowing it out with compressed air, use the pump to circulate some new ATF through the cooler. This will ensure that all solvent has been purged from the cooler. If you don't have a drill-powered pump, an alternative method is to use a hand-type pump, such as the kind that come with large containers of gear oil.

Before assuming your cooler is now good to go, check to see if there is a leak. Generally speaking, a leak will cause transmission fluid in the engine coolant and/or coolant in the transmission fluid (which

will generally show up as fluid that looks like a strawberry milkshake). To test the cooler, securely plug the end of one of the cooler lines, then apply compressed air at about 30 psi to the other line. Remove the radiator cap and look for bubbles in the engine coolant. Any bubbles at all are an indication there is a leak and the cooler will need to be repaired or the radiator replaced. Continue to apply pressure for ten minutes or so while you watch the radiator opening.

Flushing and inspecting the torque converter

Note: *We recommend routinely replacing the torque converter at overhaul time. Torque converters generally are well worn by overhaul time, and it would be a shame to destroy a newly overhauled transmission by re-installing a failing converter that's sending pieces of metal throughout the transmission. Remanufactured torque converters are generally available at a reasonable price.*

After removing the transmission and placing it on your workbench, remove the torque converter. The torque converter is easily removed from the transmission by supporting it securely and pulling it straight out of the front pump **(see illustration)**. Immediately after removing the converter, turn it front side down so no fluid leaks out. Next, overturn the converter in a bucket or pan that can hold at least four quarts and allow the converter to drain **(see illustration)**.

If you're planning to re-use the same torque converter, it's important to flush it thoroughly so no burned fluid, metal particles or clutch material wind up in your newly rebuilt transmission. Transmission shops have a machine that flushes the converter with solvent while it spins the turbine to assure good agitation that will break loose particles of gunk. You can simulate this operation at home (though not nearly as well) by filling the converter with solvent and using snap-ring pliers to spin the turbine (the last splined hub you see when looking down the opening) as best you can. After letting the converter sit for about an hour, spin the turbine with the pliers and drain the solvent, then repeat the whole operation until the solvent comes out clean. If any metal particles come out of the converter, the converter must be replaced. Finally, repeat the procedure with new ATF.

First check the drive studs on the converter. There should be four welded-on studs that allow the driveplate to be bolted to the converter. If the base of any stud is cracked, or the stud is loose or has damaged threads, it's best to replace the converter rather than try to repair the stud. Since the studs assure correct alignment with the driveplate, vibration can result from a damaged or deformed stud.

Next, check the converter hub for scoring or nicks **(see illustration)**. Light scoring can be removed by polishing with 600-grit sandpa-

7.33 Overturn the converter in a bucket or similar container to drain it

7.34 Inspect the hub area (arrow) carefully. This is where the front seal rides, so it must be smooth, with no ridge. The converter must be replaced if this surface has a groove or nicks that won't polish out with 600-grit sandpaper

7.35 Operation of the stator one-way clutch can be checked with large snap-ring pliers

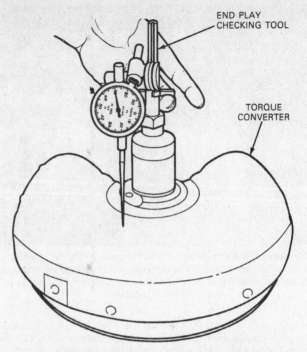

7.37 Measuring converter endplay with a special tool

per (cover the opening to make sure nothing enters the converter during polishing), but any significant scoring means the converter will have to be replaced. Since the transmission front seal rides on the converter hub, a worn or damaged hub means your freshly overhauled transmission will almost surely leak.

Check also for leaks and damage to the converter case. Any dents or cracks will necessitate converter replacement. Check very carefully and look for signs of leakage, particularly at the weld that runs the circumference of the converter and the weld that attaches the hub to the rear shell of the converter.

The first operational check is for correct functioning of the stator one-way clutch. This check can be done with a large pair of snap-ring pliers **(see illustration)** or with the transmission front pump cover (refer to the appropriate Part of Chapter 8 to remove the front pump cover). Place the converter front-side down on your workbench. Using the pump cover or snap-ring pliers, rotate the stator hub (the second splined hub you can see through the opening). It should turn freely when it's rotated clockwise, but you should feel a slight resistance when turned in the counter-clockwise direction. Also, there should be no binding or noise when the stator is rotated clockwise. It the converter fails to operate as described, replace it.

Next check converter endplay. With the converter still front-side down, hook a special tool under the turbine hub at the bottom of the converter opening **(see illustration)**. Zero the dial indicator, then pull up on the tool until the maximum reading is obtained. The reading should not exceed 0.050 inch. A less-exact way to take this measurement is to bend a small hook at the bottom of a piece of very stiff wire. Hook the wire under the turbine hub and place a steel ruler across the converter opening. Scratch a mark on the wire where ruler crosses it, then pull up on the wire and mark it again. The distance between the two marks is converter endplay. Again, the measurement should not exceed 0.050 inch.

Now check for stator-to-impeller interference. Referring to the appropriate Part of Chapter 8, remove the front pump assembly from the transmission and place it on the workbench, shaft-side up. Carefully place the converter over the shaft, twisting it to make sure the splines engage correctly. Now hold the pump assembly and rotate the converter counter-clockwise. If the converter binds or makes a scraping noise during this test, replace it.

Finally, check for stator-to-turbine interference. Referring to the appropriate Part of Chapter 8, remove the front pump and input shaft/front clutch assembly. With the converter front-side down, install the front pump assembly, making sure the splines fully engage, then install the input shaft, again making sure the splines engage correctly. Hold the converter and pump while rotating the input (turbine) shaft. The turbine should rotate freely in both directions. If there is any binding or scraping noises, the converter must be replaced.

Installation

1 Prior to installation, make sure the torque converter hub is securely engaged in the pump. It is often easiest to do this with the transmission tilted so the front is facing up (if the transmission is chained to a transmission jack, this can be done safely on the jack). Wipe some transmission fluid on the converter hub to lubricate the front seal, then carefully place the converter over the input shaft. Rotate the converter back-and-forth while supporting it in the center, and the converter should slide into place, one "click" at a time. When the converter is fully installed, the drive lugs on the converter hub will be engaged in the front pump. To verify the converter is fully engaged, continue rotating the converter back and forth until it will not drop any further into the transmission and it rotates without any wobble. Once the converter is fully engaged, secure it in place using one of the methods described in the last step of the removal procedure in this Chapter.

2 With the transmission secured to the jack, raise it into position. Be sure to keep it level so the torque converter doesn't slide out. Connect the transmission fluid cooler lines.

3 Turn the torque converter until the marks on the converter stud and driveplate are aligned.

4 Move the transmission towards the engine carefully until the dowel pins engage with the holes in the bellhousing and the studs protrude through the driveplate.

5 Install the transmission housing-to-engine bolts. Tighten them securely. Also install the dipstick tube at this time. Be sure to use a new O-ring or seal on installation.

6 Install the driveplate-to-torque converter bolts or nuts and tighten them to 30 ft-lbs. **Note:** *Install all of the bolts or nuts before tightening any of them.*

7 On rear wheel drive vehicles, Install the crossmember and lower the mount studs into their holes on the crossmember. On front wheel drive vehicles, install the sub-frame (Taurus/Sable) or the engine and transaxle mounts (Tempo/Topaz/Escort Lynx and EXP). Tighten the bolts and nuts securely.

8 Remove the jacks supporting the transmission and the engine.

9 On four-wheel drive models, secure the transfer case to the jack and raise it into position. Align the transfer case input shaft with the splines on the transmission output shaft, install a new gasket, then join the transmission and transfer case. Install the transfer case mounting

bolts and braces.
10   Install the starter motor. On four-wheel drive models, install the skid plate (if equipped).
11   Connect the vacuum hose(s) (if equipped).
12   Connect the shift linkage and TV linkage.
13   Plug in the transmission wire harness connectors.
14   Install the torque converter cover.
15   On rear wheel drive vehicles, install the driveshaft(s).
16   On front wheel drive vehicles, install the driveaxles and the steering gear. Also reinstall any front suspension components and chassis components that were removed or disconnected.
17   Connect the speedometer cable or speed sensor electrical connector.
18   Adjust the shift linkage or cable (see Chapter 6).
19   Install any exhaust system components that were removed or disconnected.

20   Lower the vehicle.
21   Fill the transmission (and transfer case on four-wheel drive models) with the recommended fluid. Add four quarts of fluid to the transmission at first, then start the engine and immediately add three more quarts of fluid (this is to replace some of the fluid that will now be in the torque converter). Holding your foot firmly on the brake, slowly shift the transmission through all the gear ranges, ending again in Park. Now check the fluid level, which will be low. Add fluid until the level is at the bottom of the operating range (cross-hatched area on the dipstick). C3 transmissions will usually take one more quart; C4 transmissions will usually take 2.6 to 3 more quarts; C5 transmissions will usually take four more quarts; C6 transmissions will usually take 4.7 to 6.5 more quarts; AOD transmissions will usually take 5.3 more quarts. If you have a deep pan, still more fluid may be required. The AXOD transaxle will usually take 5.8 more quarts. The ATX/FLC transaxle will usually take 1.5 to 2.0 more quarts.

Notes

Chapter 8 Part A
Disassembly, inspection and assembly
C3, C4 and C5 transmissions

Introduction

The C3, C4 and C5 transmissions are three-speed automatic transmissions manufactured for rear-wheel drive vehicles. The major components of these transmissions are:

a) Torque converter
b) Gear-type oil pump
c) Control valve assembly
d) Two multiple-disc clutch packs
e) Planetary gear set
f) One-way clutch
g) Intermediate and low-reverse bands

Follow the photographic sequence for disassembly, inspection and assembly. The model shown is a typical transmission of this type. Differences do exist between models and many changes have been made over the years, so perform each step in order and lay the components out on a clean work bench in the EXACT ORDER of removal to prevent confusion during reassembly. Many snap-rings and clutch plates are similar in size, but must not be interchanged. Keep the individual parts together with the component from which they were removed to avoid mix-ups. Save all old parts and compare them with the new part to ensure they are an exact match before reassembly. Pay particular attention to the stack-up of the various clutch packs. Differences do exist between models and your transmission may not match the stack-up shown. Note the exact location of the check balls in the case and/or valve body. Save all the old parts until the overhaul is complete and the transmission has been thoroughly road tested; old components can be useful in diagnosing any problems that may arise.

Basic hand tools can be used for most procedures. Although some special tools are required. Alternate procedures are shown where possible, but some procedures can only be accomplished with special tools. Read through the entire overhaul procedure before beginning work to familiarize yourself with the procedures and identify any special tools that may be needed. Thoroughly clean the exterior of the transmission before beginning disassembly.

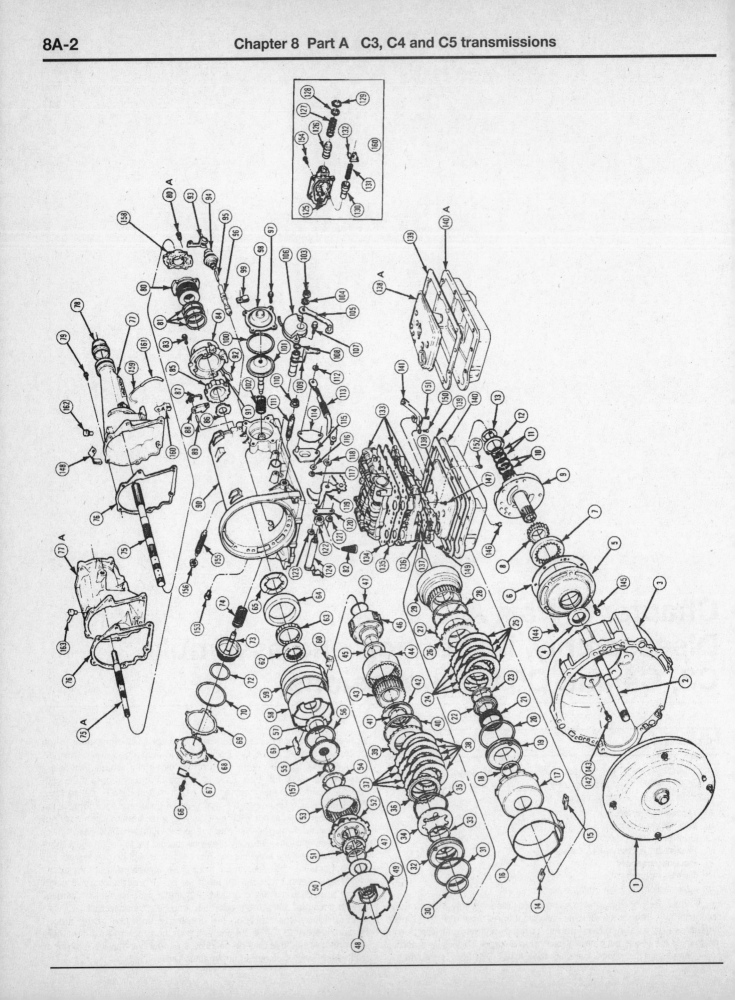

8A.1 Exploded view of a typical C4/C5 transmission

1	Torque converter
2	Input shaft
3	Converter housing
4	Oil pump seal
5	Oil pump body
6	Oil pump gasket
7	Oil pump driven gear
8	Oil pump drive gear
9	Oil pump stator support
10	Reverse clutch drum seal
11	Forward clutch drum seal
12	Thrust washer no. 1 (selective)
13	Thrust washer no. 2
14	Intermediate band apply strut
15	Intermediate band anchor strut
16	Intermediate band
17	Intermediate drum
18	Reverse clutch inner seal
19	High clutch piston
20	high clutch outer seal
21	high clutch piston spring
22	Clutch piston spring retainer
23	Retainer ring
24	Steel clutch plate
25	Friction clutch plate
26	Clutch pressure plate
27	Clutch pressure plate spring
28	Snap-ring (selective)
29	Forward clutch drum
30	O-ring
31	Forward clutch outer seal
32	Forward clutch piston
34	Forward clutch piston spring
35	Retainer ring (waved)
36	Forward clutch pressure plate
37	Steel clutch plate
38	Friction clutch plate
39	Clutch pressure plate
40	Retaining ring (selective)
41	Thrust washer no. 3
42	Retainer ring
43	Forward clutch hub
44	Output shaft ring gear
45	Thrust washer no. 4
46	Forward planetary assembly
47	Retainer ring
48	Sun gear
49	Input shell
50	Thrust washer no. 5
51	Thrust washer No. 6
52	Reverse planetary assembly
53	Output shaft ring gear
54	Thrust washer no. 7
55	Output shaft hub
56	Retaining ring
57	Thrust washer no. 8
58	Reverse band drum
59	Reverse band
60	Reverse band apply strut
61	Reverse band anchor strut
62	Overrun clutch inner race
63	One-way clutch spring assembly
63A	One-way clutch roller
64	Overrun clutch outer race
65	Thrust washer No. 9
66	Bolt
67	Identification tag
68	Intermediate band servo cover
69	Intermediate band servo cover gasket
70	Intermediate band servo cover seal
72	Intermediate band servo piston seal
73	Intermediate band servo piston
74	Intermediate band servo piston spring
75	Output shaft (4X2)
75A	Output shaft (4X4)
76	Extension gasket
77	Extension assembly (4X2)
77A	Extension assembly (4X4)
78	Extension assembly oil seal
79	Bolt
80	Governor oil collector body
80A	Governor oil screen
81	Governor seal ring
82	Pump inlet screen
83	Bolt
84	Oil distributor sleeve
85	Output shaft parking gear
86	Thrust washer no. 10
87	Parking pawl return spring
88	Parking pawl assembly
89	Pin
90	Case assembly
91	Oil distributor tube
92	Oil distributor tube
93	Clip
94	Throttle valve diaphragm
95	Throttle valve control rod
96	Throttle valve
97	Bolt
98	Reverse band servo cover
99	Clip
100	Reverse band servo cover seal
101	Low-reverse servo piston
102	Low-reverse servo piston spring
103	Nut
104	Washer
105	Downshift control lever
106	Neutral start switch
107	Screw and washer
108	O-ring
109	Manual lever
110	Nut
111	Screw
112	Retaining ring
113	Park lever rod
114	Park lever spacer
115	Park lever
116	Washer
117	Retaining ring
118	Park lever rod roller
119	Manual valve detent lever
120	Park link
121	Retaining ring
122	Nut
123	Retaining ring
124	Downshift detent lever
125	Governor valve body
126	Governor valve (primary)
127	Governor valve spring
128	Washer
129	Retaining ring
130	Governor valve (secondary)
131	Governor valve spring
132	Spring retainer
133	Main control valve assembly
134	Separator plate
135	Separator plate gasket
136	3-2 timing body separator plate (C5 only)
137	3-2 timing body separator plate gasket (C5 only)
138	Oil pan screen (4X2)
138A	Oil pan screen (4X4)
139	Oil pan gasket
140	Oil pan (4X2)
140A	Oil pan (4X4)
141	Manual valve detent spring
142	Bolt
143	Bolt
144	Screw
145	Bolt
146	Screw and washer
147	Screw
148	Clip
149	Screw
150	Screw
151	Screw
152	Screw
153	Bolt
154	Bolt
155	Screw
156	Nut
157	Retaining ring
158	Governor body
159	Vent tube
160	Clip
161	Vent hose
162	Vent assembly
163	Vent assembly elbow

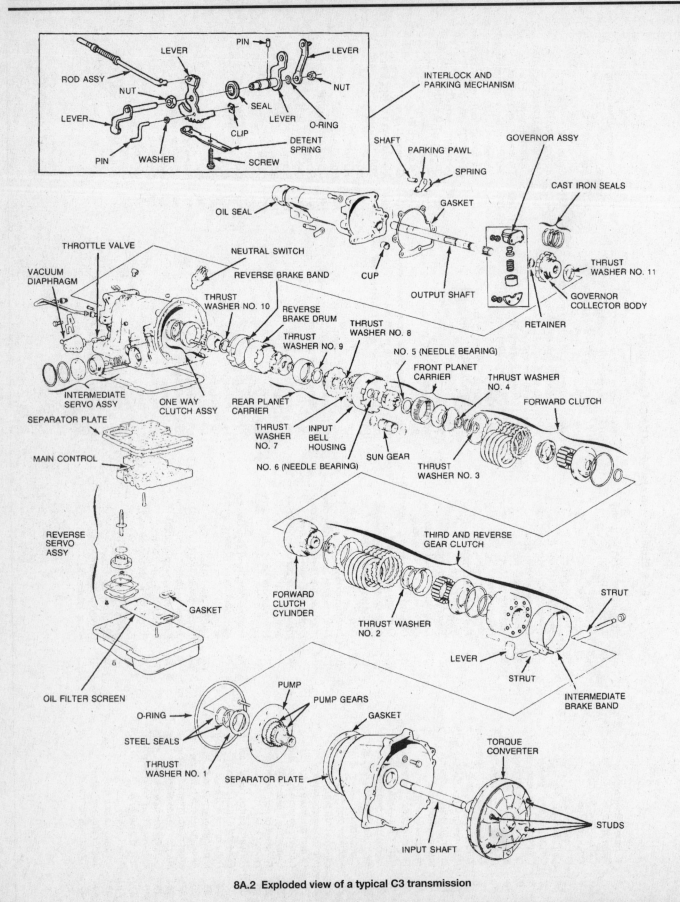

8A.2 Exploded view of a typical C3 transmission

Transmission disassembly

8A.3 Remove the seven converter housing bolts and remove the housing

8A.4 On C3 models, remove the eight converter housing bolts and remove the converter housing and front pump

8A.5 On C3 models, remove the five pump attaching bolts (arrows)

8A.6 On C3 models, remove the front oil pump assembly from the bellhousing and re-install the pump back into the case. Be sure the assembly is correctly engaged. The pump body must be below the level of the case

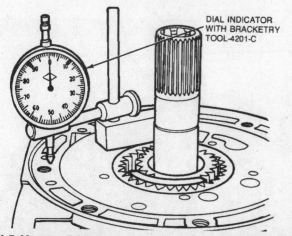

8A.7 Mount a dial indicator on the pump with the plunger resting on the transmission housing. Set the dial indicator to zero. Turn the gauge so that the plunger contacts the pump. Note the reading on the dial. This reading is the end play (C3)

DIAL INDICATOR WITH BRACKETRY TOOL-4201-C

Note

The case end play clearance should be 0.001 to 0.025 inch. If the clearance is not within specifications your local dealer parts department has no. 1 selective thrust washers available in different thickness.

8A.8 Remove the pump separator plate . . .

8A.9 . . . and remove the drive and driven gears (C3)

8A.10 Remove the four bolts retaining the intermediate servo and remove the cover and gasket

8A.11 Remove the intermediate servo piston . . .

8A.12 . . . and remove the intermediate servo piston return spring

8A.13 On C3 models, the intermediate servo cover is held in place by a snap-ring (arrow)

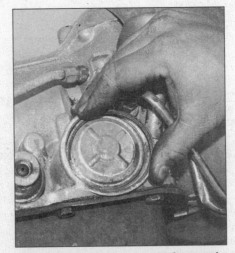

8A.14 Press the servo cover down and remove the retaining snap-ring

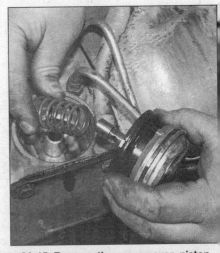

8A.15 Remove the servo cover, piston and return spring

8A.16 Remove the oil cooler line fittings at the case to clean and check the passages

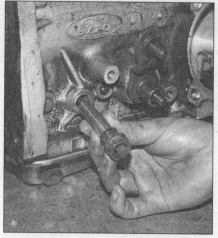

8A.17 Loosen and remove the intermediate band adjusting locknut and screw

8A.18 Using a screwdriver and a hammer, remove the rear extension housing seal. Be careful not to damage the bushing when you knock the seal out

8A.19 Remove the six extension housing bolts and remove the extension housing

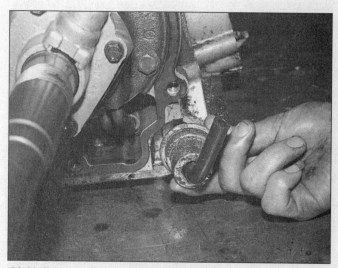

8A.20 Remove the vacuum modulator bolt and hold down clamp, and pull the vacuum modulator from the case

8A.21 Remove the modulator control rod from the vacuum modulator

8A.22 Remove the primary throttle valve from the case

8A.23 Remove the four bolts retaining the governor to the governor distributor and slide the governor off the output shaft

8A.24 Remove the four low-reverse servo cover attaching bolts and remove the cover

8A.25 Remove the low-reverse servo piston and seal. The seal is bonded to the piston - do not try to remove the seal

8A.26 Remove the low-reverse servo piston return spring

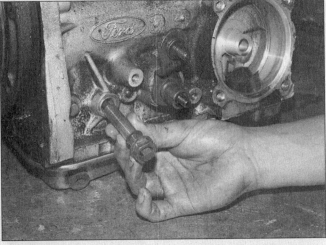

8A.27 Loosen and remove the low-reverse band adjusting locknut and screw

8A.28 Remove the transmission oil pan bolts and remove the oil pan. You can use the oil pan as a parts tray

8A.29 Remove the nine 1/4 inch bolts (arrows) retaining the valve body to the case and carefully remove the valve body

8A.30 On C3 models, remove the thirteen oil pan attaching bolts and remove the pan and gasket. The pan can be used as a small parts holding tray

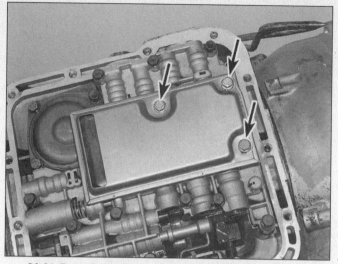

8A.31 Remove the three oil filter attaching bolts (arrows)

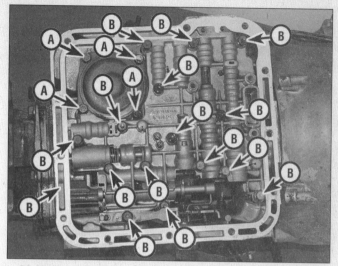

8A.32 Remove the four reverse servo attaching bolts (A), and remove the reverse servo cover. Remove the control valve body attaching bolts (B) and carefully remove the valve body

8A.33 Remove the reverse servo piston assembly . . .

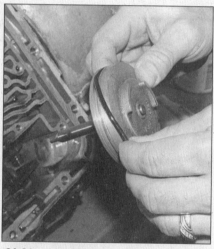

8A.34 . . . and the servo piston seals (C3)

8A.35 Remove the intermediate band anchor strut . . .

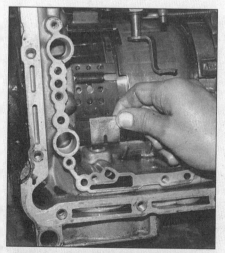

8A.36 . . . and the intermediate band apply strut

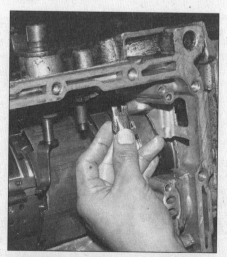

8A.37 Remove the low-reverse band apply strut . . .

8A.38 . . . and the low-reverse band anchor strut

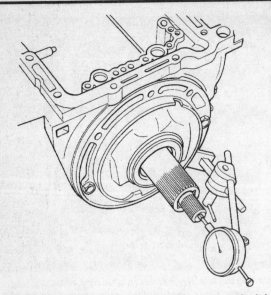

8A.39 Before you begin teardown of the gear train, it is best to take an end play check. Install a dial indicator on the front pump assembly with the dial indicator needle contacting the end of the input shaft

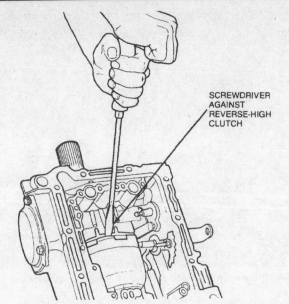

SCREWDRIVER AGAINST REVERSE-HIGH CLUTCH

8A.40 Using a screwdriver pry against a lug on the reverse-high clutch and push the gear train to the rear of the case

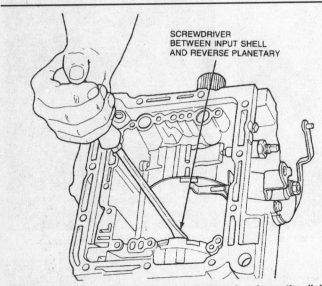

SCREWDRIVER BETWEEN INPUT SHELL AND REVERSE PLANETARY

8A.41 Make sure the input shaft is fully seated and zero the dial indicator. Using a screwdriver between the input shell and the reverse planetary assembly, pry the input shell forward and read the amount of end play on the dial indicator

8A.42 Insert a screwdriver behind the input shell and push the gear train forward, dislodging the pump from the housing. Clean any gasket material from the case left by the front pump gasket

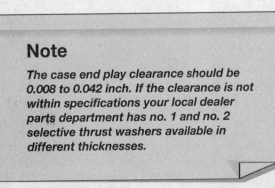

Note

The case end play clearance should be 0.008 to 0.042 inch. If the clearance is not within specifications your local dealer parts department has no. 1 and no. 2 selective thrust washers available in different thicknesses.

8A.43 Remove the input shaft from the front pump stator support assembly

8A.44 Remove the no. 1 selective thrust washer from the pump. If the washer didn't come out with the pump, remove it from the top of the reverse-high clutch. Also remove the no. 2 selective thrust washer from the end of the stator hub. If it didn't come out with the pump it will be on the forward clutch cylinder

8A.45 Remove the six bolts that attach the stator support to the pump housing

8A.46 Remove the drive gear from the pump housing

8A.47 Remove the driven gear from the pump housing

8A.48 Remove the front pump oil seal and discard it. Be careful not to damage the pump bushing. Set the pump aside for cleaning

8A.49 Remove the reverse-high clutch from the case and remove the selective snap-ring

8A.50 Remove the pressure plate, friction discs and steel plates. The number of friction discs and steel plates may vary, depending on the model of transmission, be sure to count them and replace them with the exact same number

8A.51 Using a suitable clutch spring compressor carefully compress the clutch spring and remove the retaining snap-ring.

8A.52 If you don't have a spring compressor use two C-clamps to compress the spring retainer

8A.53 Remove the spring retainer . . .

8A.54 . . . and the spring

8A.55 Remove the reverse-high piston . . .

8A.56 . . . and remove the outer seal from the piston. Remove the inner seal from the reverse-high clutch drum

8A.57 Squeeze the intermediate band ends together and remove it from the case

8A.58 Remove the forward clutch assembly from the case. Remove the four tang no. 2 selective thrust washer from the forward clutch drum. If the no. 3 thrust washer didn't come out with the forward clutch, remove it from the forward clutch hub and ring gear

8A.59 Remove the forward clutch selective snap-ring

8A.60 Remove the rear pressure plate, friction discs, steel plates and forward pressure plate. The number of friction discs and steel plates may vary, depending on the model of the transmission. Be sure to count them and replace them with the exact same number

8A.61 Remove the clutch piston non-selective snap-ring by prying it from the groove with a small screwdriver . . .

8A.62 . . . and remove the disc spring or Bellville spring

8A.63 Make note of the direction the disc spring sits on the piston

8A.64 Remove the steel clutch pressure ring . . .

8A.65 . . . and remove the piston from the drum

8A.66 Remove the outer seal from the piston and the inner seal from the forward clutch drum

8A.67 Make sure the check ball moves freely in the piston (arrow)

8A.68 Remove the no. 3 thrust washer from on top of the forward clutch hub

8A.69 Remove the forward clutch hub and ring gear from the case

8A.70 Remove the no. 4 thrust washer from the back of the forward clutch hub and ring gear

8A.71 Remove the forward planetary carrier from the case

8A.72 Remove the input shell and the sun gear assembly. The no. 5 thrust washer is part of the input shell and sun gear assembly

8A.73 Remove the no. 6 thrust washer from the input shell. If the no. 6 thrust washer is not on the input shell, remove it from the reverse planetary carrier

8A.74 Squeeze the low-reverse band ends together and remove it from the case

8A.75 Slide the inner downshift lever out of the manual shaft

8A.76 Remove the reverse planetary carrier from the case

8A.77 Remove the no. 7 thrust washer from the top of the reverse ring gear. If it isn't on top of the ring gear, look on the back of the reverse planetary carrier

8A.78 Remove the inner snap-ring from the output shaft . . .

8A.79 . . . and remove the reverse ring gear and hub from the case

8A.80 Remove the no. 8 thrust washer from the back of the reverse ring gear and hub. If the no. 8 washer isn't on the ring gear, remove it from the low-reverse drum

8A.81 Remove the low reverse drum from the case

8A.82 Remove the bolts retaining the distributor governor sleeve to the case

8A.83 Slide the output shaft out of the case with the governor distributor body attached

8A.84 Using a screwdriver, carefully pry the governor distributor sleeve and oil feed tubes from the case

8A.85 Remove the parking gear and the no. 10 thrust washer, which will fall out when then distributor sleeve is removed

8A.86 Remove the parking pawl and spring from the case

8A.87 Using a screwdriver on the inner splines, rotate the inner one-way clutch race until you can remove the race by hand. After the race is removed, remove the rollers and spring cage

8A.88 Remove the no. 9 thrust washer from the case

8A.89 Remove the six bolts retaining the outer one-way clutch race and remove the race from the case

8A.90 Remove the nut retaining the inner manual lever to the manual shaft . . .

8A.91 . . . and withdraw the outer manual lever and shaft from the case

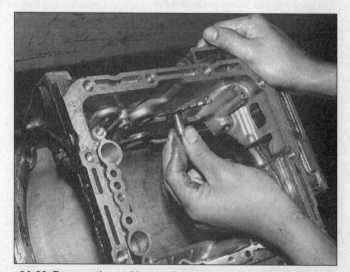

8A.92 Remove the parking pawl actuating rod and inner manual lever from the case

Component inspection and subassembly

Using an approved cleaning solvent, clean and dry all the components thoroughly, including the case. Do not use rags to wipe the components dry, lint from the rag may lodge in the oil passages causing a valve to stick.

Inspect the following transmission components and repair or replace as necessary:

a) **Case** - Inspect the exterior of the case for damage, cracks and porosity. Check the valve body surface for damage and flatness. Check all the oil passages, the accumulator bore, the speedometer bore and the governor bore for damage. Check all threaded holes for damage. Damaged threads may be repaired by drilling, tapping and installing thread inserts. Check the oil cooler line fittings for damage. Check the interior of the case for damaged retaining ring grooves. Check the case lugs for excessive wear. Check the output shaft bushing for wear. Inspect the manual linkage and the park lock linkage for damage.

b) **Forward clutch pack and high-reverse clutch pack** - Inspect the condition of the clutch plates. Check for signs of overheating. Check the friction plates for wear, pitting, cracking or flaking. Check the intermediate band for wear or damage. Check the pistons for damage. Check the return springs for damage or signs of overheating. Check the bushings for wear or damage. Check the check balls for damage and freedom of movement. Check the input shaft for scoring or damages splines.

c) **Planetary gear set** - Inspect the planetary carriers, ring gears, sun gear and drive shell for damaged teeth or splines. Check for worn bushings. Check the thrust bearings for wear or damage. Inspect the pinion gear bearings for wear or damage.

d) **Low-reverse clutch pack and one-way clutch assembly** - Inspect the condition of the clutch plates. Check for signs of overheating. Check the friction plates for wear, pitting, cracking or flaking. Check the low-reverse band for wear or damage. Inspect the one-way clutch for worn or damaged rollers. Check the springs for damage. Check the race finish for scoring, wear or damage.

e) **Output shaft and governor** - Inspect the output shaft for damages splines, scoring or worn bushing races. Check the governor for stuck valves. Check the governor distributor O-ring grooves for damage.

Oil pump assembly

Clean the oil pump components with solvent and air dry. Inspect the gears and gear pocket for scoring or damage. Check the hub for damaged sealing ring grooves. Inspect the stator shaft bushings for wear or damage. Inspect the pump cover and body faces for nicks or burrs and make sure the oil passages and lubrication holes are not restricted. Place the pump body over the cover and check for warpage.

8A.93 On C3 models, install the driven gear into the pump body with the chamfered teeth facing down, into the pump body

8A.94 On C3 models, install the drive gear with the flat side of the offset drive tang (arrows) facing away from the pump body

8A.95 On C3 models, lubricate the pump face and gears with petroleum jelly and place the steel plate over the pump face

Note

If the end play was not within specifications when originally checked, do not install the oil pump to converter housing until the endplay has been checked again and the proper no. 1 selective thrust washer is selected.

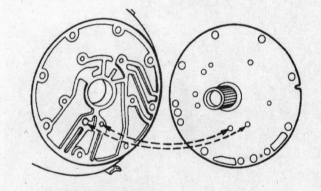

8A.96 Align the steel plate and front pump with the converter housing as shown (C3). . .

8A.97 . . . and install the pump onto the converter housing (C3)

8A.98 Tighten the five attaching bolts to 7-10 ft-lbs (C3)

8A.99 Check the pump body face for nicks, burrs or scoring

8A.100 Inspect the pump body bushing for wear or damage. If necessary see Chapter 2 for servicing

8A.101 Install the front oil pump seal, driving it in until it's flush with the housing

8A.102 Check the stator support ring lands for nicks, burrs or scoring (arrows)

8A.103 Check the stator support bushings, if necessary see Chapter 2 for servicing. Install the rear bushing with the notch aligned to the rear

8A.104 Install the stator support front bushing flush with the inner taper on the end of the stator shaft

8A.105 Check the stator support face for defects or deep scoring

8A.106 Check that the spring and valve are clean and have no build up or residue

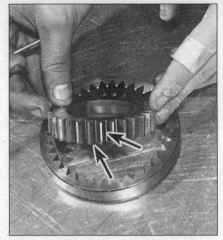

8A.107 Check the gear teeth (arrows) for chips or cracks . . .

8A.108 . . . and the gear face for excessive wear or deep scratches. If found to be defective, replace the gears as a set

8A.109 Install the driven gear into the pump body with the chamfered ends of the teeth facing down, into the pump body (toward the seal). Install the drive gear with the flat side of the offset drive tangs (arrows) facing up (away from the seal) or the converter will damage the gear. Lubricate the pump housing and gears with transmission fluid

8A.110 Position the stator support over the pump body and align the bolt holes

8A.111 Install the five bolts and tighten them to 12-20 ft-lbs

8A.112 If the front pump has to be replaced, try and match the casting numbers (arrow)

Control valve assembly

Lay the control valve assembly on a clean work surface and begin removing the valves from the valve body. Withdraw the bushings, valves and springs and lay them out on a clean lint-free towel in the EXACT order of removal. Keep them in the proper orientation to the valve body. Clean all the bushings, valves and springs. Check the valves and bushings closely for scoring, cracks or damage. Check the springs for collapsed or distorted coils. Finally check the valve body bores for scoring or damage and begin reassembly.

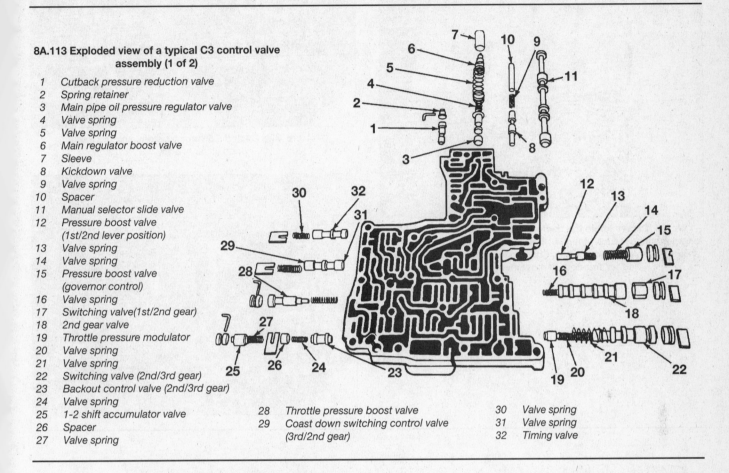

8A.113 Exploded view of a typical C3 control valve assembly (1 of 2)

1   Cutback pressure reduction valve
2   Spring retainer
3   Main pipe oil pressure regulator valve
4   Valve spring
5   Valve spring
6   Main regulator boost valve
7   Sleeve
8   Kickdown valve
9   Valve spring
10   Spacer
11   Manual selector slide valve
12   Pressure boost valve
       (1st/2nd lever position)
13   Valve spring
14   Valve spring
15   Pressure boost valve
       (governor control)
16   Valve spring
17   Switching valve(1st/2nd gear)
18   2nd gear valve
19   Throttle pressure modulator
20   Valve spring
21   Valve spring
22   Switching valve (2nd/3rd gear)
23   Backout control valve (2nd/3rd gear)
24   Valve spring
25   1-2 shift accumulator valve
26   Spacer
27   Valve spring

28   Throttle pressure boost valve
29   Coast down switching control valve
       (3rd/2nd gear)

30   Valve spring
31   Valve spring
32   Timing valve

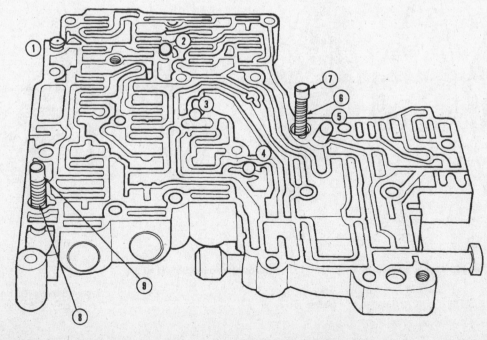

8A.114 Checkball location for the control valve body (2 of 2)

1   Intermediate servo release puck
2   Torque demand check ball
3   Manual 1, manual 2 and reverse check ball
4   High clutch and reverse servo circuit check ball
5   TV coast boost check ball
6   Valve spring
7   Pressure relief throttle valve
8   Valve spring
9   Governor pressure relief valve

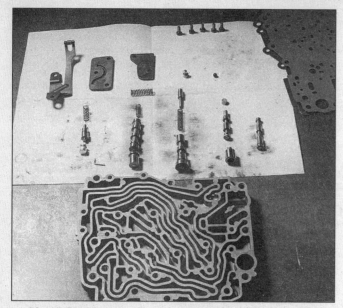

8A.115 Disassemble the control valve assembly and lay the components out on a clean lint-free towel. Clean and inspect the valves, bushings and springs. Check each valve for nicks, burrs and for freedom of movement in its bore

8A.116 The C4 and C5 transmissions use the same control valve body . . .

8A.117 . . . but the C5 has an added timing body (arrow) in place of the oil filter

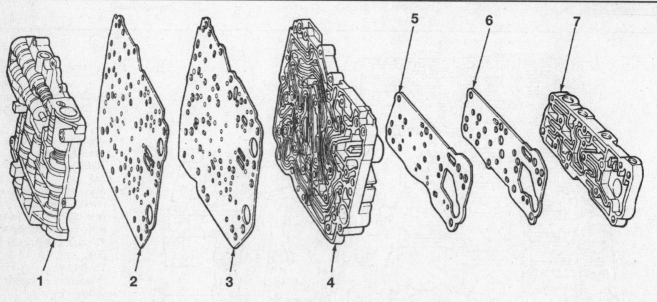

8A.118 Exploded view of a typical C4/C5 control valve assembly (1 of 3)

1 Upper body	4 Lower body	6 Separator plate (C5 only)
2 Separator plate	5 Gasket (C5 only)	7 Timing body (C5 only)
3 Gasket		

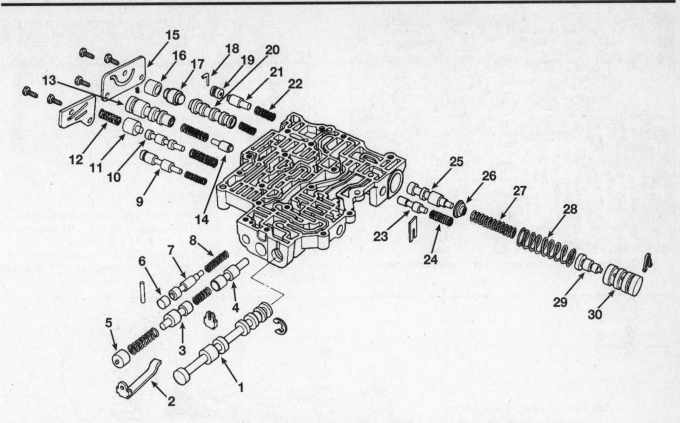

8A.119 Exploded view of a typical C4/C5 control valve assembly (2 of 3)

1	Manual control valve	11	1-2 transition valve	21	Intermediate servo accumulator valve
2	Retainer	12	Valve spring	22	Valve spring
3	Low servo modulator valve	13	2-3 shift valve	23	Line coast boost valve
4	Throttle downshift valve	14	Throttle modulator valve	24	Valve spring
5	Retainer plug	15	Retainer plate	25	Main oil pressure regulator valve
6	Plug	16	Cup	26	Retainer
7	Throttle pressure boost valve	17	1-2 shift valve	27	Valve spring
8	Valve spring	18	Pin	28	Valve spring
9	Cut-back valve	19	Retainer	29	Main oil pressure boost valve
10	2-3 back-out valve	20	D-2 valve	30	Sleeve

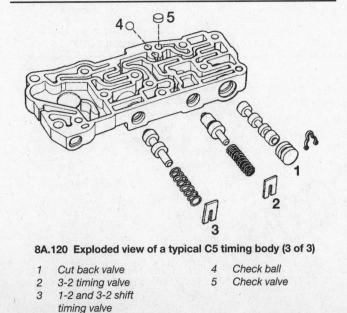

8A.120 Exploded view of a typical C5 timing body (3 of 3)

1	Cut back valve	4	Check ball
2	3-2 timing valve	5	Check valve
3	1-2 and 3-2 shift timing valve		

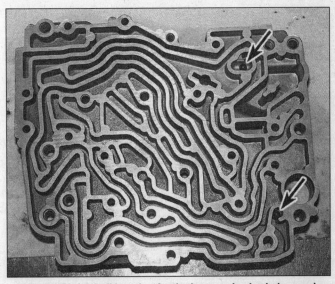

8A.121 Check ball location for the lower valve body (arrows)

8A.122 Check ball location for the upper valve body (arrow)

Note

Use petroleum jelly when installing the check balls to prevent them from falling out of the correct passage.

Governor valve assembly

Lay the governor assembly on a clean work surface and begin removing the screws and retaining clips from the body and counter weight. Lay them out on a clean lint-free towel in the EXACT order of removal. Keep them in the proper orientation to the governor body. Clean the valves and body. Check all the parts for dirt and wear and scoring.

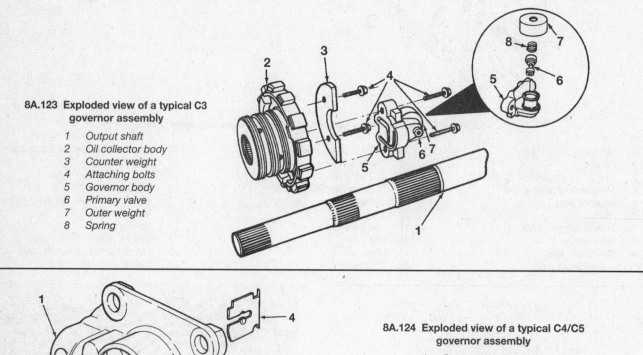

8A.123 Exploded view of a typical C3 governor assembly

1   Output shaft
2   Oil collector body
3   Counter weight
4   Attaching bolts
5   Governor body
6   Primary valve
7   Outer weight
8   Spring

8A.124 Exploded view of a typical C4/C5 governor assembly

1   Governor body
2   Secondary valve
3   Secondary valve spring
4   Spring retainer plate
5   Primary valve
6   Primary valve spring
7   Washer
8   Snap-ring

Reverse-high clutch assembly

8A.125 Install the reverse clutch inner square-cut seal on the drum

8A.126 Install the outer seal on the piston. Lubricate the seals with petroleum jelly

8A.127 Carefully press the piston into the reverse drum until seated. To prevent possible damage to the seals, use a seal installation tool (see Chapter 2)

8A.128 Install the reverse piston return spring(s) and retainer

Note

The C3 transmission uses 20 reverse-high clutch return springs in place of the one large spring used on C4 and C5 models.

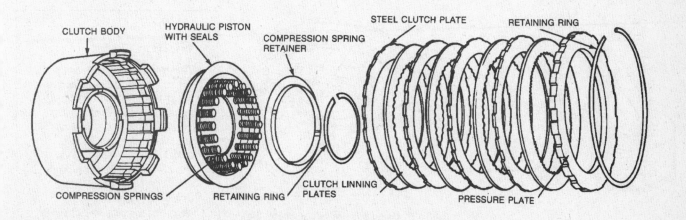

8A.129 Exploded view of a typical C3 reverse-high clutch assembly

8A.130 Using a suitable clutch spring compressor, carefully compress the clutch spring retainer and install the retaining snap-ring

8A.131 If you don't have a spring compressor use two C-clamps to compress the spring retainer.

8A.132 Install a steel plate into the drum, against the piston

8A.133 Soak the clutch friction plates in automatic transmission fluid for fifteen minutes. Install a clutch friction plate against the steel plate. Alternately install steel plates and friction plates to equal your original clutch pack

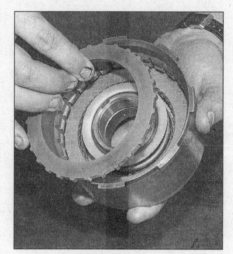

8A.134 Install the thick flat pressure plate . . .

8A.135 . . . and the selective snap-ring. Make sure the snap-ring is fully seated in the groove

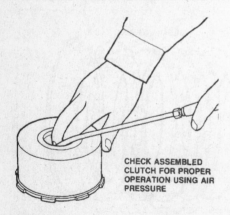

CHECK ASSEMBLED CLUTCH FOR PROPER OPERATION USING AIR PRESSURE

8A.136 Using air pressure check the operation of the of the clutch pack, it should apply smoothly and have no leaks when air is applied

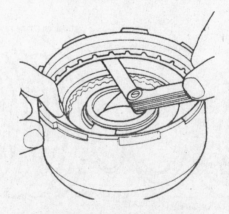

8A.137 Using a feeler gauge check the clearance between the selective snap-ring and the pressure plate. When making the check, push down lightly on the pressure plate

Note

The reverse-high clutch pressure plate-to-selective snap-ring clearance should be 0.051-0.079 inch for C3 models, 0.050- 0.071 inch for C4 models and 0.025-0.050 inch for C5 models. If the clearance is not within specifications your local dealership parts department has selective snap-rings in available in different thickness.

Forward clutch assembly

8A.138 Install the forward clutch inner seal on the drum

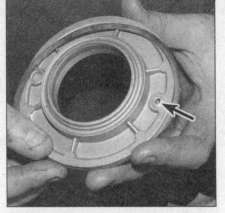

8A.139 Install the outer piston seal on the piston. Inspect the piston check ball and make sure it's clean and moves freely (arrow). Lubricate the piston and seals with petroleum jelly

Note

The C3 transmission uses a rubber cushion in the piston as well as the inner and outer piston seals.

8A.140 Carefully push the piston into the reverse drum until seated. To prevent possible damage to the seals, use a seal installation tool (see Chapter 2)

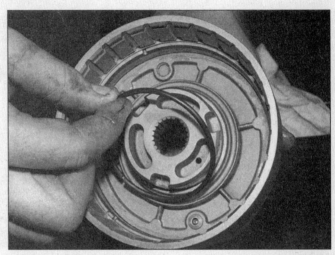

8A.141 Install the steel pressure ring into the groove in the piston

8A.142 Install the reverse piston Bellville return spring into the drum . . .

8A.143 . . . and install the non selective retaining snap-ring

Note

The C3 transmission uses 15 small springs, spring retainer and retaining snap-ring instead of the Bellville spring. There is no forward pressure plate used and the clutch pack is assembled with a steel plate against the piston and then a friction plate.

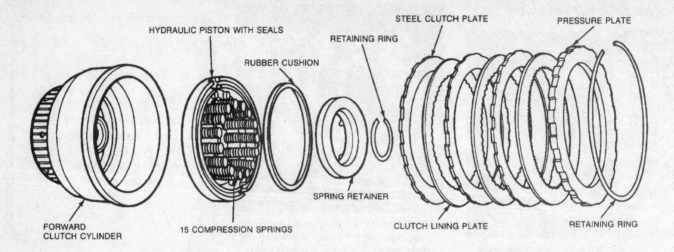

HYDRAULIC PISTON WITH SEALS

RUBBER CUSHION

STEEL CLUTCH PLATE

PRESSURE PLATE

RETAINING RING

FORWARD CLUTCH CYLINDER

15 COMPRESSION SPRINGS

SPRING RETAINER

CLUTCH LINING PLATE

RETAINING RING

8A.144 Exploded view of a typical C3 forward clutch assembly

8A.145 Lubricate no. 3 thrust washer with petroleum jelly and install it on the forward clutch hub

8A.146 Install the forward pressure plate against the Bellville spring, with the flat side up

8A.147 Soak the forward clutch friction plates in automatic transmission fluid for fifteen minutes. Install a clutch friction plate against the pressure plate

8A.148 Install a steel plate against the friction plate. Alternately install friction plates and steel plates to equal your original clutch pack.

8A.149 Install the thick, flat rear pressure plate . . .

8A.150 . . . and install the selective snap-ring. Make sure the snap-ring is fully seated in the groove

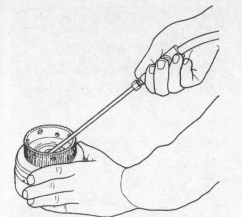

8A.151 Using air pressure, check the operation of the of the clutch pack. It should apply smoothly and have no leaks when air is applied

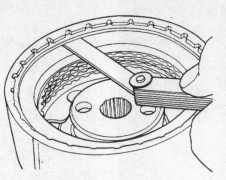

8A.152 Using a feeler gauge, check the clearance between the selective snap-ring and the pressure plate. When making the check, push down lightly on the pressure plate

Note

The forward clutch pressure plate-to-selective snap-ring clearance should be 0.055-0.083 inch for C3 models and 0.025-0.050 inch for C4 and C5 models. If the clearance is not within specifications your local dealership parts department has selective snap-rings in available in different thickness.

Transmission assembly

An automatic transmission is a precision fit piece of equipment. Install each component as shown, do not force any component into place. If it doesn't fit properly, find out why and rectify the situation. Maintain a clean work place and lubricate all moving parts as they are installed. Lubricate thrust washers and bearings with automatic transmission fluid or petroleum jelly. Use petroleum jelly to retain thrust washers and check balls in their proper location as the component is installed.

8A.153 Lubricate the two intermediate servo piston seals with petroleum jelly and install the seal in the piston grooves

8A.154 Lightly lubricate the servo cover and the intermediate piston with transmission fluid . . .

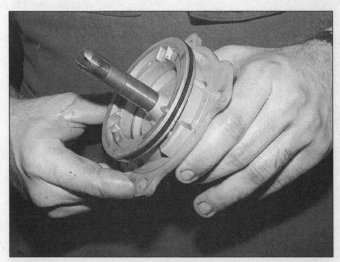

8A.155 . . . and carefully install the piston into the servo cover, turning and pushing at the same time. If at any time the piston feels like it's binding, stop and remove it to prevent damage to the seals

8A.156 Using gasket adhesive, attach the servo cover gasket to the case and install the intermediate servo spring

8A.157 Install the servo cover and piston assembly into the case . . .

8A.158 . . . and tighten the four attaching bolts to 16-22 ft-lbs

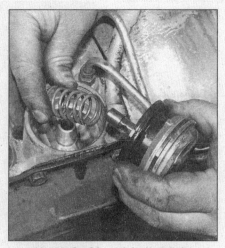

8A.159 On C3 models, install the intermediate servo return spring, piston, and cover into the case. Push the servo cover past the retaining groove . . .

8A.160 . . . and install the retaining snap-ring

8A.161 Install the low-reverse servo return spring into the case

8A.162 Lubricate the servo piston and apply rod with clean transmission fluid and carefully install the servo piston in the case

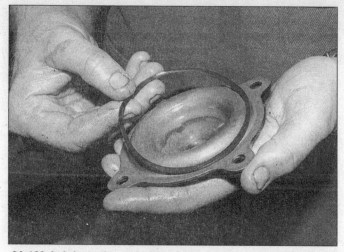

8A.163 Lubricate the seal with petroleum jelly and place the seal on the servo cover

8A.164 Install the cover on the case with the four attaching bolts. Tighten the bolts to 16-22 ft-lbs

8A.165 On C3 models, install the reverse servo piston, gasket and cover into the case. Tighten the four attaching bolts to 7-10 ft-lbs

8A.166 Install the low-reverse band adjusting screw into the case. Turn the adjusting screw by hand only a few turns (just enough to hold the low-reverse anchor strut and band in position)

8A.167 Place the manual shaft seal into the case and using the appropriate seal installer, seat the seal into the case (a deep socket can also be used as a driver)

8A.168 Lubricate the outer manual shaft with transmission fluid and install the manual shaft into the case

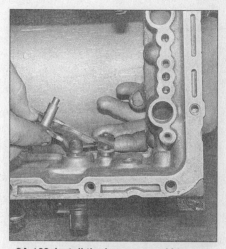

8A.169 Install the inner manual lever on the manual shaft

8A.170 Install the nut that retains the inner manual lever to the manual shaft (arrow) and tighten the nut to 12-16 ft-lbs

8A.171 Install the inner downshift lever and shaft into the manual shaft

8A.172 Install the downshift shaft O-ring onto the end of the manual shaft to retain the downshift shaft and lever in place

8A.173 Install the one-way clutch outer race into the case and align the bolt holes. Install the six attaching bolts (arrows) and tighten the bolts evenly to 13-20 ft-lbs

8A.174 Lubricate the no. 10 thrust washer with petroleum jelly and place on the parking gear

8A.175 Place the parking gear and thrust washer on the case

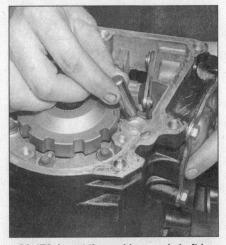

8A.176 Insert the parking pawl shaft in the case . . .

8A.177 . . . and slide the parking pawl over the shaft

8A.178 Position the hooked end of the return spring (A) into the case groove and the long end of the return spring (B) on the parking pawl

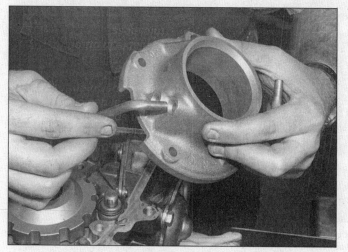

8A.179 Press the oil feed tubes into the governor distributor sleeve . . .

8A.180 . . . install the governor distributor sleeve over the parking gear and press the oil feed tubes into the case (arrows)

8A.181 Install the four governor distributor sleeve attaching bolts (arrows) and tighten them to 12-20 ft-lbs

8A.182 Lubricate the no. 9 thrust washer with petroleum jelly and place it in the center of the one-way clutch outer race at the bottom of the case

8A.183 Install the one-way clutch spring assembly into the outer race . . .

8A.184 . . . and carefully install the inner one-way clutch race, with the polished, machined face against the thrust washer

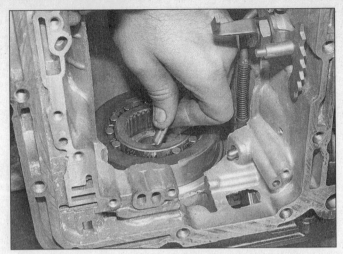

8A.185 Install the one-way clutch rollers one at a time . . .

8A.186 . . . until all 12 rollers are in the proper position (arrows)

8A.187 Soak the low-reverse band in automatic transmission fluid for fifteen minutes. Install the low-reverse band . . .

8A.188 . . . and center the band in the case

8A.189 Install the large low-reverse anchor strut into the case. Lock the anchor strut (narrow) end in the band. The band adjusting screw should fit in the hole on the wide end of the anchor strut

8A.190 With one finger, push the low-reverse band away from the low-reverse servo piston rod. Install the apply strut against the band and servo piston rod

8A.191 Once installed, the band apply strut and anchor strut should hold the band in place

8A.192 Install the low-reverse clutch drum into the case, the low-reverse band should be loose enough for the drum to fit inside of it

8A.193 Use petroleum jelly to retain the no. 8 thrust washer (arrow) on top of the low-reverse drum

8A.194 Install the three oil rings on the governor distributor (arrows). Check the oil rings for free rotation in the ring grooves and lubricate them with petroleum jelly

8A.195 Carefully install the output shaft into the case. If the governor oil distributor sticks or binds, do not force it in. Remove the output shaft and find the problem

8A.196 Once the governor oil distributor is installed in the distributor sleeve, rotate the case, front end up, and check that the output shaft is fully seated in the low-reverse drum

8A.197 Install the reverse ring gear and hub onto the output shaft and seat it on the no. 8 thrust washer

8A.198 Install the reverse ring gear retaining snap-ring over the output shaft

8A.199 Make sure it's fully seated in the output shaft groove (arrow)

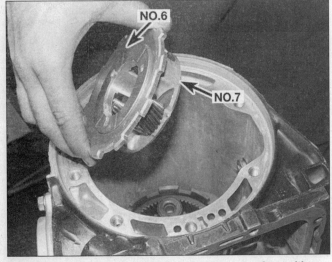

8A.200 Lubricate the no. 6 and no. 7 thrust washers with petroleum jelly. Place the no. 7 thrust washer on the bottom of the reverse planetary carrier and the no. 6 thrust washer on top of the reverse planetary carrier

8A.201 Install the reverse planetary carrier over the output shaft, meshing the pinion gears with the reverse ring gear. The tabs on the planetary carrier fit into the slots on the low-reverse drum (arrow)

8A.202 Lubricate the no. 4 thrust washer with petroleum jelly and place it on the front planetary carrier

8A.203 Install the front planetary carrier into the forward clutch ring gear and hub

8A.204 Lubricate the no. 3 thrust washer with petroleum jelly and place on the forward clutch drum

8A.205 Align the forward clutch friction plate splines and install the forward clutch hub and drum into the forward clutch. Hold the forward clutch, while turning and pressing down on the forward clutch hub until the clutch hub engages all the forward clutch plates

8A.206 Install the forward clutch assembly into the reverse-high clutch. Hold the reverse-high clutch, while turning and pressing down on the forward clutch until the clutch hub is seated in the reverse-high clutch

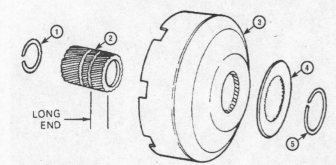

LONG END →

8A.207 Exploded view of the sun gear and input shell assembly

1	Forward snap-ring	4	No. 5 thrust washer-
2	Sun gear		wear plate
3	Input shell	5	Rear snap-ring

8A.208 Install the input shell and sun gear assembly over the forward clutch assembly . . .

8A.209 . . . and lock the tabs of the reverse-high clutch into the input shell (arrow)

8A.210 Slowly lower the gear train into the case . . .

8A.211 . . . until the input shell seats on the no. 6 thrust washer

8A.212 Install the input shaft into the gear train

8A.213 Soak the intermediate band in automatic transmission fluid for fifteen minutes. Install the intermediate band into the case. Insert the lugs through the clearance hole (arrow) and rotate the band into position

8A.214 Install the intermediate band adjusting screw into the case

8A.215 Install the apply strut into the servo piston rod and lock it against the intermediate band

8A.216 Holding the intermediate band against the servo apply strut, install the anchor strut on the band

8A.217 Turn the adjusting screw in until the anchor and apply struts hold the band in place

8A.218 Install the no. 1 selective thrust washer over the stator support. Use petroleum jelly to retain it in place during installation

Note

If the end play was not within specifications when checked prior to disassembly, replace the no. 1 selective thrust washer on the C3 and the no. 1 and 2 selective thrust washers on C4 and C5 models with one of the proper thickness.

8A.219 Install the four sealing rings on the stator support (arrows)

8A.220 Make sure the sealing ring ends are locked (arrow) and in the proper grooves. Install the no. 2 selective thrust washer, using petroleum jelly to retain it on the end of the stator support

8A.221 Install two alignment studs into the case and place the pump gasket on the case. Make sure case surface is cleaned of all old gasket material before placing the new gasket on the case

8A.222 Carefully lower the pump into the case. If the input shaft will not easily slide over the stator support, remove the input shaft and check the bushings for nicks or burrs - DO NOT FORCE IT

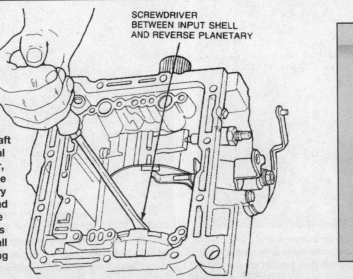

Note
On C3 models install the oil pump, with the converter housing, into the case and tighten the eight attaching bolts to 27-39 ft-lbs.

8A.223 Press down on the pump to seat it. If the pump does not seat smoothly or flush with the case, remove the pump and check for interference. DO NOT FORCE IT. Place the converter housing on the pump and install the attaching bolts. Tighten the bolts to 20 ft-lbs

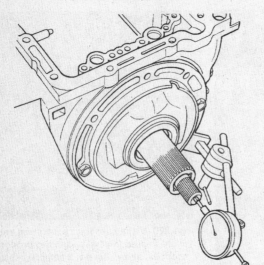

8A.224 Install a dial indicator onto the front pump assembly, with the dial indicator needle contacting the end of the input shaft

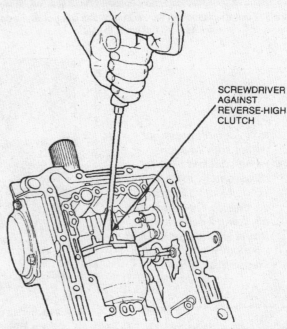

SCREWDRIVER AGAINST REVERSE-HIGH CLUTCH

8A.225 Using a screwdriver, pry against a lug on the reverse-high clutch and push the gear train to the rear of the case

SCREWDRIVER BETWEEN INPUT SHELL AND REVERSE PLANETARY

8A.226 Make sure the input shaft is fully seated and zero the dial indicator. Using a screwdriver, between the input shell and the reverse planetary assembly pry the input shell forward and read the amount of end play on the dial indicator. If the end play is within specifications, tighten all the converter housing attaching bolts to 20-35 ft-lbs

Note
The case end play clearance should be 0.008 to 0.042 inch. If the clearance is not within specifications your local dealer parts department has no. 1 and 2 selective thrust washers available in different thickness.

8A.227 Slowly lower the control valve assembly on the case. Align the slot in the manual valve with the post on the inner manual valve

8A.228 Check the contact between the detent spring roller and the inner manual lever (arrow)

8A.229 Install the control valve body-to-case attaching bolts (arrows). Tighten the bolts to 80-120 in-lbs

Note

On C3 models tighten the control valve body attaching bolts to 71-97 in-lbs.

8A.230 Install the governor onto the governor distributor sleeve

8A.231 Install the governor attaching bolts (arrows) and tighten them to 80-120 in-lbs. Place the extension housing gasket on the case

8A.232 Install a new extension housing seal . . .

8A.233 . . . driving it in until it's seated flush with the extension housing (arrows)

8A.234 Place the extension housing onto the case and install five of the six attaching bolts. Do not install this bolt (arrow) at this time

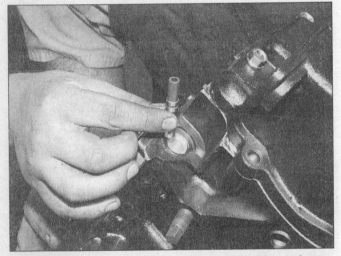

8A.235 Lubricate the vacuum modulator valve with petroleum jelly and install the valve into the case

8A.236 Apply a thin coat of petroleum jelly to the vacuum control rod and insert the rod into the valve

8A.237 Install an O-ring on the vacuum modulator (arrow). Lubricate the O-ring with transmission fluid and install the vacuum modulator into the case

8A.238 Install the vacuum modulator hold-down clamp and bolt. Tighten all the extension housing bolts to 28-40 ft-lbs

8A.239 Place a new oil pan gasket on the case, making sure the old gasket material has been completely removed

8A.240 Install the oil pan attaching bolts and tighten them to 12-16 ft-lbs

8A.241 Install a new lock nut with seal, on the intermediate band and the low-reverse band adjusting screws

8A.242 Adjust the bands as follows:

a) *Low-reverse band* - tighten adjusting screw to 10 ft-lbs, then back off exactly 3 turns

b) *Intermediate band* - tighten adjusting screw to 10 ft-lbs, then back off exactly 1-1/2 turns (1980 and earlier C3); 2 turns (1981 and later C3); 1-3/4 turns (C4); 4-1/4 turns (C5) or 1-1/2 turns (C6)

c) *Tighten the lock nuts* to 40 ft-lbs while holding the adjusting screw to keep it from turning

Notes

Chapter 8 Part B
Disassembly, inspection and assembly
C6 transmission

Introduction

The C6 transmission is a three-speed automatic transmission manufactured for rear-wheel drive vehicles. The major components of this transmission are:

a) *Torque converter*
b) *Gear-type oil pump*
c) *Control valve assembly*
d) *Three multiple-disc clutch packs*
e) *Planetary gear set*
f) *One-way clutch*
g) *Intermediate band*

Follow the photographic sequence for disassembly, inspection and assembly. The model shown is a typical transmission of this type. Differences do exist between models and many changes have been made over the years, so perform each step in order and lay the components out on a clean work bench in the EXACT ORDER of removal to prevent confusion during reassembly. Many snap-rings and clutch plates are similar in size, but must not be interchanged. Keep the individual parts together with the component from which they were removed to avoid mix-ups. Save all old parts and compare them with the new part to ensure they are an exact match before reassembly. Pay particular attention to the stack-up of the various clutch packs. Differences do exist between models and your transmission may not match the stack-up shown. Note the exact location of the check balls in the case and/or valve body. Save all the old parts until the overhaul is complete and the transmission has been thoroughly road tested; old components can be useful in diagnosing any problems that may arise.

Basic hand tools can be used for most procedures. although some special tools are required. Alternate procedures are shown where possible, but some procedures can only be accomplished with special tools. Read through the entire overhaul procedure before beginning work to familiarize yourself with the procedures and identify any special tools that may be needed. Thoroughly clean the exterior of the transmission before beginning disassembly.

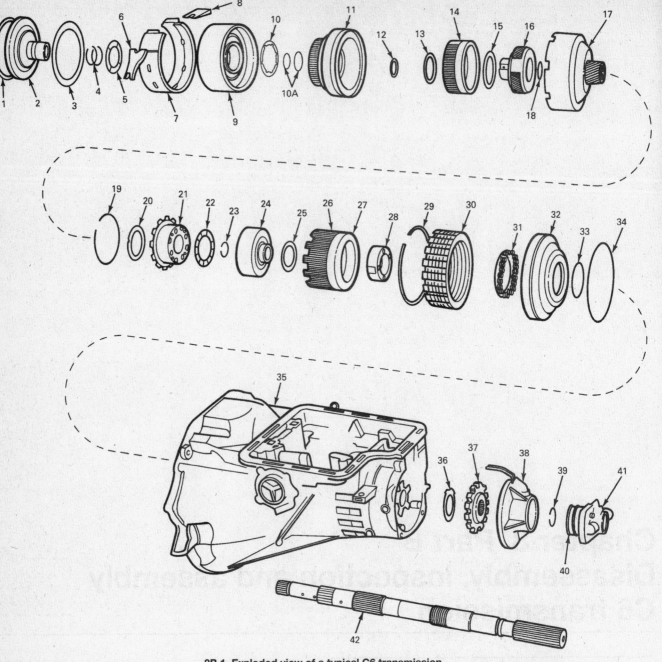

8B.1 Exploded view of a typical C6 transmission

1	Oil pump seal ring	15	Thrust washer no. 5	29	Snap-ring
2	Oil pump	16	Forward planetary assembly	30	Low-reverse clutch plates
3	Gasket	17	Input shell and sun gear assembly	31	Low-reverse piston return spring
4	Seal rings	18	Thrust washer no. 6	32	Low-reverse piston
5	Selective thrust washer no. 1	19	Snap-ring	33	Inner seal
6	Intermediate band apply strut	20	Thrust washer no. 7	34	Outer seal
7	Intermediate band	21	Reverse planetary assembly	35	Case
8	Intermediate band anchor strut	22	Thrust washer no. 8	36	Thrust washer no. 10
9	High-reverse clutch assembly	23	Retaining ring	37	Parking gear
10	Thrust washer no. 2	24	Reverse ring gear	38	Governor distributor sleeve
10A	Forward clutch seal rings	25	Thrust washer no. 9	39	Snap-ring
11	Forward clutch assembly	26	Low-reverse clutch hub	40	Governor collector
12	Thrust washer no. 3	27	One-way clutch	41	Governor
13	Thrust washer no. 4	28	One-way clutch inner race	42	Output shaft
14	Forward planetary ring gear				

Transmission disassembly

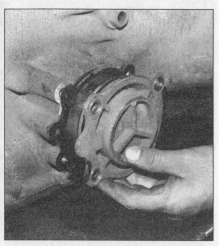

8B.2 Remove the four intermediate servo cover bolts and remove the servo cover

8B.3 Remove the intermediate servo piston from the cover. Remove the two seals from the piston and cover seal from the cover along with any gasket material sticking to the cover

8B.4 Remove the servo spring from the case and gasket

8B.5 Using a screwdriver and a hammer remove the rear extension housing seal and discard it. Be careful not to damage the bushing when you knock the seal out

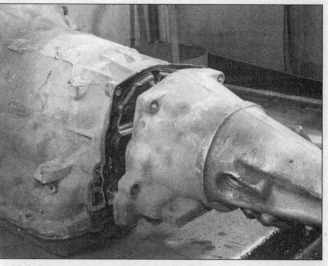

8B.6 Remove the six extension housing bolts and remove the extension housing.

Note

To remove the extension housing on flanged models (most trucks), remove the lock nut on the end of the output shaft. Using a soft-faced hammer tap the flanged yoke off of the output shaft. Remove the six extension housing attaching bolts and remove the extension housing

8B.7 Remove the four bolts that retain the governor to the governor collector and slide the governor off the output shaft

8B.8 Remove the kickdown lever nut, two neutral safety switch bolts (arrows) and remove the kickdown lever, shift lever and neutral safety switch

8B.9 Loosen and remove the band adjusting locknut and screw

8B.10 Remove the vacuum modulator bolt and hold-down clamp. Slowly pull the modulator out of the case. On some models the end of the vacuum modulator is threaded; unscrew this type from the case

8B.11 Remove the modulator rod from the vacuum modulator

8B.12 Withdraw the vacuum modulator valve from the case

8B.13 Remove the transmission oil pan bolts and remove the oil pan

8B.14 Remove the eight 1/4-inch bolts that attach the valve body to the case (arrows)

8B.15 Carefully lift the valve body assembly from the case

8B.16 Remove the intermediate band anchor strut

8B.17 Remove the intermediate band apply strut

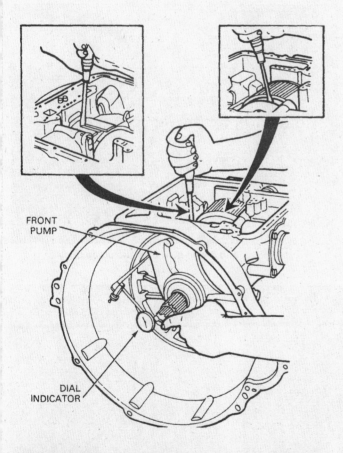

FRONT PUMP

DIAL INDICATOR

8B.18 Before you begin teardown of the gear train, it is best to take an end play check. Install a dial indicator on to the front pump assembly and position the indicator needle on the end of the input shaft. Using a screwdriver, pry the gear train rearward, press the input shaft in and zero the indicator; then pry forward and note the end play. Record the endplay for use on reassembly

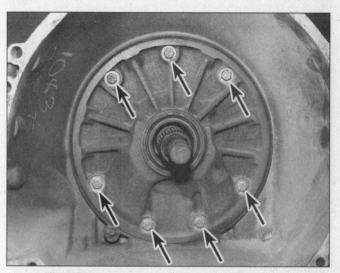

8B.19 Remove the seven front pump bolts (arrows)

8B.20 Using a large screwdriver, pry between the input shell and case to push the front pump out of the case

8B.21   Remove the front pump from the case

8B.22   Remove the input shaft from the stator support and the five bolts that retain the stator support to the pump body (arrows)

8B.23   Remove the stator support

8B.24   Remove the drive gear . . .

8B.25   . . . and driven gear from the pump body

8B.26   Remove the front pump oil seal and discard it. Be careful not to damage the pump bushing. Set the pump aside for later cleaning

8B.27   Remove the no. 1 selective thrust washer, if it's still inside the case

8B.28   Remove the reverse-high clutch assembly from the case

8B.29 Remove the selective snap-ring from the reverse-high clutch assembly

8B.30 Remove the pressure plate, friction discs and steel plates from the drum. The exact number of friction discs and steel plates may vary, depending on the year and model of your transmission; be sure to make notes so you can replace them with the same number on reassembly

8B.31 Using a suitable clutch spring compressor, carefully compress the clutch spring and remove the retaining snap-ring. If you don't have a spring compressor, use two C-clamps to compress the spring retainer

8B.32 Remove the spring retainer . . .

8B.33 . . . and the springs, making note of the spring locations

8B.34 Remove the piston from the drum. If the piston is difficult to remove, cover the piston with shop rags and place the drum, face down on the bench. Apply air pressure to the piston apply hole in the clutch hub and pop the piston out against the rags. Warning: *Always wear eye protection when using compressed air!*

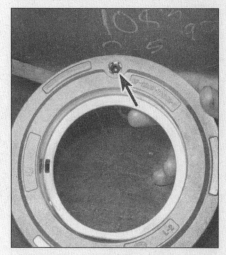

8B.35 Make sure the check ball moves freely in the piston (arrow)

8B.36 Remove the no. 2 thrust washer from the case. If you don't find it in the case it may be stuck on the reverse high clutch assembly

8B.37 Squeeze the ends of the intermediate band together and remove it from the case

8B.38 Remove the forward clutch assembly from the case

8B.39 Remove the no. 4 thrust washer from the forward clutch assembly

8B.40 Disassemble the forward clutch by removing the outer selective snap-ring

8B.41 Remove the rear pressure plate, friction plates ,steel plates, wave plate and forward pressure plate. The exact number of friction discs and steel plates may vary, depending on the year and model of your transmission; be sure to make notes so you can replace them with the same number on reassembly

8B.42 Remove the outer non selective snap-ring . . .

8B.43 . . . and remove the disc spring or Bellville spring from the drum

8B.44 Remove the steel ring from the piston . . .

8B.45 . . . and remove the piston from the drum

8B.46 Remove the outer seal from the piston and the inner seal on the forward clutch drum

8B.47 Make sure the check ball moves freely in the piston

8B.48 Remove the no.3 thrust washer, needle bearing and race

8B.49 Remove the forward clutch hub from the case

8B.50 Remove the no.5 thrust washer from the back of the forward clutch hub

8B.51 Remove the forward planetary gear assembly from the case

8B.52 Remove the input shell and sun gear assembly

8B.53 Remove the no.7 thrust washer from the input shell. The no.6 thrust washer is a steel disc that rides on the outside of the input shell and is held in place by the sun gear

8B.54 Use a screwdriver to pry the snap-ring from the case, retaining the reverse planetary gear assembly

8B.55 Remove the reverse planetary gear assembly from the case

8B.56 Remove the no. 8 thrust washer from on top of the ring gear or behind the planetary gear assembly

8B.57 Remove the snap-ring retaining the reverse ring gear to the output shaft. Note: *Models with a flanged-type output shaft (most trucks) will not have this snap-ring*

8B.58 After removing the snap-ring the reverse ring gear can be removed but don't remove it now, remove the output shaft first

8B.59 Withdraw the output shaft and governor distributor body from the case

8B.60 Remove the bolts that retain the governor distributor sleeve to the case

8B.61 Using a screwdriver, carefully pry the governor distributor sleeve and oil feed tubes from the case without bending the tubes

8B.62 Remove the parking gear and the no. 10 thrust washer, which will fall out when then distributor sleeve is removed

8B.63 Remove the parking pawl and spring from the case

8B.64 Slide the inner downshift lever out of the manual shaft

8B.65 Remove the nut that retains the inner manual lever to the manual shaft

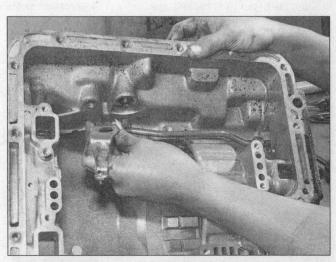

8B.66 Remove the parking pawl actuating rod and inner manual lever from the case. **Note:** *There are two types of detent spring and roller assemblies: One type is attached to the valve body and comes off with the valve body. The other type is bolted to the case and not normally removed from the case unless it's absolutely necessary*

8B.67 Withdraw the outer manual lever and shaft from the case

8B.68 Using a screwdriver, pry the manual shaft seal from the case. Be careful not to damage the seal bore with the screwdriver

8B.69 Remove the reverse ring gear from the case

8B.70 Remove the no. 9 thrust washer from the backside of the ring gear, or from inside the low-reverse clutch hub

8B.71 Pry the case snap-ring retaining low reverse clutch plates from the groove

8B.72 Remove the low-reverse clutch hub and one-way clutch assembly from the case

8B.73 Remove the one-way clutch inner snap-ring from the hub . . .

8B.74 . . . and remove the one-way clutch roller, spring and cage assembly

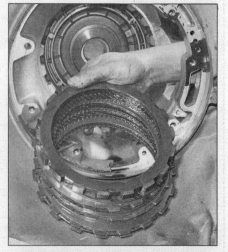

8B.75 Remove the low reverse clutch pressure plate, friction discs and steel plates from the case

8B.76 Slowly remove the five bolts, in an even manner, that retain the one-way clutch inner race to the case

8B.77 With the bolts removed, the spring pressure will push the inner race away from the case allowing the snap-ring, spring retainer and springs to fall free into the case

8B.78 Remove the one-way clutch inner race . . .

8B.79 . . . the snap-ring and spring retainer . . .

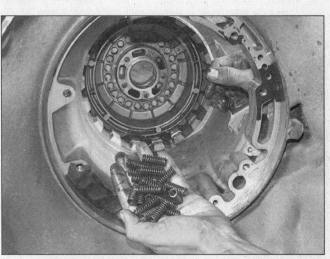

8B.80 . . . and the springs from inside the case

8B.81 Remove the low-reverse piston from the case by applying air pressure to the low-reverse clutch apply passage, forcing the piston from the case. Place shop rags inside the case to catch the piston. Caution: *Do not place your head or hands near the case when applying air pressure to the apply passage. The piston will be ejected with some force and could fly out and hit you. Always wear eye protection when using compressed air!*

8B.82 Once the piston is free, remove it from the case

Component inspection and subassembly

Using an approved cleaning solvent, clean and dry all the components thoroughly, including the case. Do not use rags to wipe the components dry, lint from the rag may lodge in the oil passages causing a valve to stick.

Inspect the following transmission components and repair or replace as necessary:

a) *Case - Inspect the exterior of the case for damage, cracks and porosity* **(see illustration).** *Check the valve body surface for damage and flatness. Check all the oil passages, the accumulator bore, the speedometer bore and the governor bore for damage. Check all threaded holes for damage. Damaged threads may be repaired by drilling, tapping and installing thread inserts. Check the oil cooler line fittings for damage. Check the interior of the case for damaged retaining ring grooves. Check the case lugs for excessive wear. Check the output shaft bushing for wear. Inspect the manual linkage and the park lock linkage for damage.*

b) *Forward clutch pack and high-reverse clutch pack - Inspect the condition of the clutch plates. Check for signs of overheating. Check the friction plates for wear, pitting, cracking or flaking. Check the intermediate band for wear or damage. Check the pistons for damage. Check the return springs for damage or signs of overheating. Check the bushings for wear or damage. Check the check balls for damage and freedom of movement. Check the input shaft for scoring or damages splines.*

c) *Planetary gear set - Inspect the planetary carriers, ring gears, sun gear and drive shell for damaged teeth or splines. Check for worn bushings. Check the thrust bearings for wear or damage. Inspect the pinion gear bearings for wear or damage.*

d) *Low-reverse clutch pack and one-way clutch assembly - Inspect the condition of the clutch plates. Check for signs of overheating. Check the friction plates for wear, pitting, cracking or flaking. Inspect the one-way clutch for worn or damaged rollers. Check the springs for damage. Check the race finish for scoring, wear or damage.*

e) *Output shaft and governor - Inspect the output shaft for damages splines, scoring or worn bushing races. Check the governor for stuck valves. Check the governor distributor O-ring grooves for damage.*

8B.83 Inspect the case carefully for cracks and damaged bolt holes. Installing an incorrect bolt or over-tightening can cause a case to crack (arrow)

Oil pump assembly

Clean the oil pump components with solvent and air dry. Inspect the gears and gear pocket for scoring or damage. Check the hub for damaged sealing ring grooves. Inspect the stator shaft bushings for wear or damage. Inspect the pump cover and body faces for nicks or burrs and make sure the oil passages and lubrication holes are not restricted. Place the pump body over the cover and check for warpage.

8B.84 Inspect the pump body bushing for wear or damage. If necessary see Chapter 2 for servicing. When installing a new bushing, align the slot in the bushing . . .

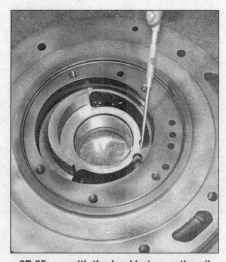

8B.85 . . . with the land between the oil passages. Check the pump body gear area for wear, nicks, burrs or scoring

8B.86 Install the front oil pump seal, driving it in until it's flush with the housing

8B.87 Check the stator support bushings, if necessary see Chapter 2 for servicing. Install the rear bushing with the notch aligned to the rear

8B.88 Install the stator support front bushing flush with the inner taper on the end of the stator shaft

8B.89 Check the stator support face for any defects or deep scoring at the gear contact surfaces

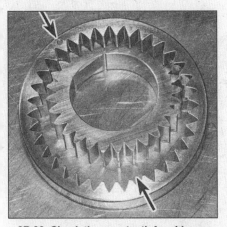

8B.90 Check the gear teeth for chips or cracks and the gear face for excessive wear or deep scratches. If found to be defective, replace the gears as a set. The mark on the gear and the chamfered end of the teeth (arrows) must face into the pump body during assembly (toward the seal)

8B.91 Lubricate the pump housing and gears with transmission fluid and install the gears into the pump body

8B.92 The drive gear must be installed with the flat side of the offset notches (arrow) to the rear of the pump (away from the seal) or the converter will damage the gear

8B.93 Position the stator support over the pump body and align the bolt holes

8B.94 Bring the pump body up to the stator support, install the five bolts and tighten them to 12-16 ft-lbs

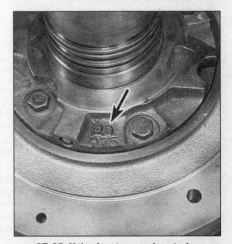

8B.95 If the front pump has to be replaced you should try and match casting numbers (arrow)

Control valve assembly

Lay the control valve assembly on a clean work surface and begin removing the valves from the valve body. Withdraw the bushings, valves and springs and lay them out on a clean lint-free towel in the EXACT order of removal. Keep them in the proper orientation to the valve body. Clean all the bushings, valves and springs. Check the valves and bushings closely for scoring, cracks or damage. Check the springs for collapsed or distorted coils. Finally check the valve body bores for scoring or damage and begin reassembly.

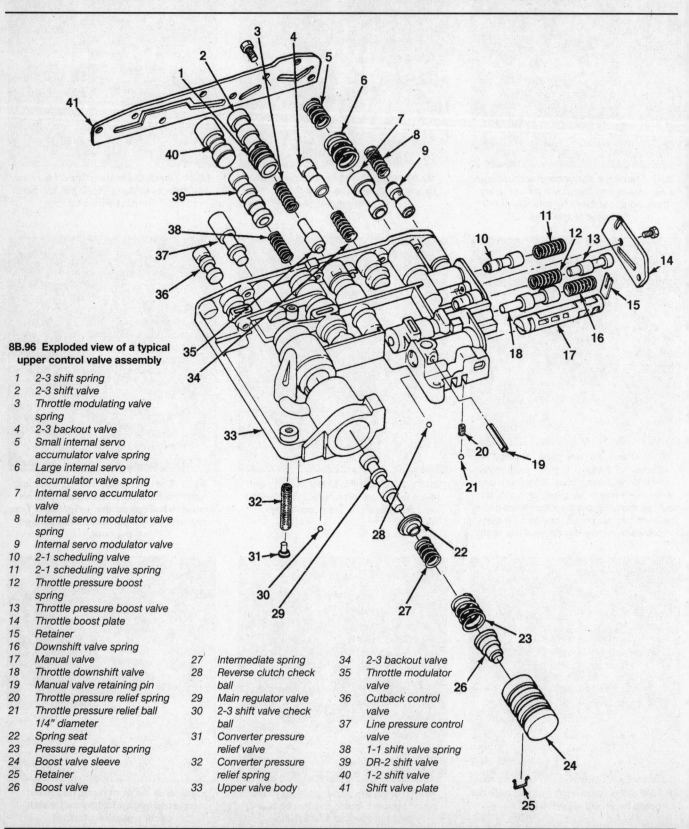

8B.96 Exploded view of a typical upper control valve assembly

1	2-3 shift spring
2	2-3 shift valve
3	Throttle modulating valve spring
4	2-3 backout valve
5	Small internal servo accumulator valve spring
6	Large internal servo accumulator valve spring
7	Internal servo accumulator valve
8	Internal servo modulator valve spring
9	Internal servo modulator valve
10	2-1 scheduling valve
11	2-1 scheduling valve spring
12	Throttle pressure boost spring
13	Throttle pressure boost valve
14	Throttle boost plate
15	Retainer
16	Downshift valve spring
17	Manual valve
18	Throttle downshift valve
19	Manual valve retaining pin
20	Throttle pressure relief spring
21	Throttle pressure relief ball 1/4" diameter
22	Spring seat
23	Pressure regulator spring
24	Boost valve sleeve
25	Retainer
26	Boost valve

27	Intermediate spring
28	Reverse clutch check ball
29	Main regulator valve
30	2-3 shift valve check ball
31	Converter pressure relief valve
32	Converter pressure relief spring
33	Upper valve body

34	2-3 backout valve
35	Throttle modulator valve
36	Cutback control valve
37	Line pressure control valve
38	1-1 shift valve spring
39	DR-2 shift valve
40	1-2 shift valve
41	Shift valve plate

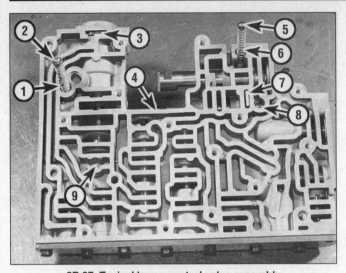

8B.97 Typical lower control valve assembly

1   Converter pressure relief spring
2   Converter pressure relief valve
3   Pressure boost valve sleeve
4   Downshift valve and spring
5   Throttle pressure relief ball 1/4 inch diameter
6   Throttle pressure relief spring
7   Downshift valve retainer
8   Reverse clutch check ball
9   2-3 shift check valve

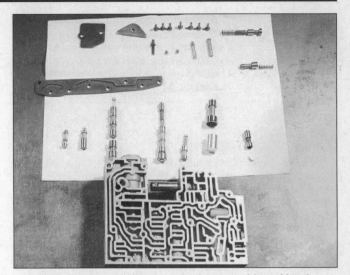

8B.98 Disassemble the control valve assembly and lay the components out on a clean lint-free towel. Clean and inspect the valve body components. Check each valve for nicks or burrs

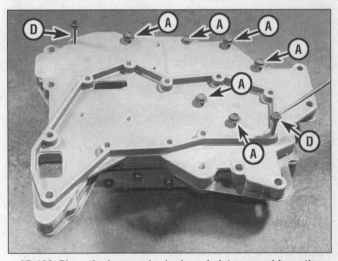

8B.100 Place the lower valve body and plate assembly on the upper valve body and install the six 7/8-inch long attaching screws (A) finger tight. Leave the two 1-5/8 inch long screws (D) loose until the filter is installed

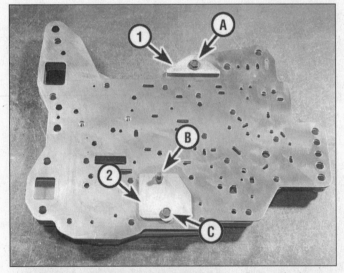

8B. 99 Carefully place the separator plate gasket on the lower valve body. Place the separator plate on top of the gasket and align the bolt holes. Install the number (1) reinforcement plate and 7/8-inch attaching screw (A) finger tight. Install the number (2) reinforcement plate and the 5/8-inch stud attaching screw (B) and the 5/16-inch attaching screw (C) finger tight

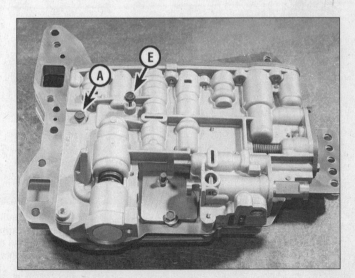

8B.101 Flip the valve body over and install the 7/8-inch screw (A) and the 1-3/8-inch long attaching screw (E) finger tight. Tighten all the screws to 40-55 in-lbs

8B.102 Remove the screw (D) from the lower valve body and install the gasket and filter screen. Start the screw (D) and the eight 1-1/4 inch long attaching screws (F). Tighten the (D) and (F) screws to 40-55 in-lbs

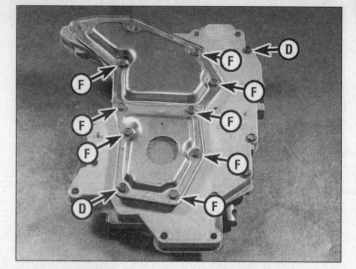

Governor valve assembly

Lay the governor assembly on a clean work surface and begin removing the screws and retaining clips from the body and counter weight. Lay them out on a clean lint-free towel in the EXACT order of removal. Keep them in the proper orientation to the governor body. Clean the valves and body. Check all the parts for dirt and wear and scoring. **Note:** *See Chapter 8, Part A for exploded view.*

Reverse-high clutch assembly

8B.103 Install the reverse clutch inner seal on the drum and install the outer piston seal on the piston. Lubricate the piston and seals with clean petroleum jelly. Carefully push the piston into the reverse drum until seated. To prevent possible damage to the seals, use a seal installation tool (see Chapter 2)

8B.104 Install the reverse piston return springs . . .

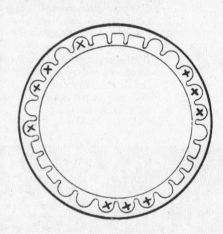

8B.105 . . . into the pockets marked with an X

8B.106 Install the spring retainer over the springs

8B.107a Using a suitable clutch spring compressor, carefully compress the clutch springs and install the retaining snap-ring

8B. 107b If you don't have a spring compressor, use two C-clamps to compress the spring retainer

8B.108 Install a steel plate into the drum, against the piston

8B.109 Soak the reverse clutch friction plates in automatic transmission fluid for fifteen minutes. Install a clutch friction plate against the steel plate. Alternately install steel plates and friction plates to equal your original clutch pack

8B.110 Install the thick flat pressure plate . . .

8B.111 . . . and the selective snap-ring. Make sure the snap-ring is fully seated in the groove

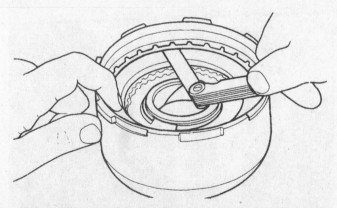

8B.112 Using a feeler gauge check the clearance between the selective snap-ring and the pressure plate. When making the check, push down lightly on the pressure plate

Note

The reverse-high clutch pressure plate-to-selective snap-ring clearance should be 0.022-0.036 inch. If the clearance is not within specifications your local dealership parts department has selective snap-rings in available in different thicknesses.

Forward clutch assembly

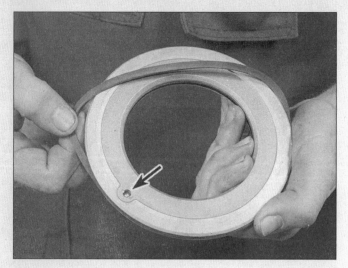

8B.113 Install the forward clutch inner seal on the drum. Install the outer piston seal on the piston. Inspect the piston check ball and make sure it's clean and moves freely (arrow). Lubricate the piston and seals with clean petroleum jelly. Carefully push the piston into the reverse drum until seated. To prevent possible damage to the seals, use a seal installation tool (see Chapter 2)

8B.114 Install the steel pressure ring into the groove in the piston

8B.115 Install the reverse piston Bellville return spring into the drum . . .

8B.116 . . .and install the non selective retaining snap-ring

8B.117 Install the forward pressure plate with the beveled side against the Bellville spring and the flat side up

8B.118 Soak the forward clutch friction plates in automatic transmission fluid for fifteen minutes. Install a clutch friction plate against the pressure plate

8B.119 Install a steel plate against the friction plate. Alternately install friction plates and steel plates to equal your original clutch pack

8B.120 Install the thick, flat rear pressure plate . . .

8B.121 . . . and install the selective snap-ring. Make sure the snap-ring is fully seated in the groove

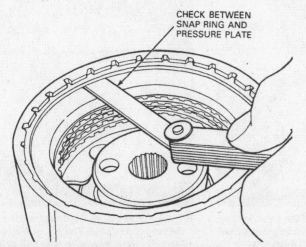

CHECK BETWEEN
SNAP RING AND
PRESSURE PLATE

8B.122 Using a feeler gauge check the clearance between the selective snap-ring and the pressure plate. When making the check, push down lightly on the pressure plate

Note

The forward clutch pressure plate-to-selective snap-ring clearance should be 0.021-0.046 inch. If the clearance is not within specifications, your local dealership parts department has selective snap-rings available in different thicknesses.

Transmission assembly

An automatic transmission is a precision fit piece of equipment. Install each component as shown, do not force any component into place. If it doesn't fit properly, find out why and rectify the situation. Maintain a clean work place and lubricate all moving parts as they are installed. Lubricate thrust washers and bearings with automatic transmission fluid (ATF) or petroleum jelly. Use petroleum jelly to retain thrust washers and check balls in their proper location as the component is installed. Dip all friction plates in ATF before installation.

8B.123 Lubricate the inner low-reverse piston seal with clean petroleum jelly and install the seal in the piston groove

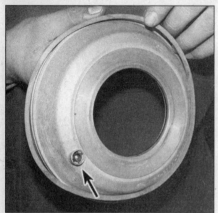

8B.124 Lubricate the outer seal with clean petroleum jelly and install the seal in the outer piston seal groove. Make sure the check ball in the piston can move freely (arrow)

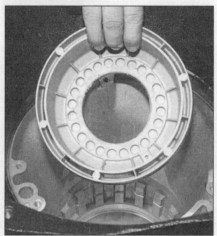

8B.125 Lightly lubricate the bottom of the case and low-reverse piston with transmission fluid . . .

8B.126 . . . and carefully install the piston into the case, turning and pushing at the same time. If at any time the piston feels like it's binding stop and remove it to prevent damage to the seals

8B.127 From inside the case, install the one-way clutch inner race

8B.128 From the rear of the case, install the five attaching bolts and tighten them evenly to 18-25 ft-lbs

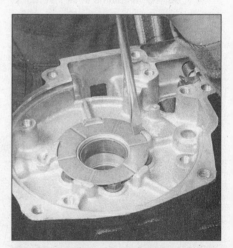

8B.129 Install the no. 10 thrust washer on the rear of the case. The thrust washer should cover the one-way clutch bolt heads. Once the thrust washer is aligned properly, stake the case tabs to retain the thrust washer in the case. Lubricate the thrust washer with clean petroleum jelly

8B.130 Place the parking gear over the no. 10 thrust washer and install the parking pawl shaft into the case

8B. 131 Slide the parking pawl onto the parking pawl shaft . . .

8B.132 . . . and install the return spring. Position the straight end of the return spring (A) into the case groove and the hooked end of the return spring (B) on the parking pawl

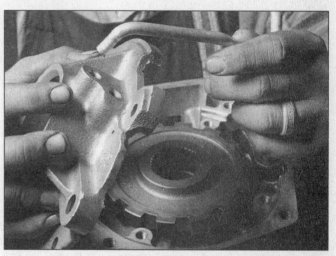

8B.133 Press the oil feed tubes into the governor distributor sleeve . . .

8B.134 . . . install the governor distributor sleeve over the parking gear and press the oil feed tubes into the case (arrows)

8B.135 Install the four governor distributor sleeve attaching bolts (arrows) and tighten them to 12-16 ft-lbs

8B.136 Install the parking pawl actuating rod guide plate . . .

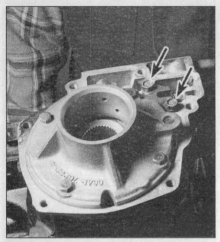

8B.137 . . . with the two guide plate attaching bolts (arrows). Tighten the bolts to 12-16 ft-lbs

8B.138 Install the outer seal on the intermediate servo piston . . .

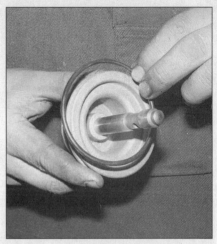

8B.139 . . . and the round inner seal in the large groove. Lubricate both seals with clean petroleum jelly

8B.140 Install the square-cut seal into the groove in intermediate servo cover . . .

8B.141 . . . and install the gasket to the face of the intermediate servo cover

8B.142 Lubricate the seals with clean petroleum jelly and the inside of the cover with transmission fluid. Install the intermediate servo piston into the intermediate cover

8B.143 Press the piston in until fully seated into the cover

8B.144 Install the intermediate servo piston return spring in the case . . .

8B.145 . . . and install the servo cover assembly with the apply pin through the return spring

8B.146 Press the servo cover down until flush with the case and install the four attaching bolts (arrows). Tighten the bolts to 14-20 ft-lbs

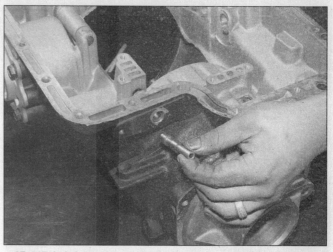

8B.147 Lubricate the vacuum modulator valve with petroleum jelly and install the valve into the case

8B.148 Apply a thin coat of petroleum jelly to the vacuum control rod and insert the rod into the valve

8B.149 Install an O-ring on the vacuum modulator (arrow). Lubricate the O-ring with transmission fluid and install the vacuum modulator into the case

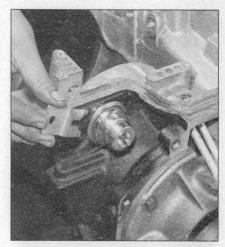

8B.150 Install the vacuum modulator hold-down clamp and bolt. Tighten the bolt to 8-12 ft-lbs

Note

Early model vacuum modulators are screwed into the case and require no hold-down clamp. Use an open-end wrench on the hex portion of the modulator body. Do not try to turn the modulator by hand, as you can damage the diaphragm.

8B.151 Place the manual shaft seal into the case . . .

8B.152 . . . and using the appropriate seal installer, seat the seal into the case (a deep socket can also be used as a driver)

8B.153 Lubricate the outer manual shaft with transmission fluid and install the manual shaft into the case

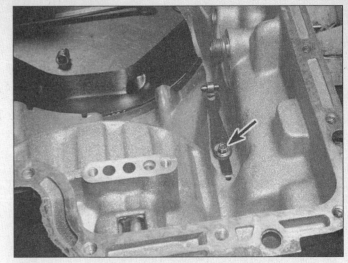

8B.154 Install the detent spring and roller in the case. Tighten the attaching bolt to 90-120 in-lbs (arrow)

Note

On some models the detent spring and roller assembly is bolted to the valve body and installed with the valve body.

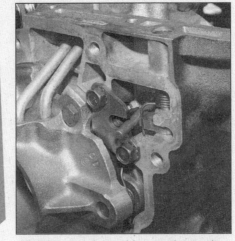

8B.155 Insert the parking pawl actuating rod into the guide plate

8B.156 Attach the inner manual lever and parking pawl actuating rod to the outer manual shaft

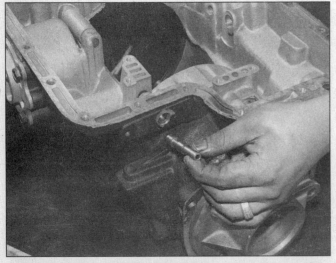

8B.157 Install the nut that retains the inner manual lever to the outer manual shaft and tighten the nut with a 7/8-inch end wrench to 12-16 ft-lbs

8B.158 Check the engagement of the detent roller on inner manual lever. The roller should hold in each notch of the manual lever and click to the next notch smoothly

8B.159 Install the inner downshift lever and shaft into the outer manual shaft

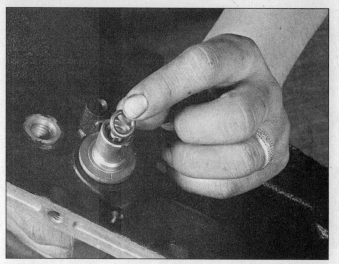

8B.160 Install the downshift shaft O-ring in the end of the outer manual shaft to retain the downshift shaft and lever in place

8B.161 Install the low-reverse piston return springs . . .

8B.162 . . . and place the spring retainer over the springs

8B.163 Install the non-selective retaining snap-ring on the inner one-way clutch race

8B.164 Using a large blade screwdriver, place the tip of the screwdriver on the retaining snap-ring. Use your hand to tap the screwdriver handle and slowly work your way around the snap-ring until the snap-ring is fully seated on the inner race

Note

A special low-reverse spring compressor is available to compress the low-reverse return spring, allowing easier installation of the snap-ring; use the tool, if available (see Chapter 2).

8B.165 Install a steel plate into the case and onto the low-reverse piston

8B.166 Soak the clutch friction plates in automatic transmission fluid for fifteen minutes. Install a clutch friction plate against the steel plate. Alternately install friction plates and steel plates to equal your original clutch pack

8B.167 Install the thick, flat rear pressure plate . . .

8B.168 . . . and install the non-selective snap-ring . . .

8B.169 . . . making sure the snap-ring is fully seated in the case groove (arrows)

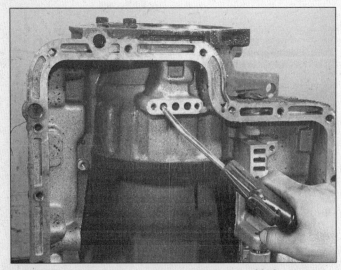

8B.170 Air check the low-reverse clutch assembly for proper operation. Apply air pressure to the apply passage; you should hear the piston apply firmly against the clutch pack. Warning: *Always wear eye protection when using compressed air!*

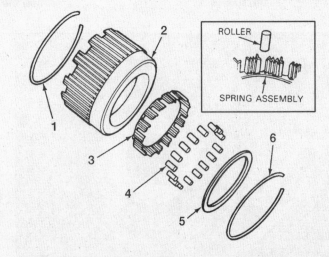

8B.171 Exploded view of the low-reverse clutch hub and one-way clutch

1	Snap-ring	4	Rollers
2	Low-reverse clutch hub	5	Bushing
3	Spring assembly	6	Snap-ring

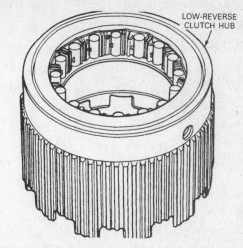

LOW-REVERSE CLUTCH HUB

8B.172 Assemble the one-way clutch on the low-reverse clutch hub

8B.173 Install the low-reverse clutch hub and one-way clutch into the case. Rotate the hub clockwise as you press the one-way clutch over the inner race. The one-way clutch must <u>only</u> rotate clockwise and lock-up in the counterclockwise direction for proper operation

8B.174 The low-reverse clutch hub must mesh with the low-reverse friction plates (arrow) and fully seat in the case

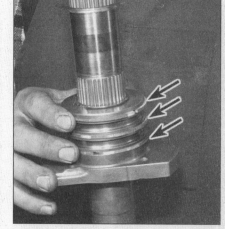

8B.175 Lubricate the three seal rings with petroleum jelly and install the rings on the governor collector body (arrows)

8B.176 Lubricate the distributor sleeve with petroleum jelly and install the output shaft and governor collector body into the case

8B.177 Place the no. 9 thrust washer on the back of the reverse ring gear and apply petroleum jelly to retain it in place. Install the reverse ring gear over the output shaft, slide it down the shaft engaging the splines

8B.178 Install the reverse ring gear-to-output shaft snap-ring over the output shaft . . .

8B.180 Install the no. 8 thrust washer on the backside, and the no. 7 thrust washer on the top of the reverse planetary gear set. Apply petroleum jelly to both thrust washers to retain them in place. Place the planetary gear set over the output shaft and slide it down the shaft, meshing the pinion gears with the reverse ring gear

8B.179 . . . and seat it in the output shaft groove (arrow). The output shaft is secured by this snap-ring

8B.181 Install the non selective snap-ring into the groove in the reverse clutch hub. This snap-ring secures the planetary gear set assembly to the reverse clutch hub

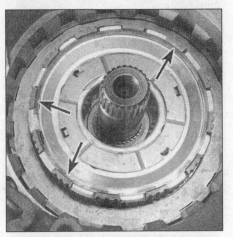

8B.182 Make sure the snap-ring is fully seated in the reverse clutch hub groove (arrows)

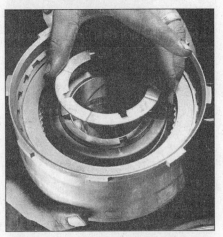

8B.183 Lubricate the no. 2 thrust washer with petroleum jelly and install the no. 2 washer on the reverse-high clutch hub

8B.184 Install the forward clutch assembly into the reverse high clutch, engaging the splines with the friction discs

8B.185 Rotate the reverse-high drum while lowering the forward hub until the forward hub is fully seated in the reverse high drum

8B.186 Lubricate the no. 3 thrust washer needle bearing race with petroleum jelly and install the race on the forward clutch drum

8B.187 Lubricate the no.3 thrust washer needle bearing with petroleum jelly and place it on the race in the forward clutch drum

8B.188 Lubricate the no. 4 thrust washer with petroleum jelly and install it on the forward clutch hub. Install the forward clutch hub into the forward clutch assembly, engaging the splines with the friction discs

8B.189 Rotate the forward hub back and forth while holding the reverse high drum to engage the friction discs. Continue until the forward hub has engaged all the friction discs and is fully seated in the forward clutch

8B.190 Lubricate the no. 5 thrust washer and the no. 3 needle bearing outer race with petroleum jelly and install them on the forward planetary gear set

8B.191 Place the forward planetary into the forward clutch hub and ring gear, engaging the planetary pinion gears with the ring gear

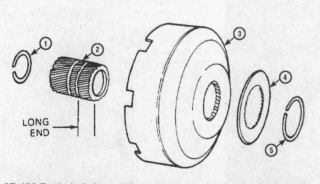

LONG END →

8B.192 Exploded view of the sun gear and input shell assembly

1	Forward snap-ring	4	No. 6 thrust washer-
2	Sun gear		wear plate
3	Input shell	5	Rear snap-ring

8B.193 Install the input shell and sun gear assembly over the forward clutch assembly . . .

8B.194 . . . . engaging the tabs of the reverse-high clutch into the input shell (arrows)

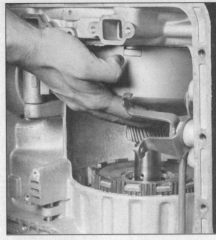

8B.195 Slowly lower the gear train into the case until the input shell seats on the no. 7 thrust washer

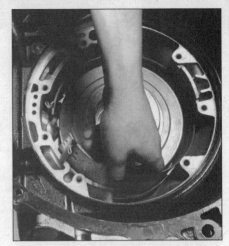

8B.196 Install the intermediate band around the reverse-high drum

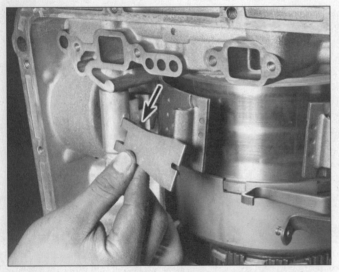

8B.197 Place the narrow end of the apply strut against the servo (arrow) . . .

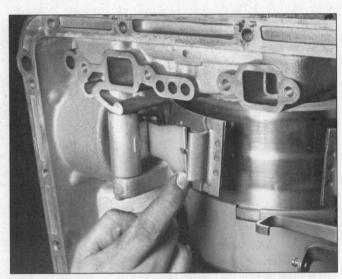

8B.198 . . . and lock the wide end into the band

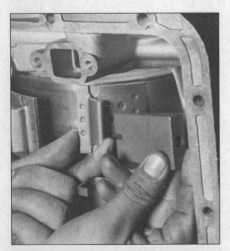

8B.199 Install the anchor strut narrow end into the band

8B.200 Install the band adjusting screw into the case . . .

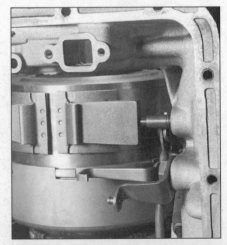

8B.201 . . . until the end of the adjusting screw locks in the anchor

8B.202 Install the front pump O-ring in the groove on the pump body with the stripe facing out and lubricate it with petroleum jelly

8B.203 Install the no.1 selective thrust washer on the stator support using petroleum jelly to retain it in place during installation

> **Note**
> *If the end play was not within specifications when checked prior to disassembly, replace the original no.1 selective thrust washer with a thicker or thinner thrust washer, as required, to bring the endplay within specifications*

8B.204 Install the two locking seal rings on the stator support

8B.205 Make sure the seal ring ends are properly locked and in the grooves. Lubricate the seal rings with petroleum jelly

8B.206 Install two front pump alignment studs into the case (arrows)

8B.207 Make sure the case surface is cleaned of all old gasket material and place a new gasket over the alignment studs. Make sure all the holes are properly aligned

8B.208 Carefully lower the pump into the case

8B.209 Press the front pump down to seat it. If the pump does not seat smoothly, or flush with the case - DO NOT FORCE IT. Remove the pump and check for interference

8B.210 Install the input shaft into the stator support, take care not to damage the bushing in the stator support. If the input shaft will not seat into the stator support, remove the input shaft and check for nicks or burrs

8B.211 Remove the two alignment studs and install the pump attaching bolts (arrows). Tighten the bolts to 16-25 ft-lbs

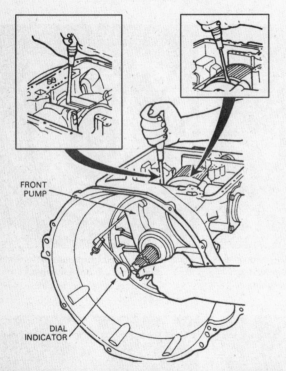

FRONT
PUMP

DIAL
INDICATOR

8B.212 Install a dial indicator on to the front pump assembly and position the indicator needle on the end of the input shaft. Using a screwdriver, pry the gear train rearward, press the input shaft in and zero the indicator; then pry forward and note the end play

8B.213 Install a new lock nut, with seal, on the intermediate band adjusting screw

Note

The end play should be 0.008 to 0.044 inch. If the clearance is not within specifications, remove the front pump and change the no. 1 selective thrust washer with a thicker or thinner thrust washer, as required. Your local dealer parts department has selective thrust washers available in different thickness

8B.214 Adjust the intermediate band by tightening the adjustment screw to ten ft-lbs, then back the adjusting screw off exactly 1-1/2 turns. Hold the adjusting screw to keep it from turning and tighten the lock nut to 35-45 ft-lbs

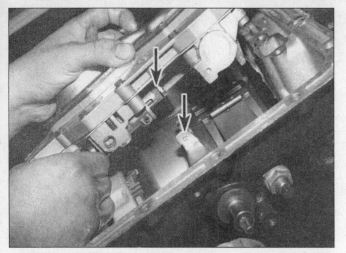

8B.215 Slowly lower the valve body on the case. Line up the slot in the manual valve with the post on the inner manual valve (arrows)

8B.216 Install the eight bolts that attach the control valve assembly to the case. Tighten the bolts to 95-125 in-lbs

8B.217 Place a new oil pan gasket on the case, making sure all the old gasket material has been removed

8B.218 Install the 17 oil pan attaching bolts and tighten them to 12-16 ft-lbs

8B.219 Install the governor and tighten the four attaching bolts to 80-120 in-lbs

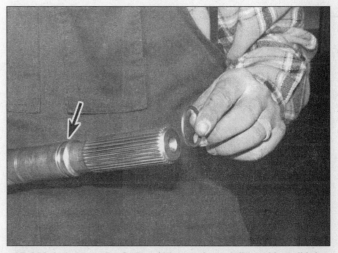

8B.220 Lubricate the O-ring with petroleum jelly and install it in the output shaft groove (arrow)

8B.221 Replace the extension housing bushing

8B.222 When the new bushing is installed, make sure the oil passage in the bushing aligns with the extension housing oil passage (arrows)

8B.223 Install a new extension housing seal, making sure it is seated flush with the extension housing (arrows)

8B.224 Install the extension housing gasket . . .

8B.225 . . . and the extension housing. Tightening the extension housing attaching bolts to 25-35 ft-lbs

Chapter 8   Part C
Disassembly, inspection and assembly
AOD transmission

Introduction

The AOD transmission is a four-speed automatic transmission manufactured for rear-wheel drive vehicles. The major components of this transmission are:

a) *Torque converter*
b) *Gear-type oil pump*
c) *Control valve assembly*
d) *four multiple-disc clutch packs*
e) *Planetary gear set*
f) *Two one-way clutch assemblies*
g) *Overdrive and low-reverse bands*

Follow the photographic sequence for disassembly, inspection and assembly. The model shown is a typical transmission of this type. Differences do exist between models and many changes have been made over the years, so perform each step in order and lay the components out on a clean work bench in the EXACT ORDER of removal to prevent confusion during reassembly. Many snap-rings and clutch plates are similar in size, but must not be interchanged. Keep the individual parts together with the component from which they were removed to avoid mix-ups. Save all old parts and compare them with the new part to ensure they are an exact match before reassembly. Pay particular attention to the stack-up of the various clutch packs. Differences do exist between models and your transmission may not match the stack-up shown. Note the exact location of the check balls in the case and/or valve body. Save all the old parts until the overhaul is complete and the transmission has been thoroughly road tested; old components can be useful in diagnosing any problems that may arise.

The AOD is a metric-dimensioned transmission; use metric tools on the fasteners. Basic hand tools can be used for most procedures. although some special tools are required. Alternate procedures are shown where possible, but some procedures can only be accomplished with special tools. Read through the entire overhaul procedure before beginning work to familiarize yourself with the procedures and identify any special tools that may be needed. Thoroughly clean the exterior of the transmission before beginning disassembly.

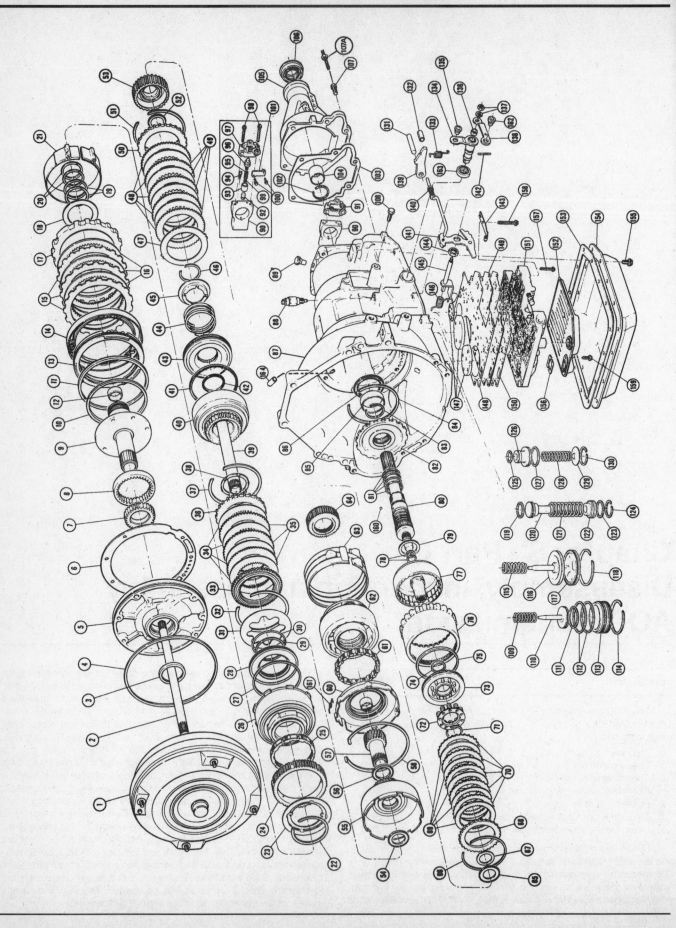

8C.1 Exploded view of a typical AOD transmission

#	Part	#	Part	#	Part
1	Torque converter	37	Reverse clutch retaining ring (selective)	121	3-4 accumulator valve return spring
2	Direct drive shaft	38	No. 2 thrust washer	122	3-4 accumulator cover
3	Front pump seal	39	Turbine shaft	123	3-4 accumulator cover seal
4	Front pump O-ring	40	Forward clutch drum	124	Retaining snap-ring
5	Front pump body	41	Forward clutch piston seal (outer)	125	2-3 accumulator valve seal (small)
6	Front pump gasket	42	Forward clutch piston seal (inner)	126	2-3 accumulator valve seal (large)
7	Front pump drive gear	43	Forward clutch piston	127	2-3 accumulator valve
8	Front pump driven gear	44	Forward clutch piston return spring	128	2-3 accumulator valve return spring
9	Front pump stator support	45	Return spring retainer	129	2-3 accumulator cover
10	Intermediate clutch piston inner lip seal	46	Retaining snap-ring	130	Retaining snap-ring
11	Intermediate clutch piston outer lip seal	47	Waved plate	131	Park pawl shaft
12	Front pump bushing	48	Forward clutch steel plate	132	Guide cup
13	Intermediate clutch piston	49	Forward and reverse clutch friction plate	133	Park pawl return spring
14	Intermediate clutch piston return springs & retainer	50	Forward and reverse clutch pressure plate	134	Manual lever
15	Intermediate clutch steel plates	51	Retaining snap-ring (selective)	135	Grommet
16	Intermediate clutch friction plates	52	No. 3 needle bearing (forward clutch)	136	Throttle lever oil seal
17	Intermediate clutch pressure plate	53	Forward clutch hub	137	Attaching nut lock washer
18	No. 1 thrust washer (selective)	54	No. 4 needle bearing	138	Throttle lever (outer)
19	Stator support seal rings (reverse clutch)	55	Reverse sun gear & drive shell assembly	139	Park pawl
20	Stator support seal rings (forward clutch)	56	No. 5 needle bearing	140	Park pawl actuating rod
21	Overdrive band	57	Forward sun gear	141	Manual lever (inner)
22	Intermediate one-way clutch retaining ring	58	Center support retaining ring	142	Roll pin
23	Intermediate one-way clutch retaining plate	59	Reverse band assembly	143	Detent spring
24	Intermediate one-way clutch outer race	60	Center support planetary	144	Nut
25	Intermediate one-way clutch assembly	61	Planetary one-way clutch cage spring and roller assembly	145	Throttle lever (inner)
26	Reverse clutch drum	62	Planetary assembly	146	Throttle tension spring
27	Reverse clutch piston seal (outer)	63	Reverse band	147	Valve body reinforcement plate
28	Reverse clutch piston	64	Direct clutch hub	148	Separator plate gasket (upper)
29	Reverse clutch piston seal (inner)	65	No. 7 needle bearing	149	Separator plate
30	Thrust ring	66	Retaining snap-ring (selective)	150	Separator plate gasket (lower)
31	Reverse clutch piston return spring	67	Thrust spacer	151	Valve body (main control)
32	Retaining snap-ring	68	Direct clutch pressure plate	152	Oil filter
33	Reverse clutch front pressure plate	69	Direct clutch friction plates	153	Oil pan gasket
34	Forward and reverse clutch friction plate	70	Direct Clutch steel plates	154	Oil pan
35	Reverse clutch steel plate	71	Retaining snap-ring	155	Bolt
36	Forward and reverse clutch rear pressure plate	72	Return spring retainer	156	Oil filter gasket
		73	Direct clutch piston	157	Bolt
		74	Direct clutch piston seal (inner)	158	Bolt
		75	Direct clutch piston seal (outer)	159	Bolt
		76	Ring gear and park gear	160	Ball (Governor drive)
		77	Direct clutch drum	161	Spring (anti clunk)
		78	Output shaft small steel seal rings	162	Grommet
		79	No. 8 needle bearing	163	Oil seal assembly
		80	Output shaft	164	Overdrive anchor pin
		81	Output shaft large steel seal rings		
		82	Output shaft hub		
		83	Retaining snap-ring		
		84	Retaining snap-ring		
		85	Rear case bushing		
		86	No. 9 needle bearing		
		87	Case assembly		
		88	Neutral start switch		
		89	Vent cap		
		90	Governor counterweight		
		91	Governor body		
		92	Governor plug		
		93	Governor sleeve		
		94	Governor oil screen		
		95	Governor valve spring		
		96	Governor valve		
		97	Governor body		
		98	Bolt (governor body to counterweight)		
		99	Clip (governor cover to governor body)		
		100	Bolt (governor cover to governor body)		
		101	Governor valve body cover		
		102	Retaining snap-ring		
		103	Extension housing bracket		
		104	Extension housing bushing		
		105	Extension housing		
		106	Extension housing seal		
		107	Bolt		
		107A	Stud		
		108	Pipe Plug		
		109	Overdrive servo piston return spring		
		110	Overdrive servo piston		
		111	Overdrive servo piston seal		
		112	Overdrive servo cover seal rings		
		113	Overdrive servo cover		
		114	Retaining snap-ring		
		115	Reverse servo piston return spring		
		116	Reverse servo piston (selective)		
		117	Reverse servo cover		
		118	Retaining snap-ring		
		119	3-4 accumulator valve seal		
		120	3-4 accumulator valve		

Transmission disassembly

8C.2 Remove the neutral start switch with a 3/4-inch wrench

8C.3 Using a screwdriver and a hammer remove and discard the rear extension housing seal. Be careful not to damage the bushing when you knock the seal out

8C.4 Remove the six extension housing bolts and remove the extension housing

8C.5 Remove the governor retainer snap-ring

8C.6 When sliding the governor off of the output shaft use a magnet to remove the governor drive ball (arrow). The ball is used to center the governor on the output shaft

8C.7 Remove the transmission oil pan bolts and remove the oil pan. Clean the inside of the oil pan and you can use it as a parts tray

8C.8 Remove the three bolts that retain the filter on the valve body (arrows). Make sure the oil filter grommet does not stick on the valve body

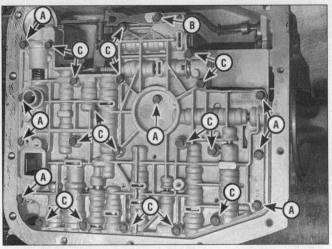

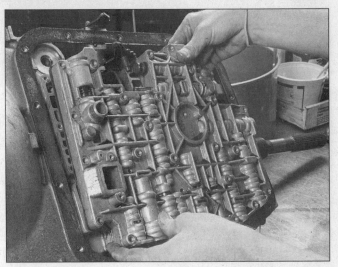

8C.9 Remove the 24 valve body bolts that attach the valve body to the case. Start by removing the eight short bolts (A); then remove the manual lever detent spring and roller assembly bolt (B) and finally the 16 long bolts (C)

8C.10 Carefully remove the valve body from the case and set it safely aside

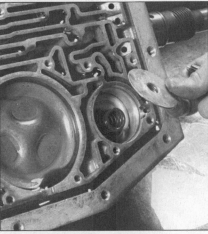

8C.11 Remove the 2-3 accumulator retaining snap-ring by prying it out of the groove with a small screwdriver

8C.12 Remove the 2-3 accumulator cover . . .

8C.13 . . . and remove the 2-3 accumulator return spring

8C.14 Remove the 2-3 accumulator piston. The piston uses two scarf-cut Teflon seal rings; inspect the seals for damage

8C.15 Remove the low-reverse servo retaining snap-ring by prying it out of the groove with a small screwdriver . . .

8C.16 . . . and remove the low-reverse servo cover

8C.17 Remove the low-reverse servo selective piston . . .

8C.18 . . . and remove the low reverse servo return spring

8C.19 Remove the overdrive servo retaining snap-ring by prying it out of the groove with a small screwdriver

8C.20 Remove the overdrive cover and piston as one unit

8C.21 Remove the overdrive piston and pin assembly from the cover

8C.22 Remove the overdrive piston return spring from the case

8C.23 Remove the 3-4 accumulator cover retaining snap-ring by prying it out of the groove with a small screwdriver

8C.24 Remove the 3-4 accumulator cover . . .

8C.25 . . . the 3-4 accumulator return spring, if equipped . . .

8C.26 . . . and the 3-4 accumulator piston

Note

Depending on model application, one of three accumulator designs will be present:

a) *There will be a spring between the cover and piston as shown.*
b) *There will be a spring beneath the piston.*
c) *there will be no spring present.*

The appearance of the piston and spring may vary among models.

8C.27 Remove the throttle tension spring from the inner throttle lever

8C.28 Remove the nut retaining the inner throttle lever to the manual shaft

8C.29 Remove the manual shaft retaining pin by prying it up with the a pair of diagonal cutters . . .

8C.30 . . . and withdraw the manual shaft from the case

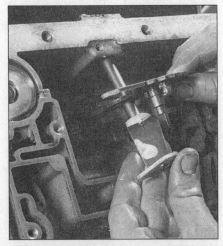

8C.31 Withdraw the inner throttle lever and shaft assembly from the case and inner manual lever

8C.32 Remove the inner manual lever and parking pawl actuating rod

8C.33 Use an open-end wrench to pry the throttle shaft seal out without damaging the case

8C.34 Withdraw the parking pawl shaft from the case . . .

8C.35 . . . and remove the parking pawl and spring

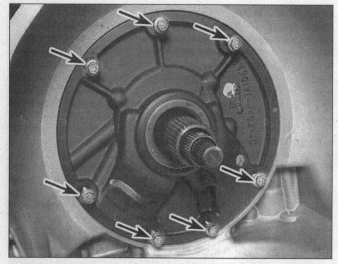

8C.36 Remove the seven front pump attaching bolts

8C.37 Withdraw the direct driveshaft from the turbine shaft

8C.38 Using two slide hammers threaded into the pump, pull the front pump out of the case

8C.39 Use a small screwdriver to carefully dislodge the locking tabs on the intermediate clutch spring retainer assembly

8C.40 Remove the spring and retainer assembly from the pump . . .

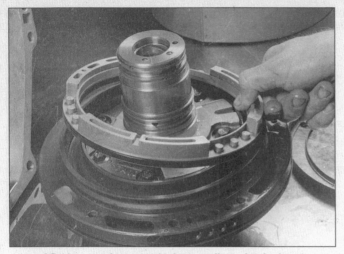

8C.41 . . . and remove the intermediate clutch piston

8C.42 Remove the no. 1 selective thrust washer from the stator support

8C.43 Remove the five stator support bolts and remove the stator support from the pump body

8C.44 Remove the drive and driven gears from the pump body

8C.45 Remove and discard the front pump oil seal. Be careful not to damage the pump bushing. Set the pump aside for later cleaning

8C.46 Firmly grasp the turbine shaft and withdraw the intermediate clutch pack, intermediate one-way clutch, reverse clutch and the forward clutch out of the case as an assembly

8C.47 Remove the intermediate clutch pack from the reverse clutch pack

8C.48 Remove the reverse clutch drum and intermediate one-way clutch from the forward clutch and turbine shaft assembly

8C.49 Remove the no. 2 thrust washer from inside the reverse clutch drum

Note

Some models may use a needle bearing assembly in place of the no. 2 thrust washer.

8C.50 Remove the reverse clutch selective snap-ring from the drum by prying it out of the groove with a small screwdriver

8C.51 Remove the pressure plate, friction discs, steel plates and apply plate from the drum. The number of friction discs and steel plates installed in the drum may vary, depending on the year and model of the transmission, be sure to replace them with the exact same number removed

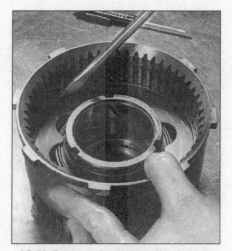

8C.52 Remove the reverse clutch wave snap-ring. If you can't pry the snap-ring out with a screwdriver it may be necessary to use a clutch spring compressor or two C-clamps to compress the return spring

8C.53 The wave snap-ring is different than any of the other snap-rings - keep it separate

8C.54 Remove the reverse clutch piston return spring . . .

8C.55 . . . the thrust spring . . .

8C.56a . . . and the reverse clutch piston from the drum

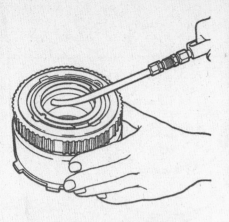

8C.56b To aid in removal of the reverse clutch piston, it may be necessary to apply air pressure to the drum. Block the opposite hole with a finger to prevent leakage. **Warning:** *Always wear eye protection when using compressed air!*

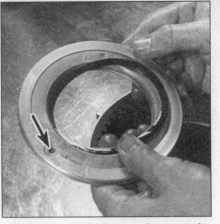

8C.57 Remove the inner and outer seals from the reverse clutch piston. Make sure the check ball in the piston moves freely (arrow)

8C.58 Flip the reverse clutch drum over, remove the intermediate one-way clutch retaining snap-ring . . .

8C.59 . . . and remove the intermediate one-way clutch retaining plate

8C.60 Remove the intermediate one-way clutch outer race . . .

8C.61 . . . and remove the intermediate one-way clutch assembly from the reverse clutch drum

8C.62 Remove the forward clutch selective retaining snap-ring from the forward clutch housing by prying it from the groove with a small screwdriver

8C.63 Remove the pressure plate, friction discs and steel plates. The number of friction discs and steel plates installed in the drum may vary, depending on the year and model of the transmission; be sure to replace them with the exact same number removed

8C.64 Remove the wave plate from the forward clutch housing

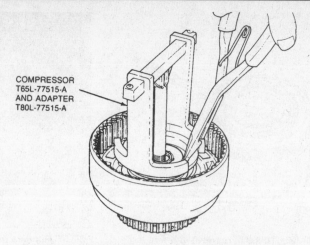

COMPRESSOR
T65L-77515-A
AND ADAPTER
T80L-77515-A

8C.65 Using a suitable clutch spring compressor carefully compress the forward clutch return spring and remove the retaining snap-ring. If a clutch spring compressor isn't available, use two C-clamps to compress the spring retainer

8C.66 Remove the snap-ring . . .

8C.67 . . . spring retainer and return spring from the forward clutch housing

8C.68 Remove the forward clutch piston from the housing . . .

8C.69 . . . and remove the inner and outer piston seals from the piston

8C.70 Reach into the case and remove the overdrive band

8C.71 Remove the forward clutch hub and the no. 3 needle bearing assembly from the case

8C.72 Remove the no. 3 needle bearing from the forward clutch hub

8C.73 Remove the no. 4 needle bearing from the top of the reverse sun gear and drive shell assembly

8C.74 Withdraw the reverse sun gear and drive shell assembly from the case

8C.75 Using a large screwdriver, pry the center support retaining ring from the case groove

8C.76 Using a large screwdriver, pry the anti-clunk spring from between the center support and the case

8C.77 Remove the forward sun gear and the no. 5 needle bearing assembly

8C.78 Remove the center support and the planetary carrier assembly together, as a unit

8C.79 Separate the center support from the planetary carrier

8C.80 Remove the planetary one-way clutch from the planetary assembly, being careful not to dislodge any rollers or springs from the cage

8C.81 Reach into the case and remove the direct clutch hub

8C.82 Grasp the end of the output shaft and withdraw the output shaft, ring gear, reverse band and direct clutch as an assembly

8C.83 Remove the reverse band from the ring gear

8C.84 Remove the no. 7 needle bearing from inside the direct clutch drum (it may have came out with the direct clutch hub)

8C.85 Also remove the thrust spacer or bearing support from inside the direct clutch drum

8C.86 Remove the output shaft hub-to-ring gear retaining snap-ring . . .

8C.87 . . . and remove the output shaft (A) from the direct clutch drum (B) and internal ring gear (C)

8C.88 Remove the no. 8 needle bearing from the direct clutch drum

8C.89 Separate the direct clutch drum from the ring gear

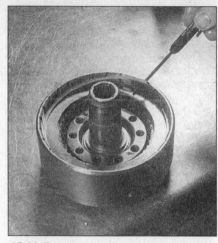

8C.90 Remove the direct clutch selective retaining snap-ring by prying it from the groove with a small screwdriver

8C.91 Remove the direct clutch pressure plate, friction discs and steel plates from the drum. The number of friction discs and steel plates installed in the drum may vary, depending on the year and model of the transmission, be sure to replace them with the exact same number removed

8C.92 Using a suitable clutch spring compressor carefully compress the direct clutch return spring and remove the retaining snap-ring. If a clutch spring compressor isn't available, use two C-clamps to compress the spring retainer

8C.93 Remove the direct clutch piston return spring and retainer assembly from the drum

8C.94 Remove the direct clutch piston from the drum and remove the inner and outer seals from the piston

8C.95 Remove the inner piston seal from the direct drum hub. Note the direction the seal lip is facing

8C.96 Remove the case snap-ring from the case groove, if equipped

8C.97a Remove the output shaft no. 9 needle bearing from the case

8C.97b Inspect the governor bore area in the case for wear or scoring (arrow) - sleeving tools are available to repair damage in this area, but if heavily damaged replacement of the transmission case is recommended

Component inspection and subassembly

Using an approved cleaning solvent, clean and dry all the components thoroughly, including the case. Do not use rags to wipe the components dry, lint from the rag may lodge in the oil passages causing a valve to stick.

Inspect the following transmission components and repair or replace as necessary:

a) **Case** - Inspect the exterior of the case for damage, cracks and porosity. Check the valve body surface for damage and flatness. Check all the oil passages, the accumulator bore, the speedometer bore and the governor bore for damage. Check all threaded holes for damage. Damaged threads may be repaired by drilling, tapping and installing thread inserts. Check the oil cooler line fittings for damage. Check the interior of the case for damaged retaining ring grooves. Check the case lugs for excessive wear. Check the output shaft bushing for wear. Inspect the manual linkage and the park lock linkage for damage.

b) **Intermediate clutch pack, intermediate one-way clutch and reverse clutch pack** - Inspect the condition of the clutch plates. Check for signs of overheating. Check the friction plates for wear, pitting, cracking or flaking. Check the overdrive band for wear or damage. Check the pistons for damage. Check the return springs for damage or signs of overheating. Check the bushings for wear or damage. Inspect the one-way clutch for worn or damaged rollers. Check the springs for damage. Check the race finish for

scoring, wear or damage. Check the check balls for damage and freedom of movement. Check the input shaft for scoring or damages splines.

c) **Planetary gear set** - Inspect the planet carriers, ring gears, sun gear and drive shell for damaged teeth or splines. Check for worn bushings. Check the thrust bearings for wear or damage. Inspect the pinion gear bearings for wear or damage. Inspect the one-way clutch for worn or damaged rollers. Check the springs for damage. Check the race finish for scoring, wear or damage.

d) **Forward clutch pack and direct clutch pack** - Inspect the condition of the clutch plates. Check for signs of overheating. Check the friction plates for wear, pitting, cracking or flaking. Check the pistons for damage. Check the return springs for damage or signs of overheating. Check the bushings for wear or damage. Check the low-reverse band for wear or damage.

e) **Output shaft and governor** - Inspect the output shaft for damages splines, scoring or worn bushing races. Check the governor for stuck valves. Check the governor distributor O-ring grooves for damage.

Oil pump assembly

Clean the oil pump components with solvent and air dry. Inspect the gears and gear pocket for scoring or damage. Check the hub for damaged sealing ring grooves. Inspect the stator shaft bushings for wear or damage. Inspect the pump cover and body faces for nicks or burrs and make sure the oil passages and lubrication holes are not restricted. Place the pump body over the cover and check for warpage.

8C.98 Remove the front pump body bushing (see Chapter 2). Align the notch in the pump body bushing . . .

8C.99 . . . with the land in the pump body

8C.100 Use the proper bushing installation tools to seat the bushing in the pump body

8C.101 Install the front oil pump seal

Note

On models built before 10/01/85 the oil pump drain-back hole in the pump cover was drilled too close to the oil seal sealing surface, allowing the oil to leak around the seal. To repair this problem apply a bead of silicone around the sealing edge of the oil pump seal before you install the seal.

8C.102 Check the stator support lands for nicks, burrs or scoring (arrows)

8C.103 Check the stator support face for defects or deep scoring

8C.104 Check the spring and valve, making sure the passage is clean and not restricted

8C.105 Remove the stator support bushings (if necessary) and using the correct size bushing installation tools, install new bushings (see Chapter 2)

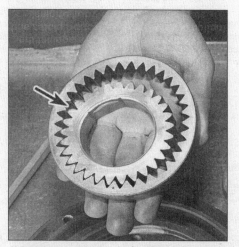

8C.106 Inspect the pump gears for wear or damage; if necessary, replace the gears as a set. The chamfers on the tips of the gear teeth (arrow) must face down into the pump body when installed

8C.107 Install the driven gear into the pump body with the reference mark facing down, into the pump body

8C.108 Install the drive gear into the pump body with the flat side of the offset drive tang facing up. Lubricate the pump gears with transmission fluid

8C.109 Position the stator support onto the pump body and install the bolts. Tighten the bolts to 12-16 ft-lb

8C.111 Snap the return spring retainer assembly into place on the pump body using even pressure

8C.110 Install the inner and outer intermediate clutch piston seals with the seal lips facing into the bore. Lubricate the piston seals and pump body with petroleum jelly. Using seal protectors, install the piston in the pump body. Seat the piston to the bottom of the bore by exerting even thumb pressure on the piston. Caution: *The piston bleed hole must be located at 12:00 o'clock position (toward top of transmission)*

Control valve assembly

Lay the control valve assembly on a clean work surface and begin removing the valves from the valve body. Withdraw the bushings, valves and springs and lay them out on a clean lint-free towel in the EXACT order of removal. Keep them in the proper orientation to the valve body. Clean all the bushings, valves and springs. Check the valves and bushings closely for scoring, cracks or damage. Check the springs for collapsed or distorted coils. Finally check the valve body bores for scoring or damage and begin reassembly.

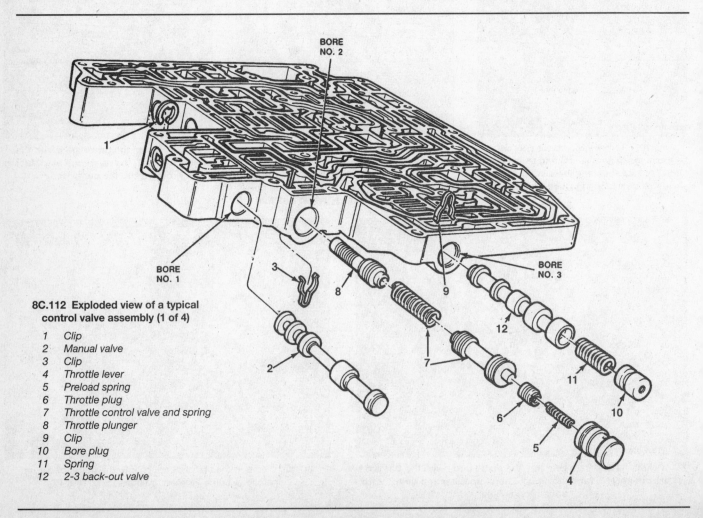

8C.112 Exploded view of a typical control valve assembly (1 of 4)

1 Clip
2 Manual valve
3 Clip
4 Throttle lever
5 Preload spring
6 Throttle plug
7 Throttle control valve and spring
8 Throttle plunger
9 Clip
10 Bore plug
11 Spring
12 2-3 back-out valve

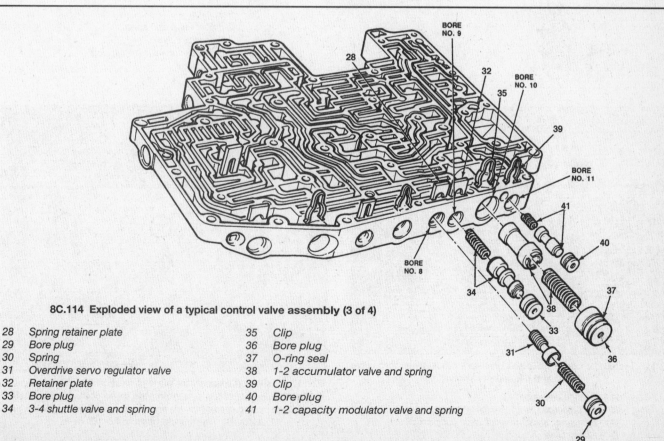

8C. 113 Exploded view of a typical control valve assembly (2 of 4)

13	Spring retainer plate
14	Bore plug
15	Orifice control valve and spring
16	Spring retainer plate
17	2-3 capacity modulator valve and spring
18	Clip
19	Sleeve
20	Plug
21	3-4 shift valve and spring
22	3-4 TV modulator valve and spring
23	Retainer plate
24	TV limit valve and spring
25	Clip
26	Bore plug
27	1-2 shift valve and spring

8C.114 Exploded view of a typical control valve assembly (3 of 4)

28	Spring retainer plate		35	Clip
29	Bore plug		36	Bore plug
30	Spring		37	O-ring seal
31	Overdrive servo regulator valve		38	1-2 accumulator valve and spring
32	Retainer plate		39	Clip
33	Bore plug		40	Bore plug
34	3-4 shuttle valve and spring		41	1-2 capacity modulator valve and spring

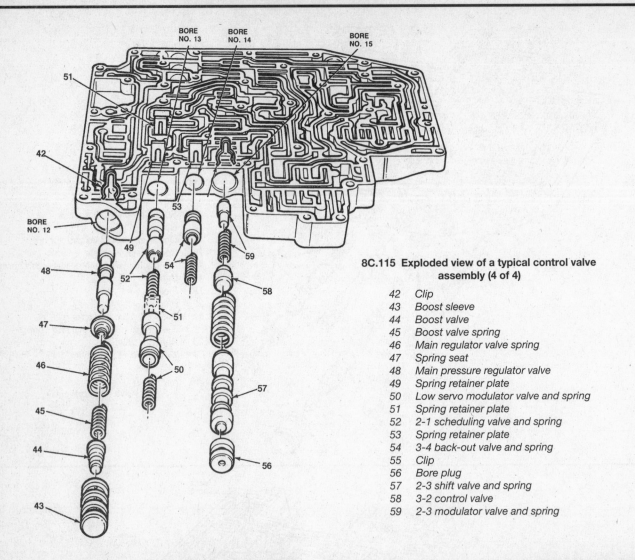

8C.115 Exploded view of a typical control valve assembly (4 of 4)

42	Clip
43	Boost sleeve
44	Boost valve
45	Boost valve spring
46	Main regulator valve spring
47	Spring seat
48	Main pressure regulator valve
49	Spring retainer plate
50	Low servo modulator valve and spring
51	Spring retainer plate
52	2-1 scheduling valve and spring
53	Spring retainer plate
54	3-4 back-out valve and spring
55	Clip
56	Bore plug
57	2-3 shift valve and spring
58	3-2 control valve
59	2-3 modulator valve and spring

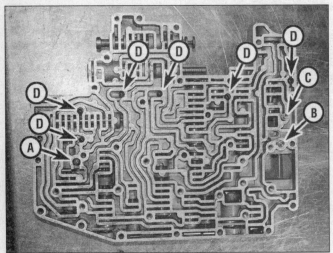

8C.116 Install the check balls and pressure relief valves into valve body at the locations shown

A   Orange check ball
B   TV pressure relief valve (short stem)
C   Converter pressure relief valve (long stem)
D   Check balls

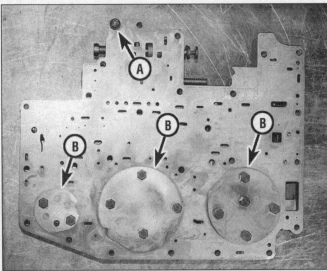

8C.117 Position the separator plate gasket on the valve body and install the separator plate, aligning the three components. Install the detent spring guide bolt (A) and the reinforcement plates and bolts (B). Tighten the bolts to 80-100 in-lb

Note

The upper and lower main control valve body gaskets have been redesigned for the 1980-86 model years. The new gasket has an additional slot, which helps prevent contamination of the 3-4 shift valve.

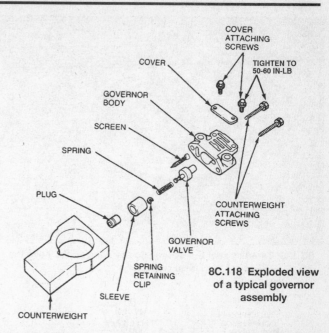

8C.118 Exploded view of a typical governor assembly

Governor valve assembly

Lay the governor assembly on a clean work surface and remove the screws from the governor body. Lay the components out on a clean lint-free towel in the EXACT order of removal, keeping them in the proper orientation to the governor body. Clean the screen, valve and body. Check all the parts for damage, wear or scoring.

Direct clutch assembly

8C.119 Install the direct clutch inner piston seal onto the direct clutch drum hub using seal protector Ford tool no. T80L-77234-A, or equivalent. Lubricate the seal and the installer with petroleum jelly, slide the seal down the installer and into the groove

8C.120 When the inner piston seal is installed correctly, the seal will be seated in the groove with the lip facing down, into the bore (arrow)

8C.121 Inspect the direct clutch piston check ball (arrow), making sure that it is clean and moves freely. Install the outer piston seal onto the piston with the seal lip facing into the direct clutch drum bore

8C.122 Using Ford tool no. T80L-77254-A, or equivalent, install the piston into the direct clutch drum. Lubricate the piston seal and the lip seal protector before installing the piston

8C.123 Carefully seat the piston into the drum and remove the seal protector

8C.124 Install the piston return spring and retainer assembly, seating the springs over the posts. Place the snap-ring over the hub

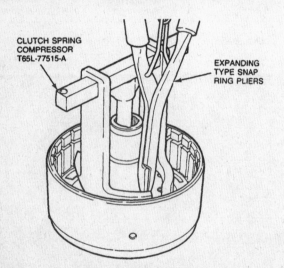

8C.125 Using a suitable clutch spring compressor carefully compress the clutch spring and install the retaining snap-ring. If a clutch spring compressor isn't available, use two C-clamps to compress the spring retainer

8C.126 Make sure the retaining snap-ring is fully seated into the hub groove

8C.127 Install the direct clutch pack into the drum, starting with a steel plate

8C.128 Soak the direct clutch friction plates in automatic transmission fluid for fifteen minutes. Install the remaining direct clutch plates, alternating friction plates and steel plates to equal your original clutch pack

8C.129 Install the direct clutch pressure plate onto the last friction plate

8C.130 Install the direct clutch selective snap-ring, seating it into the groove

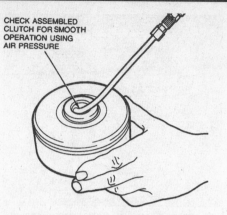

8C.131 Using air pressure, check the operation of the of the clutch pack; it should apply smoothly and have no leaks when pressure is applied. **Warning:** *Always wear eye protection when using compressed air!*

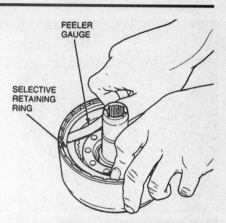

8C.132 Using a feeler gauge, check the clearance between the selective snap-ring and the pressure plate. When making the check, push down lightly on the pressure plate

Note

The direct clutch pack clearance should be held between 0.047 to 0.057 inch for 3.8L V6 engines and 0.050 to 0.067 inch for 5.0L and 5.8L V8 engines. If the clearance is not within specifications, replace the selective snap-ring with a thicker or thinner snap-ring, as required. Selective snap-rings are available at a dealership parts department in different thicknesses.

Reverse clutch assembly

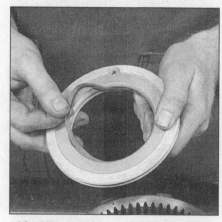

8C.133 Install the inner square-cut seal onto the reverse clutch piston. When using square-cut seals the direction of installation does not matter

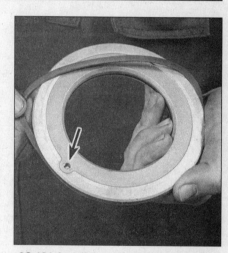

8C.134 Install the outer square-cut seal. Inspect the piston check ball and make sure it's clean and moves freely (arrow)

8C.135 Before installing the reverse clutch piston, coat the piston seals with petroleum jelly. Install inner seal protector (Ford tool no. T80L-77403-B, or equivalent) over the reverse clutch drum hub

8C.136 Place the outer seal protector (Ford tool no. T80L-77403-A, or equivalent) over the reverse clutch piston and install the piston into the reverse clutch drum. Press the piston down until fully seated and remove the seal protectors

8C.137 Install the thrust ring over the hub and onto the reverse clutch piston

8C.138 Install the Bellville return spring, making sure the spring is installed with the tips down against the thrust ring (arrows)

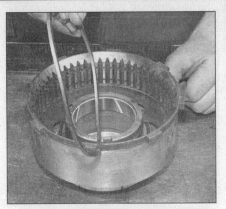

8C.139 Install the thick non-selective wave snap-ring into the reverse clutch drum with the points down next to the return spring

8C.140 Using a suitable clutch spring compressor or two C-clamps, compress the return spring and seat the wave snap-ring into the groove. If a clutch spring compressor is not available, the easiest way to install the wave snap-ring is with a hammer and a screwdriver. Install the snap-ring into the drum as close as possible to the groove in the drum. Place the screwdriver blade on the snap-ring and tap it down, seating the snap-ring into the groove

8C.141 Install the reverse clutch apply plate into the drum with the dished side against the return spring and the flat side facing up

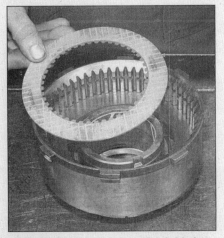

8C.142 Soak the reverse clutch friction plates in automatic transmission fluid for fifteen minutes. Install a clutch friction plate against the apply plate

8C.143 Install a steel plate against the friction plate. Alternate friction plates and steel plates to equal your original clutch pack

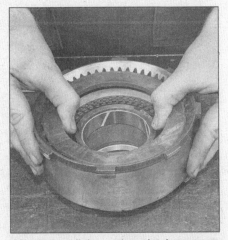

8C.144 Install the reverse clutch pressure plate into the drum against the last friction plate

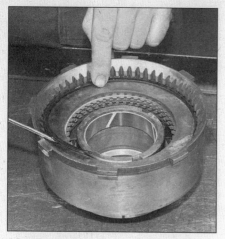

8C.145 Install the reverse clutch selective snap-ring, seating it in the groove

8C.146 Flip the reverse clutch drum over and install the intermediate one-way clutch assembly onto the inner race

8C.147 Install the outer race over the intermediate one-way. Place the race over the one-way clutch assembly and press down on the race while turning it counterclockwise until fully seated. Lubricate the one-way clutch with transmission fluid

8C.148 Install the retaining plate over the hub . . .

8C.149 . . . and install the non-selective snap-ring, seating it in the groove

8C.150 The intermediate one-way clutch outer race should only turn counterclockwise and lock in the clockwise direction

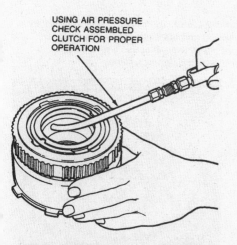

8C.151 Using air pressure, check the operation of the of the reverse clutch pack. Apply air to the oil feed hole - the clutch pack should operate smoothly and have no leaks. Warning: *Always wear eye protection when using compressed air!*

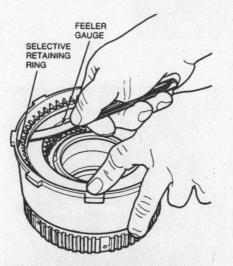

8C.152 Using a feeler gauge, check the clearance between the selective snap-ring and the pressure plate. When making the check, push down lightly on the pressure plate

Note

The clearance should be held between 0.030 to 0.056 inch for 3.8L V6 engines and 0.040 to 0.075 inch for 5.0L and 5.8L V8 engines. If the clearance is not within specifications, replace the selective snap-ring with a thicker or thinner snap-ring, as required. Selective snap-rings are available at a dealership parts department in different thicknesses.

Forward clutch assembly

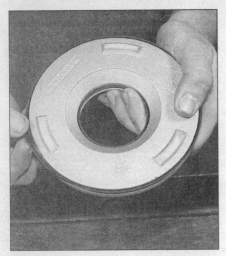

8C.153 Install the inner and outer lip seals on the forward clutch piston with the seal lips facing into the housing bore

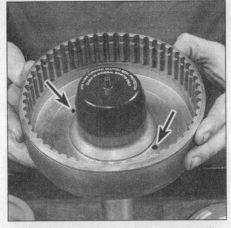

8C.154 Inspect the housing check balls (arrows). Make sure they are clean and move freely in the clutch drum. Install the inner lip seal protector (Ford tool no. T68P-7D158-A, or equivalent) on the clutch hub. Lubricate the piston seals and protector with petroleum jelly

8C.155 Install the outer lip seal protector (Ford tool no. T80L-77140-A, or equivalent) onto the forward clutch piston. Lubricate the piston seal and protector with petroleum jelly. Press the piston down into the forward clutch drum until fully seated and remove the seal protectors

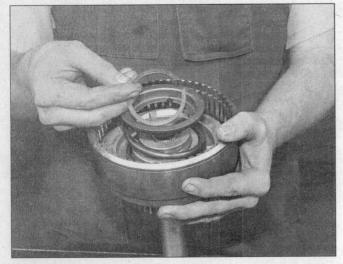

8C.156 Install the piston return spring, retainer and snap-ring over the forward clutch hub

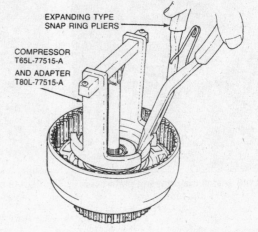

8C.157 Using a suitable clutch spring compressor, carefully compress the clutch spring and install the retaining snap-ring. If a spring compressor is not available, use two C-clamps to compress the spring retainer

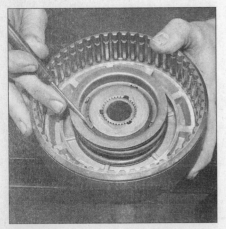

8C.158 Make sure the retaining snap-ring is fully seated into the hub groove

8C.159 Install the forward clutch wave plate into the drum

8C.160 Install the forward clutch pack, starting with a steel plate placed against the wave plate

8C.161 Soak the forward clutch friction plates in automatic transmission fluid for fifteen minutes. Install a clutch friction plate against the steel plate. Alternate steel plates and friction plates to equal your original clutch pack

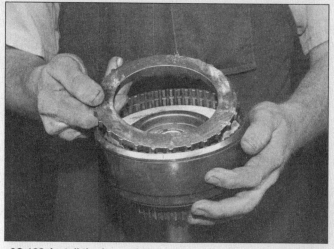

8C.162 Install the forward clutch pressure plate against the last friction plate

8C.163 Install the forward clutch selective snap-ring, seating it in the groove

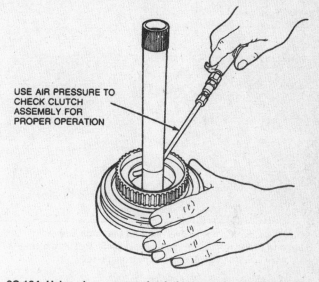

USE AIR PRESSURE TO CHECK CLUTCH ASSEMBLY FOR PROPER OPERATION

8C.164 Using air pressure, check the operation of the forward clutch pack; it should apply smoothly and have no leaks when pressure is applied. Warning: *Always wear eye protection when using compressed air!*

FEELER GAUGE

SELECTIVE RETAINING RING

8C.165 Using a feeler gauge check the clearance between the selective snap-ring and the forward clutch pressure plate. When making the check, push down lightly on the pressure plate

Note

The clearance should be held between 0.040 to 0.071 inch for 3.8L V6 engines and 0.050 to 0.089 inch for 5.0L and 5.8L V8 engines. If the clearance is not within specifications, replace the selective snap-ring with a thicker or thinner snap-ring, as required. Selective snap-rings are available at a dealership parts department in different thicknesses.

Transmission assembly

An automatic transmission is a precision fit piece of equipment. Install each component as shown, do not force any component into place. If it doesn't fit properly, find out why and rectify the situation. Maintain a clean work place and lubricate all moving parts as they are installed. Lubricate thrust washers and bearings with automatic transmission fluid or petroleum jelly. Use petroleum jelly to retain thrust washers and check balls in their proper location as the component is installed. Dip all friction plates in automatic transmission fluid before installation. Clean all attaching bolts with a wire brush, and coat the threads with Teflon thread and pipe sealant.

8C.166 Install the large output shaft seal rings in the grooves in the output shaft (arrows)

8C.167 Be careful not to over-expand the rings and make sure each end of the ring locks together properly. Retain the rings in their grooves with petroleum jelly

8C.168 Install the small output shaft Teflon seal rings into the grooves in the output shaft (arrows)

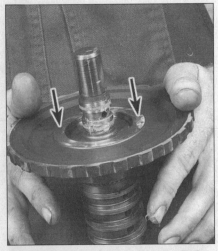

8C.169 Make sure the ends of the Teflon seal rings overlap and retain the rings in their grooves with petroleum jelly. Check the bearing surface on the output shaft hub for pits or scoring (arrows)

8C.170 Lubricate the thrust spacer with petroleum jelly and place it over the direct clutch hub

8C.171 Lubricate the no. 7 needle bearing with petroleum jelly and place it over the direct clutch hub onto the thrust spacer

8C.172 Align the friction plate splines and install the direct clutch hub into the direct clutch pack

8C.173 Apply petroleum jelly on the no. 8 needle bearing and install it on the direct clutch drum

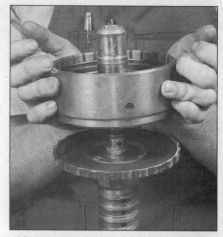

8C.174 Place the direct clutch on to the output shaft. Be careful not to damage the Teflon seals when seating the drum. Make sure the drum turns freely on the output shaft

8C.175 Place the ring gear over the direct clutch drum, engaging it into the output shaft hub

8C.176 Turn the assembly over and install the hub-to-ring gear non-selective snap-ring. Seat the snap-ring fully in the groove

8C.177 Install the parking pawl shaft through the case and into the parking pawl

8C.178 Attach the parking pawl return spring to the pawl and hook it on the case

8C.179 Install the inner manual lever and the parking pawl actuating rod as an assembly

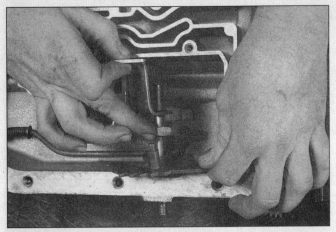

8C.180 Install a new manual lever shaft seal in the case. Install the inner throttle lever and shaft assembly with the manual lever attaching nut placed on the shaft. Insert the shaft through the inner manual lever and shaft seal. Be careful not to damage the seal

8C.181 Lubricate the outer manual lever and shaft assembly with petroleum jelly and install it in the case without damaging the shaft seal. Attach the inner manual lever to the outer manual shaft and tighten the lock nut to 19-27 ft-lbs

8C.182 Install the manual lever retaining pin into the case and tap it down. DO NOT drive the pin below the pan gasket surface

8C.183 Lubricate the no. 9 needle bearing with petroleum jelly . . .

8C.184 . . . and install it into the bottom of the case

8C.185 Install the output shaft assembly into the case seating assembly on the No. 9 needle bearing. Make sure it turns smoothly on the bearing

8C.186 Install the case non-selective snap-ring, if equipped

8C.187 Seat the snap-ring into the case groove with a large screwdriver (not all models are equipped with a case snap-ring)

8C.188 Install the reverse band into the case, seating it against the lower band anchor pins

8C.189 Lubricate the reverse servo piston seal with transmission fluid and install the piston and return spring into the case bore

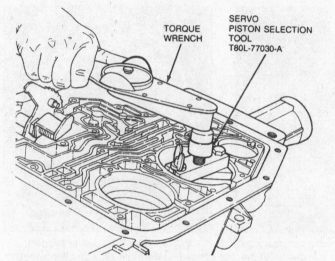

8C.190 If it was necessary to replace the low-reverse servo piston, use the following steps to determine the length of the new apply pin: Install servo piston selection tool (Ford tool no. T80L-77030-A, or equivalent). Tighten the band apply bolt on servo piston selection tool to 50 in-lbs

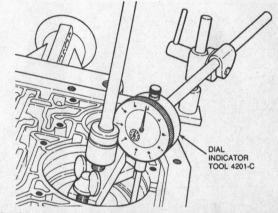

8C.191 Attach a dial indicator (TOOL-4201-C, or equivalent) and position the indicator stem on the flat portion of the piston. Zero the dial indicator. Thread the bolt out of the selector tool until the piston stops against the bottom of the tool. Read the amount of piston travel on the dial indicator. If the travel is 0.112-0.237 inch, the piston length is within specifications. If the travel is not within specification, selective pistons are available in various lengths from your dealership parts department

Note

Check the outer edge of the reverse servo bore for nicks or burrs which might have been raised during removal and installation of the snap-ring. Use hand pressure, or a hammer handle, to depress the low reverse servo piston and return spring into the bore past the snap-ring groove. Check to see if the apply pin locks into the reverse band.

8C.192 Install the reverse servo cover . . .

8C.193 . . . and the retaining snap-ring

8C.194 Install the planetary one-way clutch in the planetary carrier

8C.195 Install the planetary carrier into the case

8C.196 Make sure the planetary carrier is seated fully into the direct clutch hub

8C.197 Install the no. 5 needle bearing onto the forward sun gear; use petroleum jelly to retain the needle bearing on the sun gear

8C.198 Install the forward sun gear into the case, meshing the sun gear with the planetary pinion gears

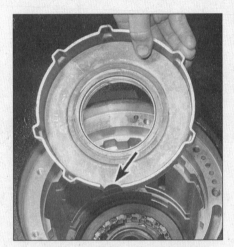

8C.199 Install the center support, engaging the inner race into the planetary one-way clutch. Align the notch in the center support (arrow) with the overdrive band anchor pin as you lower the center support into the case

8C.200 Install the center support retaining ring with its turned-up ends pointing up

8C.201 Seat the center support retaining ring in the case groove with the ends positioned as shown (arrows)

8C.202 Install the anti-clunk spring between the center support and the case. The end of the spring locks into the hole in the side of the case (arrows)

8C.203 When the anti-clunk spring is properly seated it will rest slightly below center support (arrow)

8C.204 Install the drive shell and reverse sun gear assembly into the case. Make sure the sun gear is seated and meshes properly into the planetary pinions

8C.205 Use petroleum jelly to retain the no. 4 needle bearing to the drive shell

8C.206 Install the no. 2 thrust washer on the reverse clutch drum with petroleum jelly

8C.207 Place the reverse clutch assembly over the turbine shaft and onto the forward clutch. Slowly lower and rotate the reverse clutch until you feel all the reverse clutch plates seat onto the reverse clutch hub

8C.208 Install the no. 3 needle bearing on the forward clutch hub, retaining it with petroleum jelly. Install the forward hub into the forward clutch drum, turning the hub until it splines into all the clutch plates and seats into the drum

8C.209a Holding the turbine shaft firmly, set the reverse clutch and forward clutch assembly into the case. Rotate the assembly as you lower it in place, locking it into the input shell

8C.209b Install the overdrive band around reverse clutch drum, seating it on the anchor pin (arrow)

Note

The overdrive band anchor pin on vehicles built prior to 9/30/86 has a been improved with a new step design to prevent wear and oil leakage from the case.

8C.210 Inspect the overdrive servo piston and cover for nicks or burrs. Install new seals on the overdrive servo cover and piston and lubricate with petroleum jelly. Carefully install the piston into the cover using a turning motion to prevent damage to the seal

8C.211 Inspect the servo piston bore for nicks or burrs. Install the piston return spring and servo assembly into the case bore

8C.212 Before you install the piston retaining snap-ring, the servo apply pin must line up on the overdrive band. After the overdrive band is properly engaged with the anchor pin and apply pin (arrows), install the servo retaining snap-ring

8C.213 Install the intermediate clutch pressure plate into the case

8C.214 Soak the intermediate clutch friction plates in automatic transmission fluid for fifteen minutes. Install a clutch friction plate against the pressure plate

8C.215 Install a steel plate against the friction plate. Alternate steel plates and friction plates to equal your original clutch pack

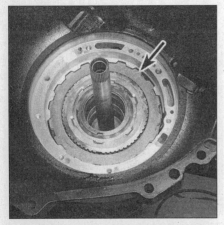

8C.216 Install the intermediate clutch selective steel plate last (arrow)

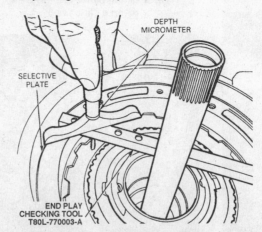

DEPTH
MICROMETER

SELECTIVE
PLATE

END PLAY
CHECKING TOOL
T80L-770003-A

8C.217 Measure the intermediate clutch clearance using a depth micrometer and end play gauge bar (Ford tool no. D80P-4201-A and T80L-77003-A, or equivalent). Position the end play gauge bar across the pump case mounting surface. Set the depth micrometer over the intermediate clutch and read the depth to the selective plate

> **Note**
>
> *The depth at the intermediate clutch separator should be (1.634-1.636 inch for 5.8L and 5.0L V8 engines and 1.629-1.640 inch for 3.8L V6 engines. If the clearance is not within specifications, your local dealership parts department has selective plates available in different thickness.*

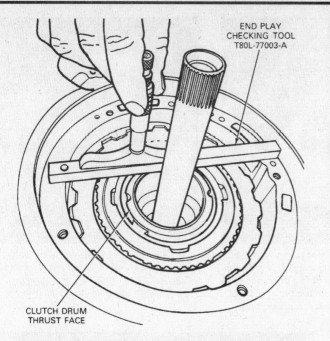

8C.219 Install alignment studs, made from M8-1.25 mm bolts, to align the front pump gasket and aid in installing the front pump (arrows)

Depth	Washer No.	Washer Size	Washer Color
(1.483-1.500 inch)	1	0.050-0.054 inch	Green
(1.501-1.517 inch)	2	0.068-0.072 inch	Yellow
(1.518-1.534 inch)	3	0.085-0.089 inch	Natural
(1.535-1.551 inch)	4	0.102-0.106 inch	Red
(1.552-1.568 inch)	5	0.119-0.123 inch	Blue

8C.218 Check the transmission end play using a depth micrometer and end play gauge bar (Ford tool no. D80P-4201-A and T80L-77003-A, or equivalent). Position the end play gauge bar across the pump case mounting surface. Set the depth micrometer over the clutch drum and measure the depth to the thrust face. Use the measurement to find the correct no. 1 selective thrust washer from the chart

8C.220 Make sure all of the old gasket material is removed from the case surface before placing the new gasket in position

8C.221 Use petroleum jelly to retain the correct no. 1 selective thrust washer (determined from the end play check) on the front pump

8C.222 Install the square cut front pump O-ring in the groove on the front pump body and lubricate with petroleum jelly

8C.223 Carefully lower the pump and stator support over the turbine shaft. Take care not to damage the bushing in the stator support and slowly set the pump into the case

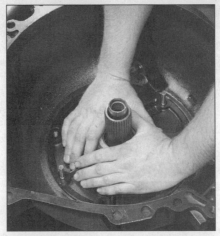

8C.224 Once the front pump is in the correct position lightly press down on the pump to seat it. If the pump does not seat smoothly or flush with the case, remove the pump and check for interference

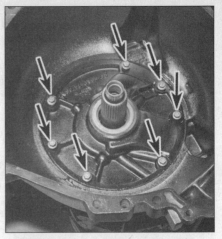

8C.225 Install the seven pump bolts, coating the threads with Ford Threadlock Sealer E0AZ-19554-A, or equivalent. Tighten the bolts to 16-20 ft-lbs

8C.226 Check the 2-3 and 3-4 accumulator case bores for nicks and burrs (arrows)

8C.227 Lubricate the scarf-cut Teflon seals with petroleum jelly

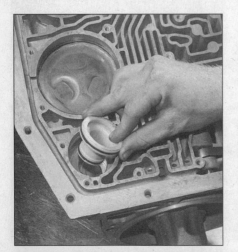

8C.228 Install the 2-3 accumulator piston into the case bore . . .

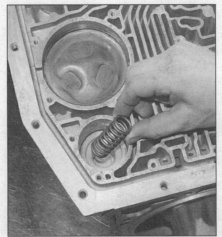

8C.229 . . . and install the accumulator spring into the piston

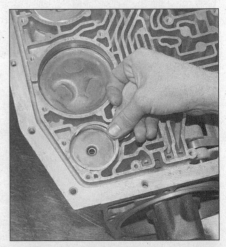

8C.230 Install the piston cover and retaining snap-ring

8C.231 Carefully install a new seal on the 3-4 accumulator piston and install the piston into the case bore

8C.232 Install the accumulator spring over the 3-4 accumulator piston

8C.233 Carefully install a new seal on the 3-4 accumulator cover and install the cover

8C.234 Press the cover down into the case bore and install the retaining snap-ring

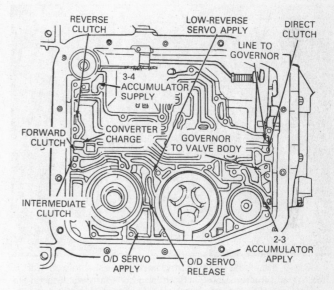

8C.235 Location of the component apply passages. As a final check of the operation of the servos and clutches, apply air pressure to the indicated apply passages (it may be necessary to cover another passage to prevent leakage)

8C.236 Install two alignment studs in the case (arrows) and place the valve body to case gasket over the studs

8C.237 Carefully place the valve body over the alignment studs (arrow)

8C.238 Slowly lower the valve body down into position. When the valve body is properly installed, the TV lever should contact the TV valve and the manual lever should fit between the manual valve lands (arrows)

8C.239 Remove the two alignment studs and install the eight short valve body bolts (arrows). Tighten the bolts finger tight

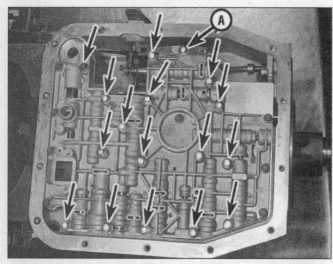

8C.240 Install the detent spring and roller assembly and its bolt (A), and the remaining sixteen long bolts (arrows). Starting in the middle of the valve body and working out in a spiral pattern, tighten the valve body bolts to 80-100 in-lbs

8C.241 Place the hooked end of the throttle tension spring against the TV lever arm and the straight end against the V-notch in the separator plate (arrows)

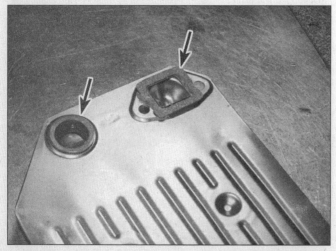

8C.242 Install the filter grommet and gasket on the oil filter. Lubricate the inside of the grommet with petroleum jelly

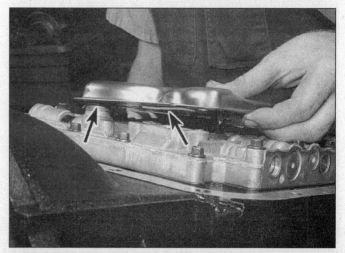

8C.243 Place the oil filter on the valve body, making sure the gasket and grommet do not slip during installation (arrows)

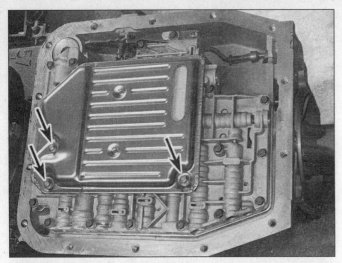

8C.244 Install the filter attaching bolts and tighten the bolts to 80-100 in-lbs (arrows)

8C.245 Install a new oil pan gasket, aligning all the bolt holes

8C.246 Install the oil pan and tighten the fourteen attaching bolts to 6-10 ft-lbs

8C.247 Install the governor onto the output shaft with the oil feed holes facing the front of the transmission (arrows)

8C.248 Place the governor drive ball into the hole in the output shaft (arrow). Align the round keyway with the drive ball and slide the governor over the drive ball

8C.249 Install the governor retaining snap-ring into the groove

8C.250 Install the extension housing gasket onto the
transmission case

8C.251 Install the extension housing, with a new rear seal, and
tighten the attaching bolts to 16-20 ft-lbs

8C.252 Install a new O-ring on the neutral start switch

8C.253 Install the switch into the case and tighten it to 8-11 ft-lbs

Chapter 8 Part D Disassembly, inspection and assembly ATX/FLC transaxles

Introduction

The ATX and FLC are three-speed automatic transaxles manufactured for front-wheel drive vehicles. The major difference between the ATX and FLC transaxles is the torque converter. The FLC uses a hydraulically locking torque converter. The major components of this transaxle are:

a) Torque converter
b) Gear-type oil pump
c) Control valve assembly
d) Low-intermediate band
e) Three separate multiple disc clutch packs (direct, intermediate and reverse)
f) One-way clutch
g) Planetary gear set
h) Final drive gear set
i) Differential unit

Follow the photographic sequence for disassembly, inspection and assembly. The model shown is a typical transaxle of this type. Differences do exist between models and many changes have been made over the years, so perform each step in order and lay the com-ponents out on a clean work bench in the EXACT ORDER of removal to prevent confusion during reassembly. Many snap-rings and clutch plates are similar in size, but must not be interchanged. Keep the individual parts together with the component from which they were removed to avoid mix-ups. Save all old parts and compare them with the new part to ensure they are an exact match before reassembly. Pay particular attention to the stack-up of the various clutch packs. Differences do exist between models and your transaxle may not match the stack-up shown. Note the exact location of the check balls in the case as well as the valve body. Save all the old parts until the overhaul is complete and the transaxle has been thoroughly road tested; old components can be useful in diagnosing any problems that may arise.

The ATX/FLC is a metric-dimensioned transaxle, so use metric tools on the fasteners. Special tools are required for some procedures. Alternate methods are shown where possible, but some procedures can only be accomplished with special tools. Read through the entire overhaul procedure before beginning work to familiarize yourself with the procedures and identify any special tools that may be needed. Thoroughly clean the exterior of the transaxle before beginning disassembly.

Transaxle disassembly

Begin disassembly by mounting the transaxle on a mounting fixture attached to a sturdy workbench. Remove the torque converter and drain the fluid from the transaxle.

8D.1 Remove the oil pump driveshaft from the input shaft

8D.2 Remove the torque converter turbine sleeve

8D.3 Remove the dipstick tube bracket bolt (arrow) and pull the dipstick tube out of the transaxle - remove and discard the seal

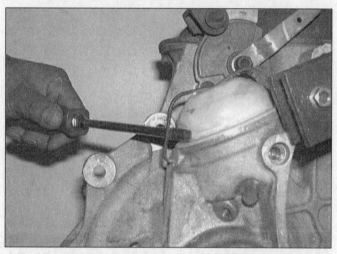

8D.4 Pry the bail off the governor cover and remove the cover

8D.5 Withdraw the governor from the case

8D.6 On models so equipped, remove the pipe plug and pull out the governor filter (on early models, the governor filter is located under the valve body)

8D.7 Remove the oil pan bolts and remove the oil pan and gasket

8D.8 Remove the bolts (arrows) and remove the oil filter and seal

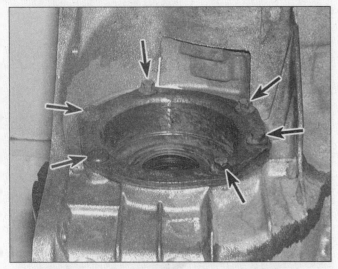

8D.9 Remove the differential bearing retainer bolts . . .

8D.10 . . . then, using two large screwdrivers or prybars, pry the bearing retainer from the case

8D.11 Remove the differential bearing shim

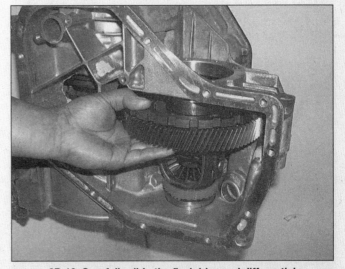

8D.12 Carefully slide the final drive and differential unit out of the case

8D.13 Remove the valve body cover bolts and remove the valve body cover and gasket

8D.14 Disconnect the throttle lever return spring from the throttle lever

8D.15 Loosen (but do not remove) the valve body bolts - there are a total of 27 bolts retaining the valve body

8D.16 Remove the main oil pressure regulator baffle plate and bolts - keep the bolts with the baffle plate to prevent mixing them with other bolts that are a different length

8D.17 Remove the control baffle plate and bolts

8D.18 Remove the detent lever spring and bolts

8D.19 Lift the valve body up, disconnect the manual valve link and remove the valve body assembly - remove and discard the gasket

8D.20 Using a screwdriver or prybar, pry the speedometer driven gear retaining pin out of the case until it can be removed with a pair of sidecutters

8D.21 Carefully drive out the speedometer drive gear with a soft-faced hammer

8D.22 Remove the oil pump retaining bolts - discard the washers (new washers are recommended for reassembly)

8D.23 Using a slide hammer, remove the oil pump assembly - make sure the oil pump thrust washer comes out with the pump

8D.24 Remove the oil pump gasket

8D.25 Remove the intermediate clutch thrust bearing

8D.26 Remove the intermediate clutch drum and shaft assembly from the case

8D.27 Remove the direct clutch thrust bearing

8D.28 Remove the direct clutch and shaft assembly

8D.29 Remove the intermediate clutch hub

8D.30 Remove the planetary assembly thrust washer

8D.31 Pry the reverse clutch snap-ring out of the case lugs and remove the snap-ring

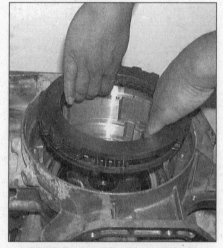

8D.32 Remove the reverse clutch pressure plate, friction plates and steel plates from the case

8D.33 Remove the planetary carrier assembly from the sun gear . . .

8D.34 . . . and remove the planetary thrust washer - it's usually stuck to the back of the planetary carrier

8D.35 Remove the reverse clutch spring assembly from the case

8D.36 Pull the reverse clutch piston straight up and out of the case

8D.37 Carefully pry around the reverse clutch cylinder at several points until it's loose, then remove the cylinder

8D.38 Using the servo removal/installation tool, push the servo cover in and remove the retaining ring

8D.39 Remove the tool and remove the servo assembly

8D.40 With the servo removed, you can now remove the low-intermediate band

8D.41 Remove the low-intermediate drum and sun gear assembly

8D.42 Remove the low-intermediate drum thrust washer

8D.43 Remove the transfer gear housing bolts (arrows)

8D.44 Carefully pry the transfer gear housing up to free it from the idler shaft - DO NOT pry down on the idler gear or damage to the idler gear teeth may result

8D.45 Remove the transfer gear housing

8D.46 Remove the transfer gear housing rear thrust bearing

8D.47 Remove the input gear . . .

8D.48 . . . the input gear bearing . . .

8D.49 . . . and the transfer gear front thrust bearing

8D.50 Hold the idler gear shaft with a hex bit and remove the nut from the shaft with an open-end wrench (arrow), then tap the idler shaft free with a soft-faced hammer and remove the idler gear and shaft from the case

Component inspection and subassembly overhaul

Using an approved cleaning solvent, clean and dry all the components thoroughly, including the case. Do not use rags to wipe the components dry, as lint from the rag may lodge in the oil passages, causing a valve to stick.

Inspect the following transaxle components and repair or replace as necessary:

a) **Case:** Inspect the exterior of the case for damage, cracks and porosity (a porous casting will cause fluid leaks). Check the valve body mating surfaces on the case and valve body for damage and flatness (use a precision straightedge to check for flatness - any warpage means the valve body or case will have to be machined or replaced). Check all the oil passages, the servo bore, the speedometer bore and the governor bore for damage. Check all threaded holes for damage (repair thread damage as described in Chapter 2). Check the oil cooler line fittings for damage. Check the interior of the case for damaged retaining ring grooves, which will mean the case will have to be replaced. Check the case lugs for excessive wear. Check the case bushing for wear and replace it if necessary. Inspect the manual linkage and the park-lock linkage for damage.

b) **Planetary gear set:** Inspect the internal gear, supports and car-

rier for damage. Check for stripped splines, cracked or broken teeth, damaged or worn thrust bearings and bushings. Check the carrier pinion gears for damaged bearings or worn washers. Check the support for damaged lugs. Inspect the sun gear for spline or tooth damage. Check the thrust washers and bushings for wear or damage.

c) **One-way clutch:** Inspect the one-way clutch for damaged rollers, broken springs or a damaged cage. Check the finish of the inner and outer races for scoring or damage.

d) **Direct, intermediate and reverse clutch assemblies:** Inspect the clutch housings for damaged splines. Inspect the check balls for looseness and the seal rings for damage. Check the clutch housings, pistons, springs, spring retainers, clutch plates, backing plates and retainer rings for wear or damage. Check for nicks or burrs in the lip seal areas. Check the housing and drum for worn bushings. Check the band apply surface for damage. Lay a steel ruler or straightedge across the surface and inspect for dishing. Inspect the band and servo for damage or wear. Check the thrust washers and bushings for wear or damage.

e) **Final drive and differential assembly:** Inspect the final drive gears for damaged teeth and worn bearing surfaces. Check the input gear and idler gear bearings for wear. Check the differential bearings, side gears, pinions and shaft for damage and wear. Inspect the speedometer and governor drive gear for damage or wear.

8D.51 Remove the oil pump thrust washer

Oil pump assembly

Disassemble the oil pump as shown in the accompanying photos. Clean and dry the cover, body and the internal components. Inspect the drive and driven gears for wear or damage; inspect the pump drive insert for damage. Inspect the gear pocket in the pump body for scoring or wear. Inspect the clutch support hub sealing ring grooves for damage. Replace any damaged components if there are any doubts about their condition.

8D.52 Remove the sealing rings from the clutch support hub

8D.53 Remove the oil pump body O-ring seal

8D.54 Remove the oil pump body retaining bolts (arrows) . . .

8D.55 . . . and separate the cover from the pump body

8D.56 Remove the pump drive insert . . .

8D.57 . . . the pump driven gear . . .

8D.58 . . . and the pump drive gear from the pump body

8D.59 After cleaning and inspecting the oil pump components, reassemble the oil pump following the reverse of the disassembly procedure; tighten the oil pump body bolts to 96 in-lbs and install new sealing rings on the clutch support hub - make sure the scarf-cut ends of the sealing rings are properly overlapped (arrows) and coat them with petroleum jelly to retain them in position

Control valve assembly

Complete disassembly of the valve body is not necessary unless the valve body has been contaminated. Clean the valve body using an approved solvent and air dry (DO NOT use rags to dry the valve body, as lint from the rag may cause a valve to stick). Check each valve for freedom of movement in its bore. If a stuck valve is encountered, remove the individual valve and components for further cleaning and inspection. Nicks and burrs may be removed by lapping the valve with a fine lapping compound.

If complete disassembly of the valve body is required, lay the valve body on a clean work bench, use clean tools to disassemble and wash the valve body with clean solvent. Remove the valves from the valve body, one at a time. Lay out the valves, springs and bushings in their proper order on a clean lint-free towel. Cleanliness and meticulous care in keeping the valves in order cannot be over-stressed. A small tap is helpful in removing any stubborn roll-pins you may encounter.

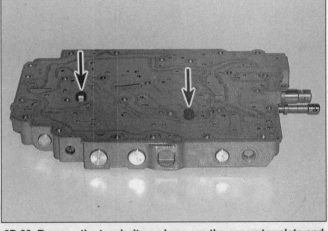

8D.60 Remove the two bolts and remove the separator plate and gasket from the valve body

8D.61 Remove the check balls (arrows) and the relief valve (A) from the valve body

8D.62 Using a small screwdriver or pick, pry each valve against spring pressure - the valve should snap back when pressure is released - check each valve for sticking

8D.63 To disassemble a typical valve assembly, push in on the bore plug or bushing and remove the clip retaining the valve and spring

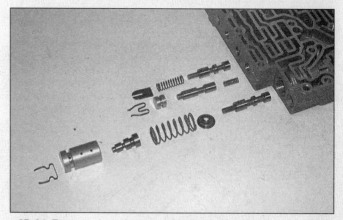

8D.64 Remove the valve assembly, keeping the components in order - clean and inspect the valves, bushings and springs, then reassemble the valve train - if the clip or roll pin does not fit securely, replace it with a new one

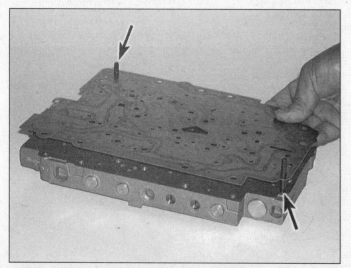

8D.65 After cleaning, inspection and reassembly of the valve body is complete, refer to the previous illustration and install the check balls and relief valve. Install two guide pins in the locations shown (arrows) and place the separator plate with a new gasket on the valve body. Tighten the two bolts to 96 in-lbs

Governor

Inspect the governor weights for freedom of movement. Check the weight springs for distortion or damage. Check the governor valve for binding. Check the governor sleeve for nicks, scoring or damage. Check the governor gear for damaged teeth. Inspect the governor screen (in the case) for contamination. Replace the governor if it does not operate smoothly or appears damaged. The drive gear can be replaced by driving out the roll pin (use a new roll pin when reassembling).

Intermediate and direct clutch assembly

When disassembling a clutch pack, keep the clutch components in the exact order as the original stack-up. Make notes on the number of plates, the installed direction and location of backing plates, apply plates, waved plates, etc. Differences may exist between your model and the model shown. The correct components for your transaxle should be in the overhaul kit, if you purchased the correct kit. Lubricate the clutch friction plates with ATF before installation. One way to accomplish this is to dip them in a shallow pan of ATF.

Before removing a piston seal, note the installed direction of the seal lip. The piston seals must be installed with the seal lip facing the correct direction. If the seal is installed with the lip facing the wrong direction, the piston will not operate properly. If unsure, a common rule-of-thumb is this; the seal lip always faces pressure. Lubricate the seal and seal bore with a thin coating of ATF prior to assembly. Refer to Chapter 2 for additional information.

Intermediate clutch

8D.66 Remove the intermediate shaft snap-ring . . .

8D.67 . . . and remove the intermediate shaft from the intermediate clutch drum

8D.68 Inspect the intermediate shaft stop ring and replace it if damaged

8D.69 Remove the intermediate clutch retaining ring . . .

8D.70 . . . and remove the pressure plate, clutch pack and waved plate from the drum

8D.71 Remove the seal rings from the intermediate clutch hub

8D.72 Using a clutch spring compressor, compress the springs and remove the retaining ring

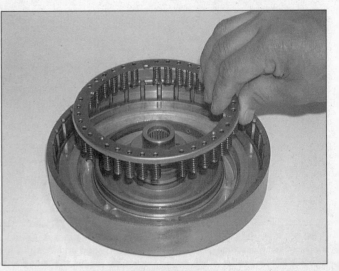

8D.73 Remove the intermediate clutch spring assembly

8D.74 Remove the intermediate clutch piston

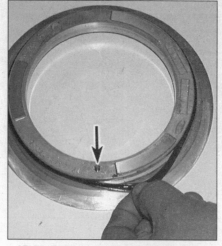

8D.75 Replace the intermediate clutch outer seal on the piston - also make sure the check ball (arrow) is not stuck in its cage

8D.76 Replace the intermediate clutch inner seal in the drum

8D.77 Install the intermediate clutch piston in the drum - rotate the piston and press down with even pressure until it's seated in the drum

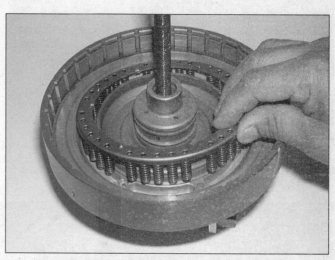

8D.78 Install the intermediate clutch spring assembly

8D.79 Compress the springs and install the retaining ring

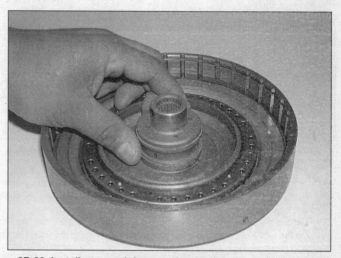

8D.80 Install new seal rings on the clutch hub - make sure the scarf-cut ends overlap properly and apply a coat of petroleum jelly to retain them in position

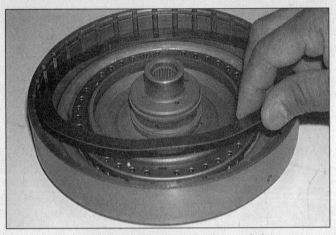

8D.81 Install the intermediate clutch waved plate . . .

8D.82 . . . followed by the clutch pack (alternate steel and friction plates) . . .

8D.83 . . . and finally the pressure plate

8D.84 Install the intermediate clutch retaining ring

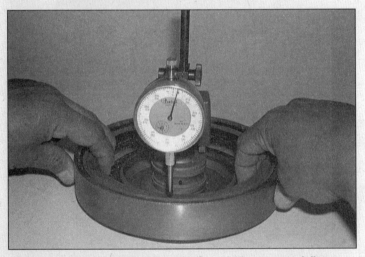

8D.85 Check the intermediate clutch pack clearance as follows:

1   Press down on the pressure plate, making sure the clutch pack is
    properly seated and the snap-ring is properly installed in the groove
2   Set up a dial indicator with the needle resting on the pressure plate,
    then zero the indicator
3   Lift the pressure plate up against the snap-ring and note the reading
    on the dial indicator. Take another reading 180-degrees from the first
    and average the readings - this is your clutch pack clearance
4   Intermediate clutch pack clearance should be 0.030 to 0.044-inch
5   If the clearance is incorrect, replace the snap-ring - selective snap-
    rings are available in thicknesses ranging from 0.049 to 0.074-inch

8D.86 Install the intermediate shaft in the clutch assembly
and install the shaft snap-ring

Direct clutch

8D.87 Remove the sun gear/one-way clutch outer race from the direct clutch assembly

8D.88 Remove the direct clutch thrust washer

8D.89 Remove the one-way clutch spring and roller assembly from the clutch assembly

8D.90 Remove the direct clutch retaining ring . . .

8D.91 . . . and remove the pressure plate, clutch pack and waved plate from the drum

8D.92 Remove the one-way clutch thrust bearing

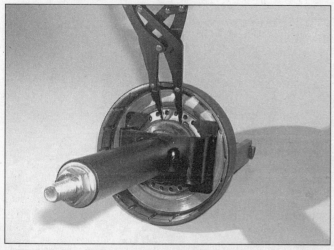

8D.93 Using a clutch spring compressor, compress the springs and remove the retaining ring

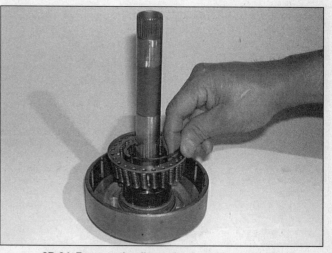

8D.94 Remove the direct clutch spring assembly

8D.95 Remove the direct clutch piston from the drum

8D.96 Replace the direct clutch outer seal on the piston

8D.97 Replace the direct clutch inner seal in the drum

8D.98 Make sure the check ball (arrow) in the direct clutch drum is not stuck in its cage

8D.99 Install the direct clutch piston in the drum - rotate the piston and press down with even pressure until it's seated in the drum

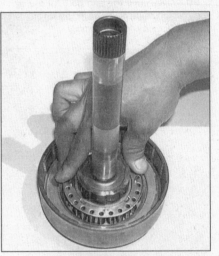

8D.100 Install the direct clutch spring assembly . . .

8D.101 . . . and place the retaining ring over the shaft

8D.102 Compress the spring assembly and install the retaining ring in the groove

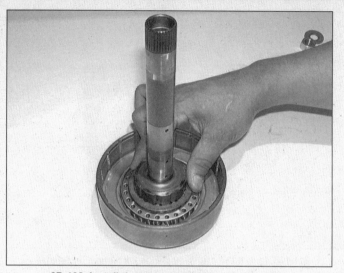

8D.103 Install the one-way clutch thrust bearing over the inner race

8D.104 Install the direct clutch waved plate . . .

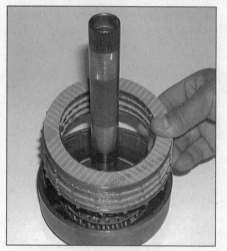

8D.105 . . . followed by the clutch pack (alternate steel and friction plates) . . .

8D.106 . . . and finally the pressure plate

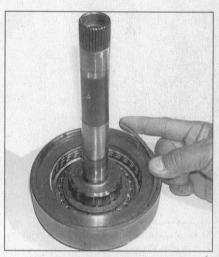

8D.107 Install the direct clutch retaining ring

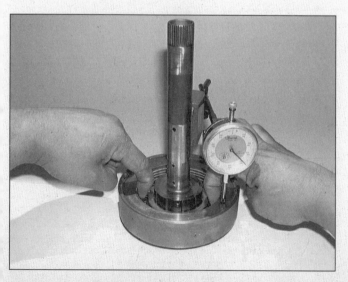

8D.108 Check the direct clutch pack clearance as follows:

1. Press down on the pressure plate, making sure the clutch pack is properly seated and the snap-ring is properly installed in the groove
2. Set up a dial indicator with the needle resting on the pressure plate, then zero the indicator
3. Lift the pressure plate up against the snap-ring and note the reading on the dial indicator. Take another reading 180-degrees from the first and average the readings - this is your clutch pack clearance
4. Direct clutch pack clearance should be 0.030 to 0.048-inch on a three friction plate clutch pack or 0.40 to 0.56-inch on a four friction plate clutch pack
5. If the clearance is incorrect, replace the snap-ring - selective snap-rings are available in thicknesses ranging from 0.050 to 0.079-inch

8D.109 Install the one-way clutch spring and roller assembly onto the inner race

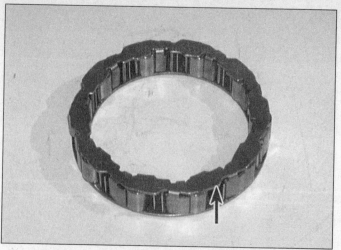

8D.110 Install the one-way clutch with this side (arrow) facing down

8D.111 Install the direct clutch thrust washer on the one-way clutch inner race with the tabs on the thrust washer against the inner race shoulders - when properly installed, the thrust washer will not rotate

8D.112 Install the sun gear/one-way clutch outer race into the direct clutch assembly - when properly installed, the sun gear/one-way clutch outer race should rotate in one direction and not the other

Reverse clutch

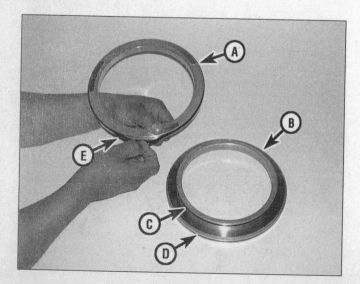

8D.113 Remove the seals from the reverse clutch cylinder and piston and install new ones, lubricating them with petroleum jelly

A　　Clutch cylinder
B　　Clutch piston
C　　Piston inner seal; lip must face down
D　　Piston outer seal; lip must face down
E　　Clutch cylinder seal; square-cut (non-directional)

Band apply servo

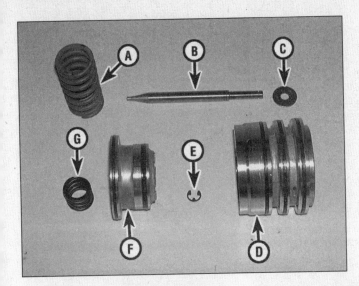

8D.114 Band apply servo details

A   Piston spring
B   Piston rod
C   Cushion spring retaining washer
D   Servo cover
E   Retaining clip
F   Servo piston
G   Cushion spring

8D.115 Remove the return spring from the piston

8D.116 Pull the servo piston out of the cover

8D.117 Pry the retaining clip from the piston rod

8D.118 Separate the piston rod, cushion spring and washer from the piston

8D.119 Carefully remove the seals from the servo cover . . .

8D.120 . . . and from the piston

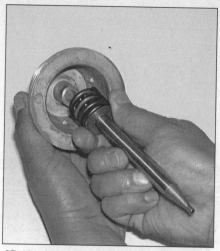

8D.121 Assemble the piston rod, cushion spring and washer to the piston . . .

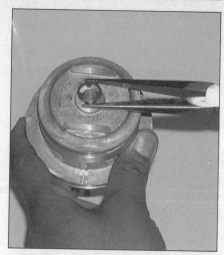

8D.122 . . . and install the retaining clip

8D.123 Install the square-cut (non-directional) seal on the piston.

Note:
If the transaxle case, band, sun gear/drum assembly, piston rod, piston or band anchor strut must be replaced, don't install the piston seals until after the piston travel has been checked and, if necessary, adjusted as described in the transaxle reassembly procedure

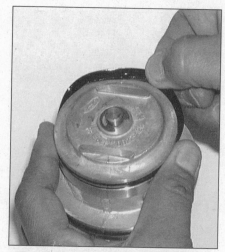

8D.124 Install the lip seal on the piston; the lip must face this end of the piston (see the Note in the previous step)

8D.125 Install new square-cut seals on the servo cover

8D.126 Apply petroleum jelly to the piston lip seal and carefully twist it into the cover

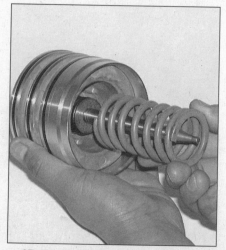

8D.127 Install the return spring onto the piston rod

Manual and throttle linkage

8D.128 Details of the manual lever and throttle linkage

A   Throttle valve outer lever
B   Neutral safety switch
C   Outer manual lever and shaft
D   Parking pawl actuating lever
E   Manual lever retaining pin
F   Parking pawl ratcheting spring
G   Inner manual lever/detent
H   Nut
I   Throttle valve inner lever

8D.129 Hold the lever to prevent it from moving, then unscrew the nut and remove the lever from the shaft

8D.130 Remove these bolts and detach the neutral safety switch

8D.131 Withdraw the manual lever retaining pin

8D.132 Unhook the ratcheting spring from the parking pawl and remove it

8D.133 Unscrew the nut on the manual lever shaft

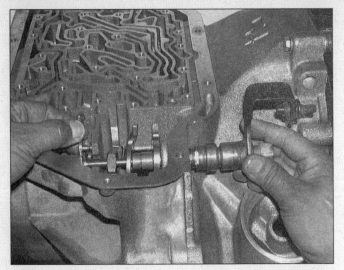

8D.134 Slide the manual lever shaft out, then remove the nut, inner manual lever and parking pawl actuating lever from the case

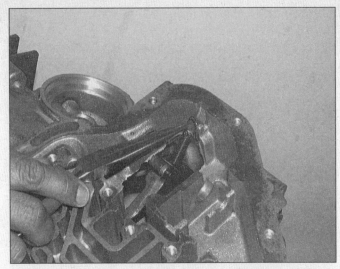

8D.135 Unhook and remove the parking pawl return spring

8D.136 Carefully pry the manual lever shaft seal from the case

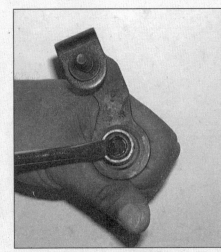

8D.137 Pry the seal out of the throttle lever shaft

8D.138 Using a seal driver or a socket with an outside diameter just slightly smaller than that of the seal, drive the new seal into the case

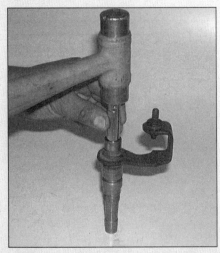

8D.139 A socket can also be used to install the seal in the throttle lever shaft

8D.140 Install the parking pawl return spring

8D.141 Install the throttle valve shaft, installing the components in the proper order (see illustration 8D.128)

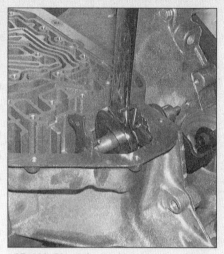

8D.142 Place the parking pawl actuator and inner manual lever/detent on the shaft and install the nut, tightening it securely (32 to 48 ft-lbs)

8D.143 Install the parking pawl ratcheting spring

8D.144 Secure the manual lever with the retaining pin

8D.145 Install the neutral safety switch and bolts, but don't tighten the bolts yet

8D.146 Install the throttle valve outer lever and nut. Tighten the nut securely while holding the lever stationary

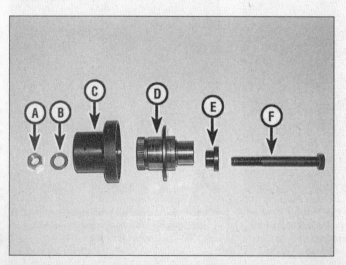

Reactor support

Before removing the reactor support, inspect it carefully. If no damage or excessive wear can be found, you can leave it in place. If it must be replaced, some special tools are required.

8D.147 Arrangement of special tools for removal of the reactor support

    A   Nut
    B   Washer
    C   Collar (T81P-70363-A5)
    D   Reactor support
    E   Sleeve (T81P-70363-A2)
    F   Bolt

8D.148 Unscrew the reactor support bolts

8D.149 Using the special tools assembled in the correct order, turn the nut . . .

8D.150 . . . while holding the bolt stationary; the support will be drawn out of the case

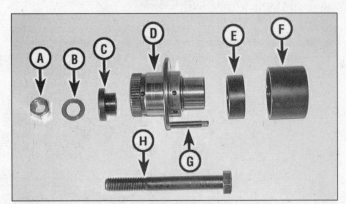

8D.151 Here's the tool arrangement of special tools for installing the reactor support

A   Nut
B   Washer
C   Sleeve (T81P-70363-A2)
D   Reactor support
E   Collar (T81P-70363-A3)
F   Adapter (T81P-70363-A4)
G   Guide pin (T81P-70363-A6)
H   Bolt

8D.152 Assemble the guide pin, bolt, sleeve and collar on the support like this . . .

8D.153 . . . and guide the reactor support into the case, making sure the slot in the support and the oil return hole in the case are lined up

8D.154 Turn the bolt while holding the nut stationary, which will pull the reactor support into the case

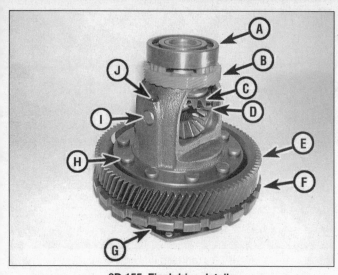

8D.155 Final drive details

A	*Bearing*
B	*Speedometer drive gear*
C	*Side gear (2)*
D	*Pinion gear (2)*
E	*Final drive gear*
F	*Parking pawl gear*

G	*Bearing (not visible in photo)*
H	*Rivet*
I	*Pinion shaft*
J	*Pinion shaft retaining pin*

Planetary gear assembly

Check the planetary gearset for wear and damage:

- Check the pins and shafts for a loose fit
- Check the shaft welds for cracking
- Check the pinion gear teeth for chipped or worn teeth
- Make sure the pinion gears rotate freely, but aren't loose on their shafts

If any undesirable conditions exist, replace the planetary gearset; individual parts aren't available.

Final drive unit

Carefully check all components of the final drive unit for damage and wear. For a thorough check, the unit should be disassembled; this is something you may want to leave to an automotive machine shop or transaxle specialist, as more special tools are required.

- Removal of the bearings requires these special tools: Screw (T84T-7025-B), Tube (T77J-7025-B), Ring (T75L-7025-G), Step plate (T81P-4220-A) and Collet (T83P-4220-AH.
- After bearing removal the speedometer drive gear can be lifted off. To remove the side gears, simply rotate them out of the differential case window (don't forget to remove the thrust washers).
- To remove the pinion gears, use a narrow punch and drive out the pinion shaft retaining pin, then remove the shaft, pinion gears and thrust bearings.
- The final drive gear can be replaced by drilling off the heads of the rivets (working on the gear side, not the case side) with a 5/16-inch drill bit. The new gear is secured by special bolts, tightened to 55 to 70 ft-lbs. Don't use any other type of bolt.

Parking pawl and band strut

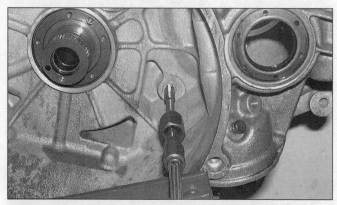

8D.156 Drill a hole in the plug covering the parking pawl/band anchor pin and tap the plug with a 3/8 inch-16 tap

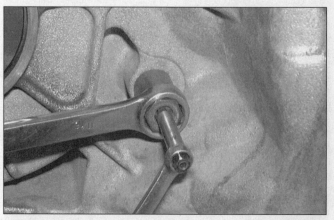

8D.157 Thread a nut onto the tap, place a spacer under the nut and thread the tap into the plug. Now tighten the nut to pull the plug out of the case

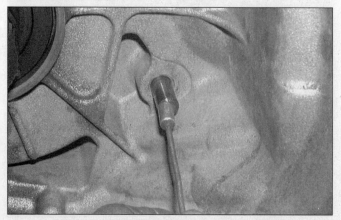

8D.158 Use a magnet to remove the anchor pin

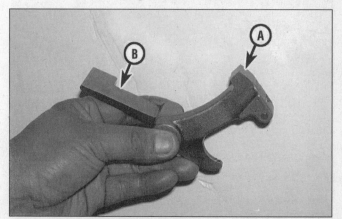

8D.159 Remove the parking pawl (A) and band strut (B) from the case. Check each component for wear or signs of damage. Replace as necessary

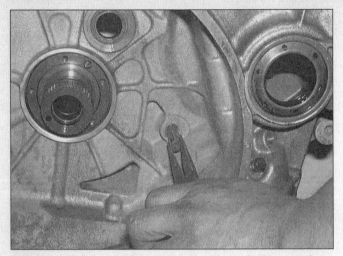

8D.160 Install the parking pawl and band strut in the case, then install the anchor pin . . .

8D.161 . . . and tap in a new plug

Transfer gear housing bearing

Check the bearing in the transfer gear housing for wear or damage. If the bearing is in need of replacement, position the transfer gear housing in the transaxle case and install the bolts (see illustration 8D.43). Remove the bearing from the housing using a slide hammer with a bearing puller attachment. To install the new bearing, remove the housing from the transaxle case and drive the bearing into place with a hammer and bearing driver (tool no. T81P-77380 or equivalent).

Transaxle assembly

An automatic transaxle is a precision piece of equipment. Install each component as shown, and do not force any component into place. If it doesn't fit properly, find out why and rectify the situation. Maintain a clean work area and lubricate all moving parts as they are installed. Lubricate thrust washers and bearings with automatic transaxle fluid (ATF) or petroleum jelly. Use petroleum jelly to retain thrust washers and check balls in their proper location as the component is installed. Dip all friction plates in ATF before installation.

8D.162 Install a new O-ring on the idler gear shaft

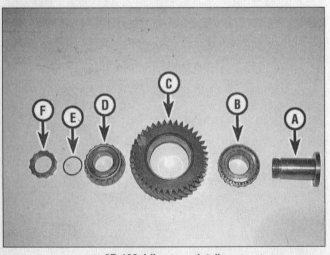

8D.163 Idler gear details

A	Idler gear shaft	D	Bearing
B	Bearing	E	O-ring
C	Idler gear	F	Nut

8D.164 Install the idler gear shaft, bearings and gear into the transaxle case. Apply a thread locking compound to the threads of the nut, then install the nut and tighten it to 80 to 100 ft-lbs. Prevent the shaft from turning by holding it with a 12mm hex bit as shown here. Note: *A 32 mm 12-point socket must be used to tighten the nut.*

8D.165 Install the transfer gear front thrust bearing

8D.166 Install the input gear needle bearing

8D.167 Install the input gear

8D.168 Install the transfer gear housing rear thrust bearing

8D.169 Rotate the band strut into its normal position. Align the transfer gear housing with the dowels in the transaxle case. Install new bolts, tightening them to 18 to 23 ft-lbs

8D.170 Install the low-intermediate drum thrust washer . . .

8D.171 . . . followed by the sun gear and low-intermediate drum assembly

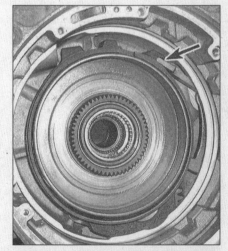

8D.172 Install the low-intermediate band, making sure it properly engages the strut (arrow)

8D.173 The servo travel will have to be checked if you've replaced the transaxle case, low-intermediate band, drum and sun gear assembly, servo piston rod, piston or band anchor strut. Place tool no. T81P- 70027-A (spring) on the piston rod and install the servo piston assembly without the seals . . .

8D.174 . . . followed by the servo selection tool (T881P-70023-A) and servo snap-ring. Tighten the bolt to 120 in-lbs

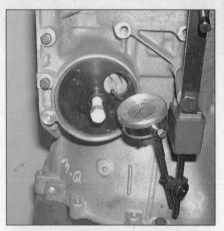

8D.175 Now mount a dial indicator as shown, zero the indicator, then unscrew the bolt until the piston stops moving. Read the indicator - if the piston travel is 0.203 to 0.247-inch, the piston rod length is fine. If travel is greater than 0.247-inch, the rod is too short; if it's less than 0.203-inch, the rod is too long

Number of grooves in rod	Rod length
None	6.313 to 6.324 inches (160.22 to 160.52 mm)
1	6.289 to 6.300 inches (159.61 to 159.90 mm)
2	6.265 to 6.276 inches (159.00 to 159.30 mm)
3	6.240 to 6.252 inches (158.39 to 158.69 mm)
4	6.216 to 6.189 inches (157.78 to 158.08 mm)
5	6.197 to 6.209 inches (157.17 to 157.47 mm)

8D.176 Piston rods are available in six different lengths. Rod lengths are measured from the end of the rod to the far end of the snap-ring groove. If your piston travel is out of range, measure the length of the existing rod and calculate the length of the replacement rod required

8D.177 With the seals installed, install the servo piston assembly and compress it with the removal/installation tool . . .

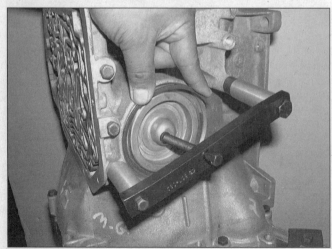

8D.178 . . . far enough to allow installation of the retaining ring

8D.179 Make sure the piston rod properly engages the band (arrow), then remove the tool

8D.180 Install the reverse clutch cylinder and gently tap it down with a hammer handle

8D.181 Push the reverse clutch piston into the seal protector tool (T81P-70402-A) . . .

8D.182 . . . then push the piston into place and remove the tool

8D.183 Assemble the thrust washer to the planetary carrier . . .

8D.184 . . . then install the planetary carrier onto the sun gear

8D.185 Install the reverse clutch spring assembly . . .

8D.186 . . . the wave spring . . .

8D.187 . . . the clutch pack . . .

8D.188 . . . and the pressure plate

8D.189 Compress the clutch pack and install the retaining ring

8D.190 Install the planetary gearset thrust washer

8D.191 Lower the intermediate clutch hub and ring gear into the case, turning it back-and-forth so it meshes with the dogs on the clutch plates

8D.192 Guide the direct clutch assembly into place

8D.193 Install the direct clutch thrust bearing

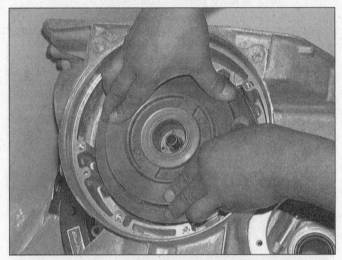

8D.194 Install the intermediate clutch drum and shaft assembly, making sure it seats completely (turn it side-to-side until it drops into place)

8D.195 Install the intermediate clutch thrust bearing

8D.196 Install two alignment pins and a new pump housing gasket

8D.197 Using a gauge bar T80L-77003-A (or equivalent) and Endplay Alignment Cup T81P-77389-A, measure the distance from the gauge bar to the intermediate clutch thrust bearing. Take two readings, 180-degrees apart, and average the two

Reading	Washer thickness required	Part ID
0.079 to 0.070-inch (2.00 to 1.77 mm)	0.055 to 0.057-inch (1.40 to 1.45 mm)	AA
0.087 to 0.079-inch (2.20 to 2.00 mm)	0.063 to 0.065-inch (1.60 to 1.65 mm)	BA
0.095 to 0.087-inch (2.41 to 2.20 mm)	0.071 to 0.073-inch (1.80 to 1.85 mm)	CA
0.070 to 0.057-inch (1.77 to 1.46 mm)	0.045 to 0.047-inch (1.15 to 1.20 mm)	EA

8D.198 Now subtract the thickness of the gauge bar and choose the correct thickness washer (measure the existing one first - it may be OK to use)

8D.199 Install the proper thickness thrust washer on the intermediate clutch drum (or you can stick it to the oil pump housing with petroleum jelly) . . .

8D.200 . . . then install the pump and carefully tap it into place with the handle of a hammer. Remove the alignment dowels and install *new* bolts and washers, tightening them to 84 to 108 in-lbs

8D.201 Guide the differential assembly into place in the transaxle case

8D.202 Lower the differential bearing shim into place

8D.203 Fit a new gasket to the differential retainer . . .

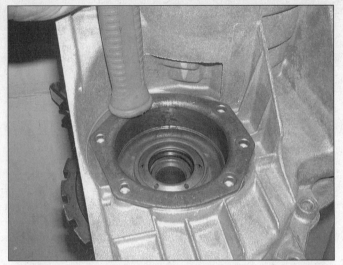

8D.204 . . . then install the differential retainer and tap it into place. Apply a non-hardening thread-locking compound to the threads of the bolts and tighten them to 15 to 19 ft-lbs

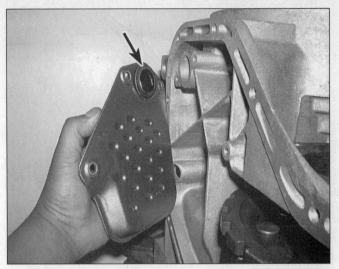

8D.205 Using a new seal, install the fluid filter. Apply a non-hardening thread-locking compound to the threads of the bolts and tighten them to 84 to 108 in-lbs

8D.206 Install a new gasket on the fluid pan. Install the pan, tightening the bolts to 12 to 17 ft-lbs

8D.207 Install a new o-ring on the speedometer gear drive assembly

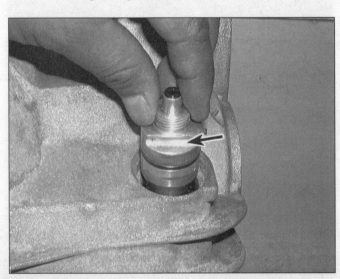

8D.208 Install the speedometer gear drive assembly into the case with the flat portion (arrow) positioned like this . . .

8D.209 . . . then tap the roll pin into place

8D.210 Install the governor filter and secure it by tapping in a new plug

8D.211 Install the governor

8D.212 Replace the O-ring on the governor cover

8D.213 Install the governor cover and tap the retaining ball into place, making sure it seats in the hole

8D.214 On early models, clean and install the governor filter under the valve body. On all models, install alignment dowels and the valve body gasket

8D.215 Remove the alignment dowel from this end of the case, then, while guiding the valve body into place, connect the "Z" link to the manual valve. Also connect the T.V. control spring to the separator plate. Note: *Make sure the roller (arrow) on the throttle valve plunger engages with the cam on the throttle lever.*

8D.216 Reinstall the alignment dowel, then install the detent spring and roller. Don't tighten the bolts yet

8D.217 Using the longer valve body bolts, install the oil pressure regulator baffle plate. Don't tighten the bolts yet

8D.218 Place the transaxle control baffle plate into position, but don't tighten the bolts yet

TORQUE CONVERTER SIDE

PUMP SIDE   10355-8D-219 HAYNES

8D.219 Tighten the valve body bolts a little at a time, in this sequence, to 72 to 96 in-lbs

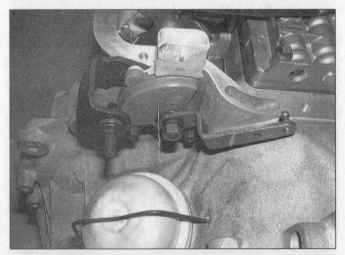

8D.220 Adjust the neutral safety switch by placing the manual valve in the neutral position and inserting a no. 43 (3/32-inch) drill bit into the hole in the switch. If the drill bit won't pass through the switch and into the case, loosen the bolts and rotate the switch until it does, then tighten the bolts securely

8D.221 Install the throttle lever return spring and hook it onto the throttle lever

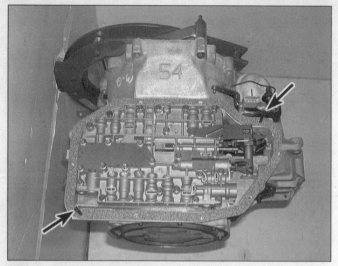

8D.222 Install two alignment dowels into the case, then install a new valve body cover gasket. Install the cover and bolts, tightening them to 84 to 108 in-lbs

8D.223 Install the oil pump driveshaft . . .

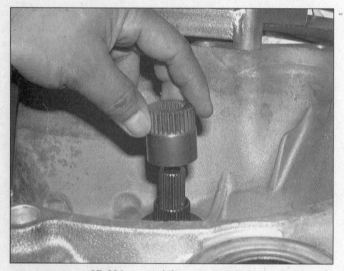

8D.224 . . . and the converter hub

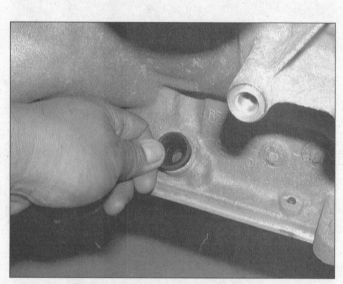

8D.225 Install a new dipstick tube seal . . .

8D.226 . . . and the dipstick tube. Tighten the dipstick tube bolts to 84 to 108 in-lbs

8D.227 Finally, attach the I.D. tag and tighten the bolt securely

Chapter 8 Part E Disassembly, inspection and assembly AXOD transaxle

Introduction

The AXOD is a four-speed automatic transaxle manufactured for front-wheel drive vehicles. The major components of this transaxle are:

a) Lock-up torque converter
b) Sprockets and drive chain assembly
c) Vane-type oil pump
d) Control valve assembly
e) Low-intermediate band
f) Overdrive band
g) Four separate multiple disc clutch packs (forward, direct, intermediate and reverse)
h) Low one-way clutch
i) Direct one-way clutch
j) Two planetary gear sets
k) Final drive

Follow the photographic sequence for disassembly, inspection and assembly. The model shown is a typical transaxle of this type. Differences do exist between models and many changes have been made over the years, so perform each step in order and lay the com-

ponents out on a clean work bench in the EXACT ORDER of removal to prevent confusion during reassembly. Many snap-rings and clutch plates are similar in size, but must not be interchanged. Keep the individual parts together with the component from which they were removed to avoid mix-ups. Save all old parts and compare them with the new part to ensure they are an exact match before reassembly. Pay particular attention to the stack-up of the various clutch packs. Differences do exist between models and your transaxle may not match the stack-up shown. Note the exact location of the check balls in the case as well as the valve body. Save all the old parts until the overhaul is complete and the transaxle has been thoroughly road tested; old components can be useful in diagnosing any problems that may arise.

The AXOD is a metric dimensioned transaxle; use metric tools on the fasteners. Special tools are required for some procedures. Alternate procedures are shown where possible, but some procedures can only be accomplished with special tools. Read through the entire overhaul procedure before beginning work to familiarize yourself with the procedures and identify any special tools that may be needed. Thoroughly clean the exterior of the transaxle before beginning disassembly.

Transaxle disassembly

Begin disassembly by mounting the transaxle on a mounting fixture attached to a sturdy workbench. Remove the torque converter and drain the transaxle fluid from the transaxle.

8E.1 Remove the two bolts (arrows) and the Park/Neutral switch

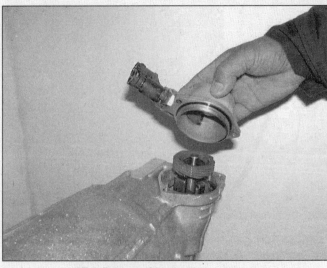

8E.2 Remove the governor cover . . .

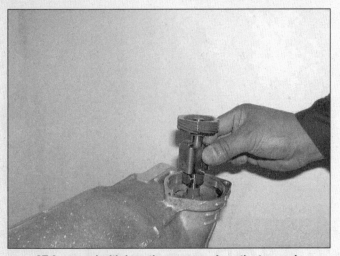

8E.3 . . . and withdraw the governor from the transaxle

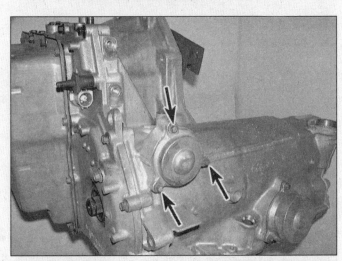

8E.4 Remove the three bolts and the overdrive servo cover

8E.5 Remove the overdrive servo piston, pin and spring - install the piston, pin and spring in the cover and keep the components together

8E.6 Remove the three bolts and the low-intermediate servo cover

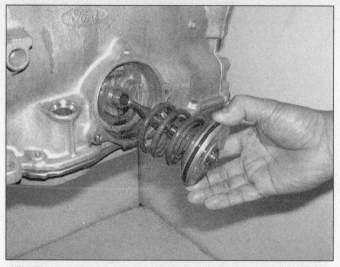

8E.7 Remove the low-intermediate servo piston, pin and spring - install the piston, pin and spring in the cover and keep the components together

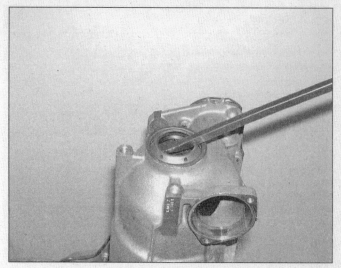

8E.8 Remove the right-side output shaft oil seal

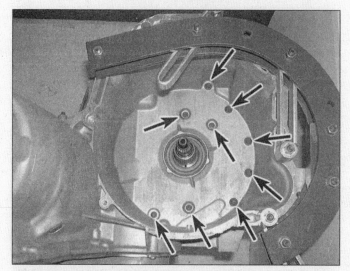

8E.9 Carefully pry out the torque converter oil seal, then remove the bolts (arrows) and the bellhousing

8E.10 Remove the valve body cover from the transaxle

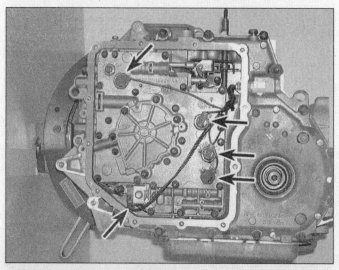

8E.11 Disconnect the electrical connectors from the pressure switches and torque converter clutch solenoid

8E.12 Press in on the tabs, disconnect the wiring harness from the case connector and remove the wiring harness

8E.13 Using a wrench on the flats of the manual lever shaft, rotate the shaft clockwise to position the manual valve in the manual Low position - the valve should be all the way in the valve body

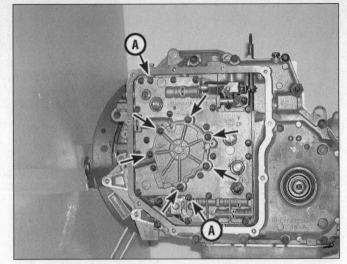

8E.14 Remove the bolts attaching the valve body to the chain cover (22 bolts total) - DO NOT remove the six oil pump cover bolts (arrows) and the bolts marked (A)

8E.15 Press the throttle valve in with one hand while rotating the valve body slightly to disconnect the manual valve link from the detent lever

8E.16 Disconnect the manual valve link from the manual valve and remove the valve body

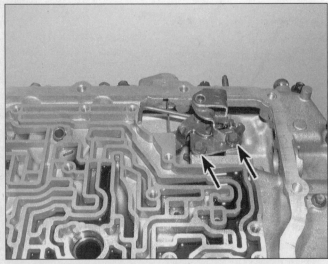

8E.17 Remove the bolts and the throttle valve linkage

8E.18 Withdraw the oil pump driveshaft from the transaxle

8E.19 Remove the C-clip from the output shaft

8E.20 Pry the metal seal protector from the output shaft oil seal . . .

8E.21 . . . and pry the output shaft oil seal from the chain cover

8E.22 Remove the chain cover bolts (arrows) and carefully remove the chain cover from the transaxle case - note the location, size and length of the various bolts so they may be returned to their original locations

8E.23 The accumulator springs are similar in appearance but must not be interchanged - apply numbered tags to the springs to identify them

A   Neutral-Drive accumulator
B   3-4 accumulator
C   1-2 accumulator

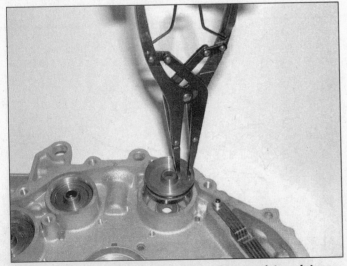

8E.24 Remove the accumulator pins and accumulator pistons

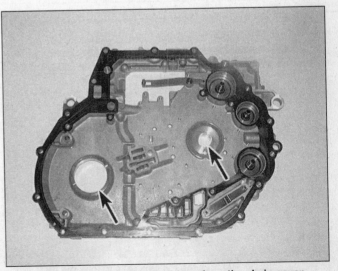

8E.25 Remove the thrust washers from the chain cover

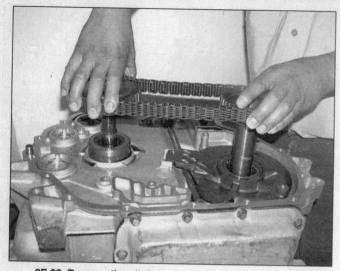

8E.26 Remove the chain and sprockets as an assembly

8E.27 Remove the sprocket support thrust washers

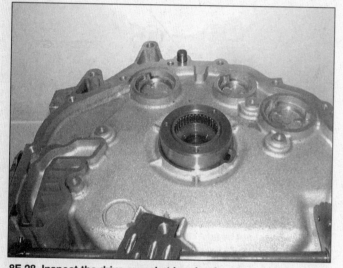

8E.28 Inspect the drive sprocket bearing for wear or damage and replace it if necessary

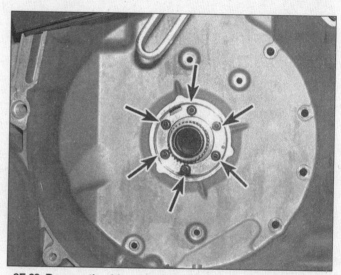

8E.29 Remove the drive sprocket support bolts and remove the drive sprocket support

8E.30 Remove the roll pins (A) and lock pin (B) from the manual shaft . . .

8E.31 . . . and withdraw the shaft from the transaxle case

8E.32 Remove the driven sprocket support

8E.33 Remove the driven sprocket support thrust washer (it may be stuck the support) - also, using a wire hook tool, retrieve the support hub thrust bearing and washer from the bottom of the drum bore

8E.34 Remove the overdrive band retainer . . .

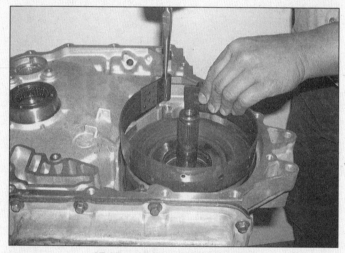

8E.35. . . and the overdrive band

8E.36 Install the clutch pack removal/installation tool, inserting the hooked end into one of the lubrication holes on the sun gear shell (arrow), position the clamp over the overdrive drum and tighten the handle; lift the forward, direct and intermediate clutch assembly out of the transaxle by the handle

8E.37 Remove the transaxle oil pan

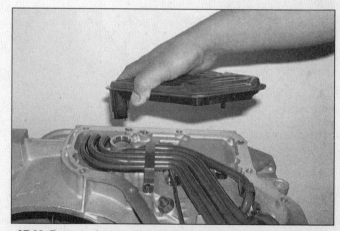

8E.38 Remove the transaxle oil filter (remove the O-rings if they remain in the case)

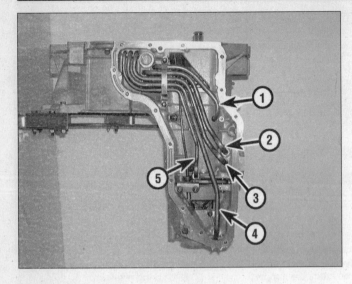

8E.39 For transaxle disassembly, the rear
lubrication oil tube and the reverse clutch
apply oil tube must be removed

1   Rear lubrication oil tube
2   Governor feed oil tube
3   Servo apply oil tube
4   Servo release oil tube
5   Reverse clutch apply oil tube

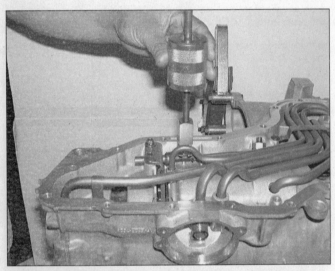

8E.40 The oil tubes are cemented into the case with Loctite -
remove the tube retaining bracket and use a small slide hammer
with a hook to pull the ends of the tubes out of the case

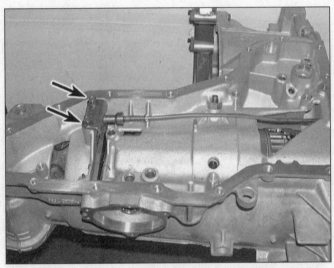

8E.41 Remove the two park rod retainer bolts and remove the
park rod from the case

8E.42 Remove the parking pawl shaft roll
pin and remove the parking pawl, shaft
and return spring from the case

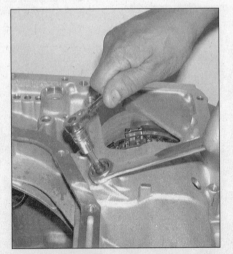

8E.43 Loosen the locknut and remove the
reverse anchor pin

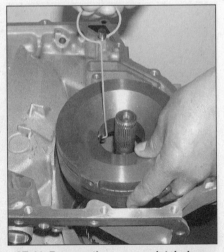

8E.44 Remove the reverse clutch drum

8E.45 Grasp the front planetary gear shaft and remove the planetary gear assembly

8E.46 Remove the low-intermediate drum and sun gear

8E.47 Remove the low-intermediate band

8E.48 Carefully pry the snap-ring out of the case lugs and remove the snap-ring

8E.49 Grasp the output shaft and lift the final drive unit from the case

8E.50 Remove the final drive ring gear

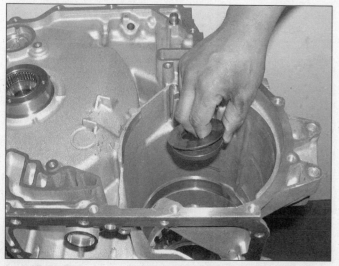

8E.51 Remove the final drive thrust bearing and washer

8E.52 Using a 3/8-inch drift, drive the rear lubrication seal out of the case - the seal must be replaced anytime the final drive unit is removed

Component inspection and subassembly overhaul

Using an approved cleaning solvent, clean and dry all the components thoroughly, including the case. Do not use rags to wipe the components dry, as lint from the rag may lodge in the oil passages, causing a valve to stick.

Inspect the following transaxle components and repair or replace as necessary:

a) *Case: Inspect the exterior of the case for damage, cracks and porosity (a porous casting will cause fluid leaks). Check the valve body mating surfaces on the case and valve body for damage and flatness (use a precision straightedge to check for flatness - any warpage means the valve body or case will have to be machined or replaced). Check all the oil passages, the servo bore, the speedometer bore and the governor bore for damage. Check all threaded holes for damage (repair thread damage as described in Chapter 2). Check the oil cooler line fittings for damage. Check the interior of the case for damaged retaining ring grooves, which will mean the case will have to be replaced. Check the case lugs for excessive wear. Check the driven sprocket support bearing for wear and replace it if necessary. Inspect the manual linkage and the park-lock linkage for damage.*

b) *Planetary gear sets: Inspect the internal gears, supports and carriers for damage. Check for stripped splines, cracked or broken teeth, damaged or worn thrust bearings and bushings. Check the carrier pinion gears for damaged bearings or worn washers. Check the support for damaged lugs. Inspect the sun gears for spline or tooth damage. Check the thrust washers and bushings for wear or damage.*

c) *One-way clutches: Inspect the low one-way clutch and the direct one-way clutch for damaged rollers, broken springs or a damaged cage. Check the finish of the inner and outer races for scoring or damage.*

d) *Forward, direct, intermediate and reverse clutch assemblies: Inspect the clutch housings for damaged splines. Inspect the check balls for looseness and the seal rings for damage. Check the clutch housings, pistons, springs, spring retainers, clutch plates, backing plates and retainer rings for wear or damage. Check for nicks or burrs in the lip seal areas. Check the housing and drum for worn bushings. Check the band apply surface for damage. Lay a steel ruler or straightedge across the surface and inspect for dishing. Inspect the band assemblies and servos for damage or wear. Check the thrust washers and bushings for wear or damage.*

e) *Differential and final drive assembly: Inspect the final drive internal gear for damaged teeth and worn bearing surfaces. Check the final drive carrier pinion gears for damaged teeth, worn bearings or worn washers. Check the thrust bearing for damage. Check the differential side gears, pinions and shaft for damage and wear.*

Oil pump assembly

Disassemble the oil pump as shown in the accompanying photos. Remove the 1-2 modulator valve train and the pressure relief ball and spring (if necessary). Lay the valves and springs out on a clean, lint-free towel in the exact order of removal to prevent confusion on assembly. Clean and dry the cover, body and all internal components. Inspect the valves and remove any burrs with a fine lapping compound; inspect the springs for damage or distortion; inspect the valve bores for damage; inspect the check balls for damage. Replace any damaged components. Inspect the pump rotor, vanes and vane ring very carefully. Replace the oil pump assembly if there are any doubts about their condition.

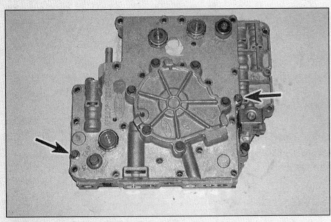

8E.53 Remove the two bolts (arrows) and separate the oil pump body from the valve body

8E.54 Remove the two bolts (arrows) and remove the separator plate and gasket

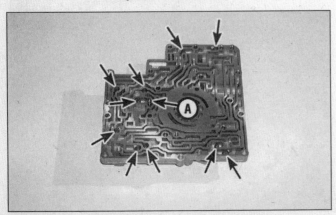

8E.55 Remove the check balls (arrows) and relief valve (A) - not all models are equipped with the check ball nearest the relief valve

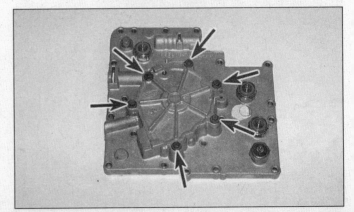

8E.56 Remove the bolts (arrows) and remove the oil pump cover

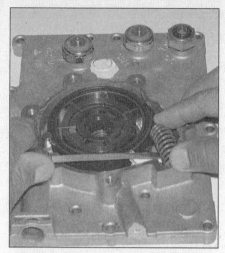

8E.57 Carefully pry the spring out of the oil pump body - be careful not to damage the oil pump body with the tool (place a piece of protective material under the tool at the leverage point)

8E.58 Remove the vane ring support pin

8E.59 Remove the O-ring retainer . . .

8E.60 . . . and the vane ring O-ring

8E.61 Remove the side seal . . .

8E.62 . . . and the side seal support

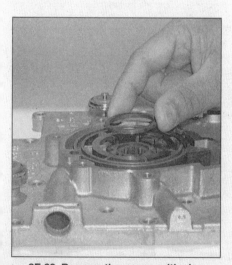

8E.63 Remove the vane positioning upper ring

8E.64 Remove the vane ring

8E.65 Remove the vanes from the rotor . . .

8E.66 . . . and remove the rotor

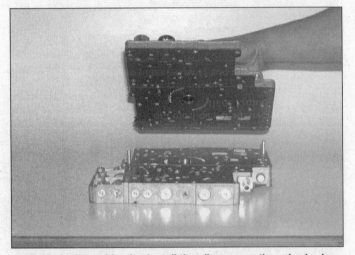

8E.67 Remove the vane positioning lower ring

8E.68 Reassemble the oil pump following the reverse of the
disassembly sequence with the following additions:

1   Install the rotor with the inside step facing up
2   Install the vanes with the shiny end toward the vane ring
3   When installing the vane positioning rings (both upper and
    lower) make sure they are positioned inside the vanes
4   Install a new side seal and vane ring O-ring seal
5   Install the check balls in the locations shown in illustration 8E.55
6   Tighten the oil pump cover and the separator plate retaining
    bolts to 96 in-lbs

8E.69   Using guide pins install the oil pump on the valve body,
tighten the two bolts to 96 in-lbs

Control valve assembly

Complete disassembly of the valve body is not necessary unless
the valve body has been contaminated. Clean the valve body using an
approved solvent and air dry (DO NOT use rags to dry the valve body,
as lint from the rag may cause a valve to stick). Check each valve for
freedom of movement in its bore. If a stuck valve is encountered,
remove the individual valve and components for further cleaning and
inspection. Nicks and burrs may be removed by lapping the valve with
a fine lapping compound.

If complete disassembly of the valve body is required, lay the valve
body on a clean work bench, use clean tools to disassemble and wash
the valve body with clean solvent. Remove the valves from the valve
body, one at a time. Lay out the valves, springs and bushings in their
proper order on a clean lint-free towel. Cleanliness and meticulous care
in keeping the valves in order cannot be over-stressed. A small tap is
helpful in removing any stubborn roll-pins you may encounter.

8E.70 Remove the two bolts (arrows) and remove the separator
plate and gasket

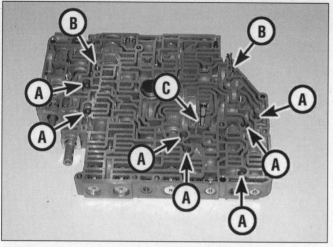

8E.71 Remove the check balls (A), the relief valves (B) and the filter (C) from the valve body

8E.72 Using a small screwdriver or pick, pry each valve against spring pressure - the valve should snap back when pressure is released - check each valve for sticking

8E.73 To disassemble a typical valve train, push in on the bore plug and remove the clip retaining the valve and spring

8E.74 It may be necessary to remove a second retaining clip to disassemble the complete valve train

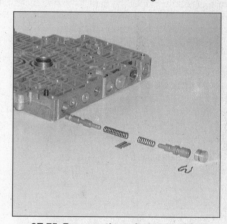

8E.75 Remove the valve assembly, keeping the components in order - clean and inspect the valves, bushings and springs, then reassemble the valve train - if the clip or roll pin does not fit securely, replace it with a new one

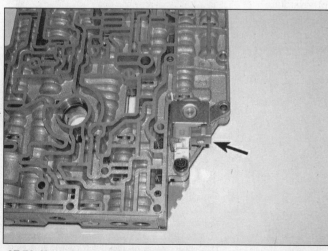

8E.76 If necessary, remove the torque converter clutch solenoid from the valve body

8E.77 After cleaning, inspection and reassembly of the valve body is complete, refer to illustration 8E.71 and install the check balls, relief valves and filter. Install two guide pins in the locations shown (arrows) and place the separator plate with a new gasket on the valve body, then tighten the two bolts to 96 in-lbs

Governor

Inspect the governor for damaged springs, seals or gear teeth. Inspect the weights for binding. Inspect the thrust bearing for wear or damage. Inspect the governor screen (in the case bore) for contamination. Replace the governor if it does not operate smoothly or appears contaminated.

Forward direct and intermediate clutch assembly

When disassembling a clutch pack, keep the clutch components in the exact order as the original stack-up. Make notes on the number of plates, the installed direction and location of backing plates, apply plates, waved plates, etc. Differences may exist between your model and the model shown. The correct components for your transaxle should be in the overhaul kit, if you purchased the correct kit. Lubricate the clutch friction plates with ATF before installation. One way to accomplish this is to dip them in a shallow pan of ATF.

Before removing a piston seal, note the installed direction of the seal lip. The piston seals must be installed with the seal lip facing the correct direction. If the seal is installed with the lip facing the wrong direction, the piston will not operate properly. If unsure, a common rule-of-thumb is this: the seal lip always faces pressure. Lubricate the seal and seal bore with a thin coating of ATF prior to assembly. Refer to Chapter 2 for additional information.

8E.78 Place the assembly on a clean workbench and remove the sun gear shell

8E.79 Remove the sun gear thrust bearing (one of two)

8E.80 Remove the intermediate clutch hub . . .

8E.81 . . . and remove the second sun gear thrust bearing

8E.82 Turn the assembly over on the bench and remove the overdrive drum

8E.83 Remove the forward clutch thrust washer

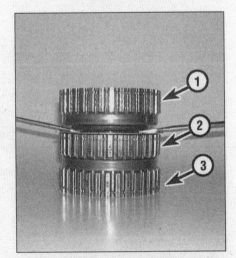

8E.84 Using two screwdrivers to apply even pressure, pry the forward clutch straight up and out of the direct clutch hub

1 Forward clutch
2 Direct clutch
3 Intermediate clutch

8E.85 Remove the direct one-way clutch . . .

8E.86 . . . and the thrust washer

Forward clutch

8E.87 Remove the forward clutch snap-ring . . .

8E.88 . . . and remove the pressure plate

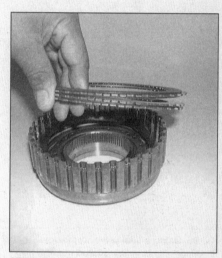

8E.89 Remove the forward clutch pack . . .

8E.90 . . . and waved plate from the forward clutch hub

8E.91 Using a clutch spring compressor, compress the clutch spring and remove the snap-ring

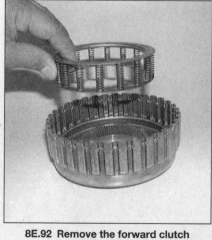

8E.92 Remove the forward clutch spring assembly

8E.93 Remove the forward clutch piston from the forward clutch hub

8E.94 Replace the outer piston seal on the forward clutch piston . . .

8E.95 . . . and the inner piston seal on the forward clutch hub

8E.96 Using a seal protector (arrow), install the forward clutch piston into the hub

8E.97 Install the forward clutch spring assembly and snap-ring, then install the waved plate, clutch pack, pressure plate and snap-ring

8E.98 **Check the forward clutch pack clearance as follows:**

1   *Press down on the pressure plate, making sure the clutch pack is properly seated and the snap-ring is properly installed in the groove*

2   *Set up a dial indicator with the needle resting on the pressure plate, then zero the indicator*

3   *Lift the pressure plate up against the snap-ring and note the reading on the dial indicator, take another reading 180-degrees from the first and average the readings - this is your clutch pack clearance*

4   *Forward clutch pack clearance should be 0.055 to 0.075-inch*

5   *If the clearance is incorrect, replace the snap-ring - selective snap-rings are available in thicknesses ranging from 0.049 to 0.104-inch*

Direct clutch

8E.99 Remove the snap-ring and remove the direct clutch pressure plate and clutch pack from the hub

8E.100 Using a clutch spring compressor, compress the clutch spring and remove the snap-ring

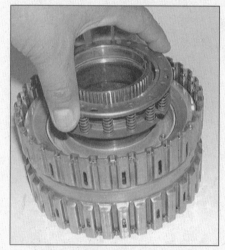

8E.101 Remove the direct clutch spring assembly

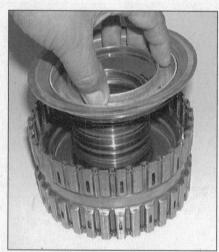

8E.102 Remove the direct clutch piston from the direct clutch hub

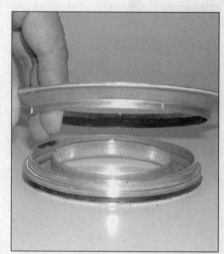

8E.103 Separate the apply ring from the direct clutch piston

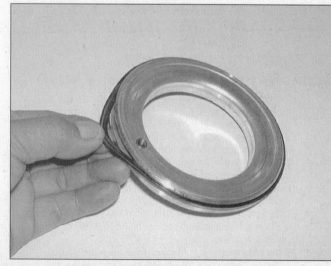

8E.104 Replace the outer piston seal on the direct clutch piston . . .

8E.105 . . . and the inner piston seal on the direct clutch hub

8E.106 Assemble the apply ring on the direct clutch piston, then using a seal protector (arrow), install the direct clutch piston into the hub

8E.107 Install the direct clutch spring assembly, aligning the notch in the spring retainer with the check ball in the piston (arrow)

8E.108 Compress the spring and install the snap-ring

8E.109 Install the direct clutch pack, pressure plate and snap-ring

8E.110 Check the direct clutch pack clearance as follows:

1   Press down on the pressure plate, making sure the clutch pack is properly seated and the snap-ring is properly installed in the groove

2   Set up a dial indicator with the needle resting on the pressure plate, then zero the indicator

3   Lift the pressure plate up against the snap-ring and note the reading on the dial indicator, take another reading 180-degrees from the first and average the readings - this is your clutch pack clearance

4   Direct clutch pack clearance should be 0.027 to 0.044-inch on a 3-plate clutch pack or 0.038 to 0.060 on a 4-plate clutch pack

5   If the clearance is incorrect, replace the snap-ring - selective snap-rings are available in thicknesses ranging from 0.049 to 0.119-inch

Intermediate clutch

8E.111 Remove the intermediate clutch snap-ring . . .

8E.112 . . . and remove the pressure plate

8E.113 Remove the intermediate clutch pack

8E.114 Using a clutch spring compressor, compress the clutch spring and remove the snap-ring

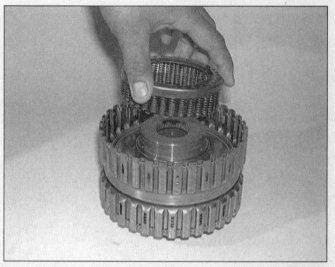

8E.115 Remove the intermediate clutch spring assembly

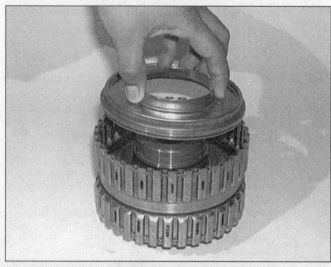

8E.116 Remove the intermediate clutch piston from the intermediate clutch hub

8E.117 Replace the outer piston seal on the intermediate clutch piston . . .

8E.118 . . . and the inner piston seal on the intermediate clutch hub

8E.119 Using a seal protector (arrow), install the intermediate clutch piston into the hub

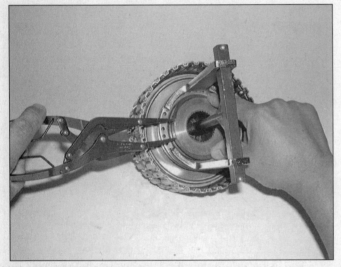

8E.120 Install the intermediate clutch spring assembly, compress the spring and install the snap-ring

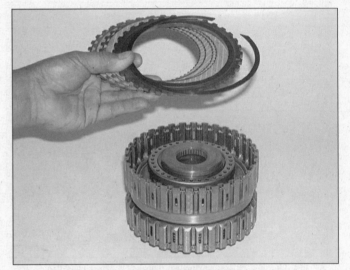

8E.121 Install the intermediate clutch pack, pressure plate and snap-ring

8E.122 Check the intermediate clutch pack clearance as follows:

1   Press down on the pressure plate, making sure the clutch pack is properly seated and the snap-ring is properly installed in the groove

2   Set up a dial indicator with the needle resting on the pressure plate, then zero the indicator

3   Lift the pressure plate up against the snap-ring and note the reading on the dial indicator, take another reading 180-degrees from the first and average the readings - this is your clutch pack clearance

4   Intermediate clutch pack clearance should be 0.035 to 0.052-inch on a 4-plate clutch pack or 0.046 to 0.067 on a 5-plate clutch pack

5   If the clearance is incorrect, replace the snap-ring - selective snap-rings are available in thicknesses ranging from 0.044 to 0.111-inch

Unit reassembly

8E.123 Install the direct clutch thrust washer, aligning the tabs on the thrust washer with the slots in the direct clutch

8E.124 Install the direct one-way clutch onto the direct clutch hub, aligning it with the clutch pack splines

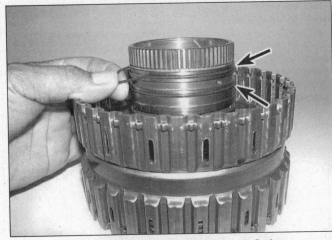

8E.125 Install the two direct clutch hub O-rings

8E.126 Install the forward clutch assembly onto the direct clutch hub - be careful not to damage the O-rings

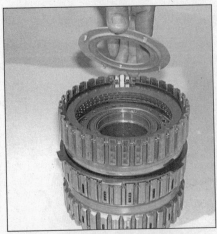

8E.127 Install the forward clutch thrust washer, aligning the tabs on the thrust washer with the slots in the forward clutch

8E.128 Install the overdrive drum onto the forward clutch, meshing the splines with the clutch pack - carefully turn the clutch assembly over

8E.129 Install the first sun gear thrust bearing onto the inside of the intermediate clutch hub, retain the thrust bearing on the hub with petroleum jelly - install the intermediate clutch hub and thrust bearing, meshing the splines with the clutch pack

8E.130 Install the second sun gear thrust bearing with the outer lip over the hub - there should be two of these thrust bearings, one on each side of the hub

8E.131 Install the sun gear and shell and place the assembly aside until final transaxle assembly

Reverse clutch

When disassembling a clutch pack, keep the clutch components in the exact order as the original stack-up. Make notes on the number of plates, the installed direction and location of backing plates, apply plates, waved plates, etc. Differences may exist between your model and the model shown. The correct components for your transaxle should be in the overhaul kit, if you purchased the correct kit. Lubricate the clutch friction plates with ATF before installation. One way to accomplish this, is to dip them in a shallow pan of ATF.

Before removing a piston seal, note the installed direction of the seal lip. The piston seals must be installed with the seal lip facing the correct direction. If the seal is installed with the lip facing the wrong direction, the piston will not operate properly. If unsure, a common rule-of-thumb is this: the seal lip always faces pressure. Lubricate the seal and seal bore with a thin coating of ATF prior to assembly. Refer to Chapter 2 for additional information.

8E.132 Remove the reverse clutch snap-ring . . .

8E.133 . . . and remove the reverse clutch pressure plate, clutch pack and waved plate from the reverse clutch drum

8E.134 Using a clutch spring compressor, compress the clutch spring, remove the snap-ring and remove the clutch spring assembly

8E.135 Remove the reverse clutch piston from the reverse clutch drum and replace the outer piston seal

8E.136 Replace the inner piston seal on the reverse clutch drum hub

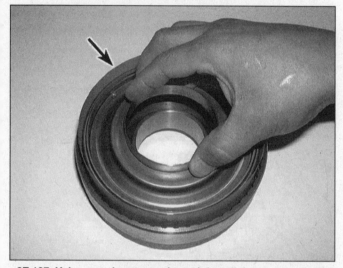

8E.137 Using a seal protector (arrow), install the reverse clutch piston into the drum

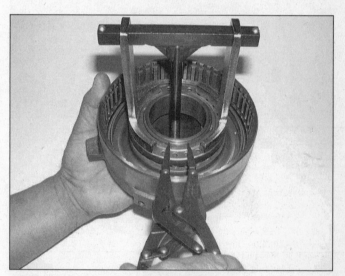

8E.138 Install the reverse clutch spring assembly, compress the spring and install the snap-ring

8E.139 Install the waved plate . . .

8E.140 . . . followed by the clutch pack . . .

8E.141 . . . and pressure plate

8E.142 Install the reverse clutch snap-ring

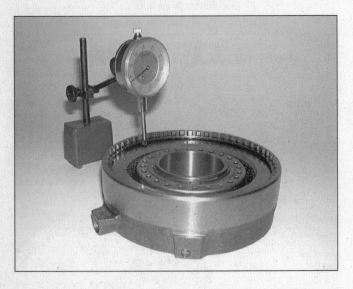

8E.143 Check the reverse clutch pack clearance as follows:

1   *Press down on the pressure plate, making sure the clutch pack is properly seated and the snap-ring is properly installed in the groove*
2   *Set up a dial indicator with the needle resting on the pressure plate, then zero the indicator*
3   *Lift the pressure plate up against the snap-ring and note the reading on the dial indicator, take another reading 180-degrees from the first and average the readings - this is your clutch pack clearance*
4   *Reverse clutch pack clearance should be 0.038 to 0.064-inch*
5   *If the clearance is incorrect, replace the snap-ring - selective snap-rings are available in thicknesses ranging from 0.059 to 0.118-inch*

Planetary gear assembly

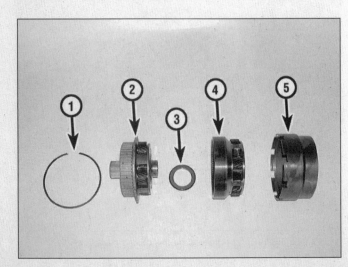

8E.144 Remove the snap-ring and disassemble the planetary gear assembly for cleaning and inspection; replace any defective components and reassemble the unit

1   *Snap-ring*
2   *Front planetary gearset*
3   *Planetary center thrust bearing*
4   *Rear planetary gearset*
5   *Ring gear*

Final drive unit

8E.145 Remove the planetary pinion shaft snap-ring

8E.146 Using a magnet, remove the planetary pinion shafts from the carrier

8E.147 Remove the planetary pinion gears from the planetary carrier

8E.148 Inspect the planetary pinion gears, needle bearings, shafts and thrust washers for wear or damage

8E.149 After removing all the planetary pinion gears, remove the planetary carrier thrust bearing (arrow) for inspection - replace any defective components and reassemble the final drive planetary gears

8E.150 Drive out the differential pinion shaft pin . . .

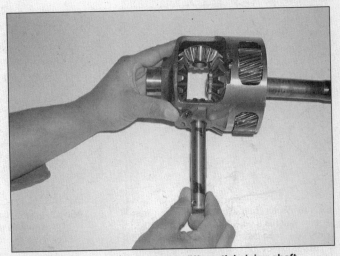

8E.151 . . . and remove the differential pinion shaft

8E.152 Rotate the output shaft and remove the differential pinion gears and thrust washers

8E.153 Inspect the differential pinion gears, thrust washers and shaft for wear or damage and replace the components as necessary

8E.154 Remove the right-side differential side gear and thrust washer

8E.155 Push the output shaft in, slide the left-hand side gear back, remove the retaining ring (arrow) and remove the left-hand side gear - inspect the differential side gears, thrust washers and output shaft for wear or damage, replace the necessary components and reassemble the output shaft and side gears into the differential case

8E.156 Mesh the differential pinion gears and washers with the side gears, 90-degrees from their installed position and rotate the output shaft until the pinion gears align with the pinion shaft bore

8E.157 Install the pinion shaft and drive in the roll pin

8E.158 Inspect the governor drive gear for wear of damage and replace it if necessary

Transaxle assembly

An automatic transaxle is a precision piece of equipment. Install each component as shown, and do not force any component into place. If it doesn't fit properly, find out why and rectify the situation.

Maintain a clean workplace and lubricate all moving parts as they are installed. Lubricate thrust washers and bearings with automatic transaxle fluid (ATF) or petroleum jelly. Use petroleum jelly to retain thrust washers and check balls in their proper location as the component is installed. Dip all friction plates in ATF before installation.

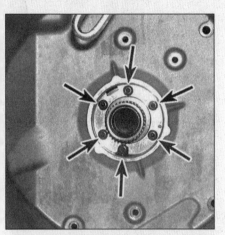

8E.159 Install the drive sprocket support; be careful, the bolt holes are offset, the support will only go on one way - tighten the bolts to 96 in-lbs

8E.160 Install the final drive thrust bearing in the case with the lip facing down

8E.161 Install the final drive ring gear in the case with the outer splines up; seat the ring gear in the case with a hammer handle or equivalent

8E.162 Install the final drive sun gear in the final drive planetary gear

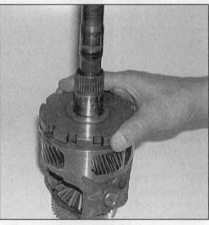

8E.163 Install the parking gear onto the sun gear

8E.164 Install the final drive planetary gear thrust bearing

8E.165 Install the rear planetary support onto the assembly

8E.166 Install the sun gear thrust bearing

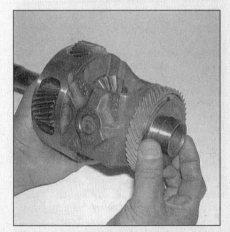

8E.167 Install the final drive thrust washer - retain the thrust washer on the unit with petroleum jelly

8E.168 Grasp the output shaft and lower the final drive assembly into the case meshing the planetary gear pinions with the ring gear

8E.169 Install the rear planetary support snap-ring, aligning one end of the snap-ring with the low-intermediate band anchor pin (arrow)

8E.170 Mount a dial indicator on the chain cover flange with the needle resting on the end of the output shaft - zero the indicator

8E.171 Working through the access hole in the case, pry the final drive unit up and read the final drive unit endplay on the indicator - final drive unit endplay should be 0.004 to 0.025-inch, if the reading is incorrect, remove the final drive unit and replace the final drive selective thrust washer - selective washers are available in sizes ranging from 0.050 to 0.065-inch

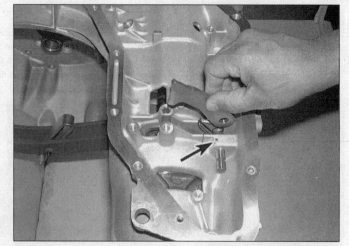

8E.172 Install the parking pawl, return spring and shaft - drive the shaft locating pin into the hole in the case (arrow)

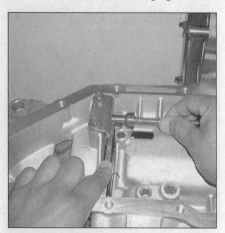

8E.173 Press down on the parking pawl and install the park rod lever, park rod and retainer

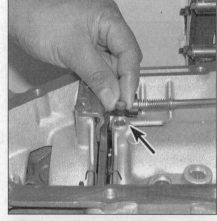

8E.174 Install the rear lubrication seal in the case (arrow) and drive the seal in with a 3/8-inch drift - make sure the seal is seated on the rear support or lubrication problems will result

8E.175 Install the low-intermediate band - make sure the band is properly engaged with the anchor pin (arrow)

8E.176 Install the low-intermediate drum/sun gear

8E.177 Install the planetary gear assembly

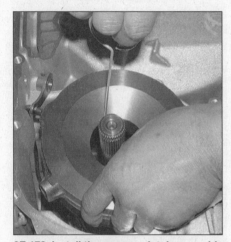

8E.178 Install the reverse clutch assembly engaging the clutch plates with the splines on the planetary unit - work the clutch assembly on the splines until all the clutch plates are engaged

8E.179 Make sure the reverse clutch assembly is fully seated before continuing - if necessary use the intermediate clutch hub to rotate the planetary unit, allowing the clutch plates to engage the splines

8E.180 Install the reverse drum anchor pin bolt, but DO NOT tighten it at this time

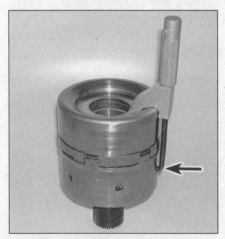

8E.181 Install the clutch pack removal/installation tool onto the clutch pack assembly; insert the hooked end into one of the lubrication holes on the sun gear shell (arrow), position the clamp over the overdrive drum and tighten the handle

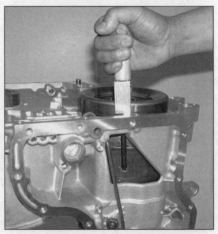

8E.182 Install the clutch pack in the case, meshing the sun gear with the planetary gears - do not remove the removal/installation tool until you're sure the assembly is fully seated

8E.183 Install the overdrive band around the overdrive drum . . .

8E.184 . . . and install the plastic overdrive band retainer with the cross facing up

Note:

Before continuing with transaxle assembly it must be determined if the two driven sprocket support thrust washers (front and rear) are the correct thickness, giving the correct driven sprocket endplay. The procedure is very tedious, so follow the procedure very carefully.

8E.185 Install the final drive loading tool and tighten the bolt, removing all endplay from the final drive unit

8E.186 Remove the Teflon seal rings from the driven sprocket support - do not install the new seals at this time

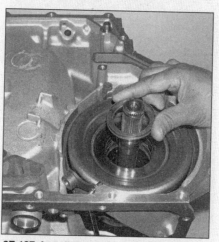

8E.187 Install the direct clutch hub thrust bearing with the outer lip facing up . . .

8E.188 . . . and install the driven sprocket support rear thrust washer

8E.189 Install the driven sprocket support, then install the driven sprocket onto the output shaft

8E.190 Using a depth gauge, determine the clearance between the driven sprocket support bolt hole surface and the case surface - if the bolt hole surface is above the case surface, position the depth gauge on the bolt hole surface with the plunger over the case surface - the clearance should not be greater than 0.008-inch; if it is, install a thinner driven sprocket support rear thrust washer

8E.191 If the bolt hole surface is below the case surface, position the depth gauge on the case surface with the plunger over the bolt hole surface - the clearance should not be greater than 0.018-inch; if it is, install a thicker driven sprocket support rear thrust washer - thrust washers are available in sizes ranging from 0.060 to 0.085-inch

8E.192 After determining the correct driven sprocket support rear thrust washer, remove the driven sprocket support, the driven sprocket support rear thrust washer and the direct clutch hub thrust bearing, install the driven sprocket support front thrust washer on the driven sprocket support aligning the tab on the thrust washer with the slot on the support (arrows) - retain the thrust washer on the support with petroleum jelly

8E.193 Install the driven sprocket support in the case and measure the clearance between the case surface and the bolt hole surface - subtract the previously recorded driven sprocket rear thrust washer measurement from this measurement; the difference should be 0.001 to 0.033-inch - if the clearance is not within the specified clearance replace the driven sprocket front thrust washer with a thinner or thicker washer as applicable - thrust washers are available in sizes ranging from 0.090 to 0.115-inch

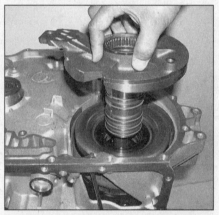

8E.194 When the correct driven sprocket support thrust washer sizes have been determined, install the front thrust washer on the support and install the five new Teflon seal rings - lubricate the thrust washer and seal rings with petroleum jelly

8E.195 Install the direct clutch hub thrust bearing and the driven sprocket support rear thrust washer over the output shaft, then install the driven sprocket support

8E.196 Install a new manual shaft seal into the case

8E.197 Install the manual shaft, drive in the roll pins (A) and install a new lock pin (B)

8E.198 Install the drive and driven sprocket thrust washers, aligning the tabs on the washers with the holes in the supports - retain the thrust washers with petroleum jelly

8E.199 Install a new cast iron seal ring on the drive sprocket input shaft - make sure the ring ends are properly locked and lubricate the ring with petroleum jelly

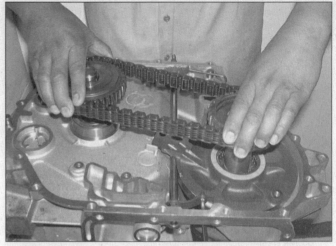

8E.200 Assemble the drive sprocket, chain and driven sprocket and install the assembly - rotate the sprockets and make sure they are seated on the sprocket supports

8E.201 Install the accumulator springs in the chain cover - make sure the springs are installed in the correct locations

1   Neutral-Drive accumulator spring
2   3-4 accumulator spring
3   1-2 accumulator spring

8E.202 Install a new chain cover gasket onto the case

8E.203 Install new seals on the accumulator pistons - the 1-2 and 3-4 accumulator pistons use a square cut seal while the Neutral-Drive accumulator piston uses an O-ring seal

8E.204 Lubricate the seals with petroleum jelly and install the accumulator pistons into their respective bores in the chain cover

8E.205 Install the accumulator piston pins

8E.206 Install the metal chain cover thrust washer (A) and the plastic drive sprocket thrust washer (B), aligning the tabs on the washers with the slots in the chain cover - retain the thrust washers with petroleum jelly

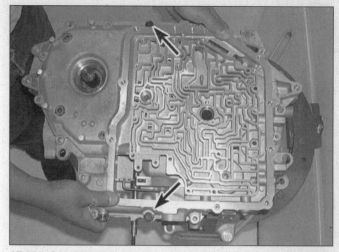

8E.207 Carefully lower the chain cover onto the case, aligning the input shaft with the bore in the chain cover (be very careful not to damage the input shaft cast iron seal ring); press the chain cover down against the accumulator springs and hand tighten two chain cover bolts (arrows)

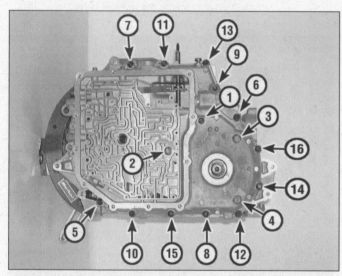

8E.208 Install the remainder of the bolts hand tight, then tighten the bolts in the sequence shown to the specified torque - tighten the 8 mm bolts to 96 in-lbs, tighten the 10 mm bolts to 24 ft-lbs and tighten the 13 mm bolts to 30 ft-lbs

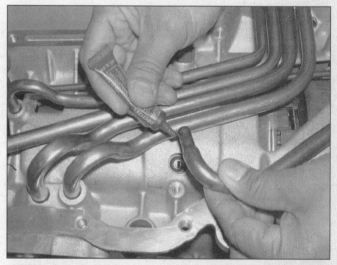

8E.209 Clean the sealer from the lubrication tubes, apply a bead of threadlocking compound to the end of the tube and tap the tube into the case - install the tube clamps

8E.210 Install the filter, with a new seal and install the filter/tube bracket (arrow)

8E.211 Install the oil pan with a new gasket - tighten the oil pan bolts to 144 in-lbs

8E.212 Install new seals on the oil pump driveshaft, lubricate the seals with petroleum jelly and install the driveshaft

8E.213 Install the throttle valve linkage and manual valve link - connect the throttle valve cable link through the hole in the case

8E.214 Install a new valve body-to-chain cover gasket and place the valve body in position, engaging the oil pump shaft with the oil pump, rotate the valve body slightly and connect the manual valve link with the manual valve

8E.215 Depress the throttle valve and lower the valve body onto the chain cover

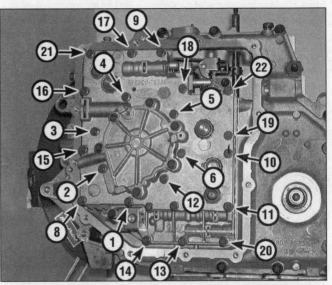

8E.216 Install the valve body bolts and tighten them in the sequence shown to 96 in-lbs - note that bolts 13, 14 and 20 in the sequence are short bolts

8E.217 Install the bulkhead connector into the case and connect the wiring harness to the bulkhead connector, pressure switches and torque converter clutch solenoid (arrows) - make sure the electrical connectors are securely connected

8E.218 Install the oil pan with a new gasket - tighten the bolts to 96 in-lbs

8E.219 Place the manual shaft in the neutral position and install the Park/Neutral switch - align the switch by inserting a 5/64-inch drill bit through the hole in the switch (arrow) and into the hole in the case, tighten the bolts to 96-in-lbs and remove the drill bit

8E.220 If a new case, band, drum, servo piston or rod has been replaced, check the servo piston travel as follows (a special overdrive and low-intermediate servo rod tool set is required) (the same procedure is used for both servos):

1   Using the special spring provided with the tool set, install the servo piston in the case without a piston seal
2   Install the tool on the case and tighten the center bolt to 10 in-lbs (overdrive servo) or 30 in-lbs (low-intermediate servo)
3   Mount a dial indicator on the case with the needle resting on the servo piston through the opening in the tool - zero the dial indicator
4   Back-off the center bolt until the piston stops and read the travel on the dial indicator - the overdrive servo the piston travel should be 0.070 to 0.149-inch; the low-intermediate servo travel should be 0.216 to 0.255-inch with the original band or 0.196 to 0.236 with a new band
5   If the piston travel is not within specifications, install a new piston rod - rods are available in different lengths

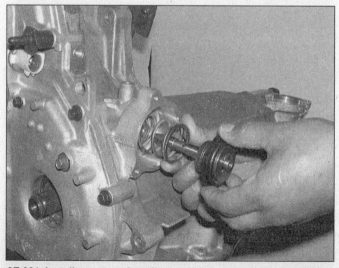

8E.221 Install a new seal on the overdrive servo piston and install the overdrive servo spring, rod and piston

8E.222 Install the overdrive servo cover with a new seal - tighten the bolts to 96 in-lbs

8E.223 Install a new seal on the low-intermediate servo piston and install the low-intermediate servo spring, rod and piston

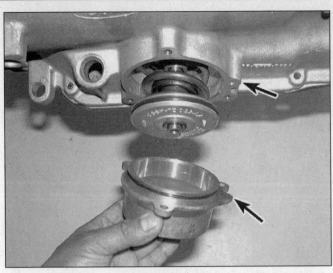

8E.224 Install the low-intermediate servo cover with a new seal, aligning the tab on the cover with the oil passage on the case (arrows) - tighten the bolts evenly to 96 in-lbs to prevent cocking the cover in the case

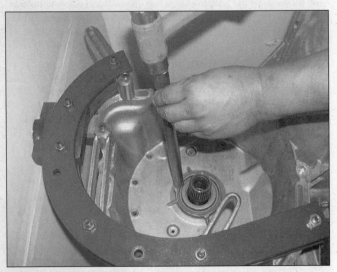

8E.225 Install a new torque converter seal and new output shaft oil seals in the transaxle case

Chapter 9
Improving your automatic transmission

The automatic transmissions covered by this manual are used in all types of vehicles, from medium-duty trucks to compact cars. They are also used for all types of driving, from highway cruising to trailer towing to high-abuse off-road driving - and all drivers expect long life from their vehicle.

When your automatic transmission was designed, engineers had to take into consideration all of these possible types of use and also keep costs low. So the transmission design is actually a compromise of adequate shifting firmness, but smooth engagement; adequate downshifts, but no excessive engine revving; adequate torque multiplication, but good fuel economy . . . and so on.

But you know best what you want from your vehicle, so isn't there a way to undo some of these compromises to get the kind of performance you want out of your automatic transmission? There absolutely is! And automatic transmission modifications are generally easy to make and can make major improvements in the type of performance you want. So read on! There's something for all types of drivers in this Chapter.

Auxiliary transmission coolers

Here's a modification everyone should consider, since it will extend transmission life in almost any application. We consider an auxiliary cooler mandatory for towing, RVs, off-road or street-performance use.

Slippage within an automatic transmission generates heat, and heat is the greatest enemy of any automatic transmission. It is often said that a 10-percent reduction in transmission heat can double the life of an automatic transmission. Heat causes fluid to break down, losing its lubricating and heat-transfer properties, and heat also causes clutch friction material to varnish, causing still more slippage. Since transmission fluid is in contact with virtually all components within an automatic transmission, cooling the fluid will ultimately cool the transmission. Stock transmission fluid coolers circulate pressurized fluid through lines (usually steel tubes) to the radiator. A separate transmission fluid chamber within the radiator bottom or side tank is in constant contact with engine coolant. Since normal engine coolant temperature is lower than normal transmission fluid temperature, the transmission fluid chamber transfers heat to the engine coolant, cooling the transmission fluid.

This "heat exchanger" works well under normal conditions, but if the engine overheats, the transmission will likewise overheat. Also, if the transmission is slipping excessively and building up excessive heat, the engine will also overheat. To overcome these problems and extend transmission life by reducing operating temperature, an auxiliary transmission cooler is called for. Also, if your engine cooling system has a tendency to overheat, installing an auxiliary transmission cooler will relieve the radiator of this additional cooling responsibility and help your engine run cooler when outside temperatures and load-carrying or performance demands on your vehicle increase.

There are two basic types of auxiliary coolers available. The first type is an extra-deep transmission pan **(see illustration)**. The concept behind this modification is that, since a deep pan can hold more transmission fluid, the additional fluid will hold and transfer more heat. Since the pan is deeper, it also exposes more metal surface to the air flowing underneath the chassis. Some deep pans also have longitudinal tubes running the length of the pan that are welded to the front and rear of the pan. This creates holes through the pan that air can flow through and cool the fluid further.

Deep pans have some drawbacks, however. First, they are most effective when the vehicle is moving down the road. When the vehicle is sitting still or moving slowly, they are much less efficient. Second, deep pans reduce ground clearance, so, on off-road vehicles or low-to-the-ground sports cars, they can be more easily damaged by contact with the ground or rocks. Finally, deep pans do not offer nearly the cooling efficiency of a large radiator-type cooler mounted at the front of the vehicle.

The radiator-type cooler, as we'll call it here, is the most popular and most effective type of auxiliary transmission cooler. These types of

9.1 Deep transmission pans are easy to install and can help lower transmission temperature, but they are generally not as effective as radiator-type auxiliary coolers

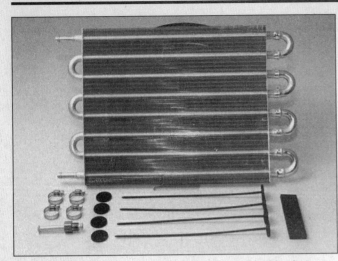

9.2a Here is the auxiliary cooler we'll install in this photo sequence. It is typical of what you'll find in auto parts stores and includes an installation kit and instructions. Before beginning installation, try to park the vehicle so its front end is pointing uphill. This will minimize fluid loss during installation. Read the instructions that come with the kit carefully - they supersede information printed here

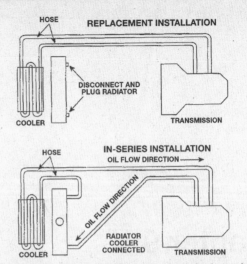

9.2b Decide if you want to use the auxiliary cooler in conjunction with the existing cooler in the radiator (bottom) or use it by itself (top). Generally, if you live in a cold climate, incorporating the existing cooler is a good idea, since it will allow the transmission to reach operating temperature faster. In a warm climate, it's best to use the auxiliary cooler by itself

9.2c If you'll be using the existing cooler, you'll need to establish which line is the outlet from the cooler. With the engine cold, start the engine and shift the transmission into gear for a moment (no more than 10 seconds). Then feel both lines - the warmer line is the inlet, so cut the other line (don't cut the line now, however - it will be cut in a later step)

9.2d Attach the hose provided in the kit to the cooler, but don't cut it (leave it in a loop). The hose clamps should be tightened only to the point where the hose rubber is pressed slightly through the slots in the clamp bands and is level with the clamp band. Do not overtighten to the point where rubber is pressed out above the band slots

coolers are available in an assortment of sizes to suit every need, from trailer towing and RV use to street/strip racing. This type of cooler uses aluminum tubing, running through heat-dissipating fins. The cooler looks somewhat like a small version of a conventional radiator and installs in front of the vehicle's radiator (or condenser, if the vehicle is air conditioned). When installing the auxiliary cooler, you can either eliminate the stock cooler (which will help the engine's cooling system work a little better in warm climates) or install it in-line with the existing cooler (which will speed warm-up in cold climates). If you eliminate the existing cooler, you must make certain the cooler will dissipate enough heat to prevent overheating. Generally, coolers are rated for the Gross Vehicle Weight (GVW) they are capable of cooling for, but bigger is usually better. Get a cooler rated well in excess of the GVW of your vehicle.

Included here is a photographic sequence of installing an auxiliary transmission cooler on a typical vehicle **(see illustrations)**. This installation is typical of what you'll encounter when installing a cooler - read the captions accompanying each photo for the complete procedure.

Inline transmission filters

The standard transmission filter located inside the transmission oil pan does an adequate job, at best, filtering the automatic transmission fluid. An inline transmission filter can be installed in a transmission cooler line, much like an auxiliary transmission cooler, to double the filtration capacity **(see illustration)**. Metallic debris is a transmission's worst enemy, and any additional filtration capability is likely to prolong the life of your transmission.

Installing an inline filter into an existing metal cooler line is a very simple operation. In fact, if you're installing an auxiliary cooler, it would be very easy to add an inline filter at the same time. Be sure to observe the proper flow direction; the filters are marked with an arrow indicating flow direction, and installing one backwards will cause a no-flow condition and damage your transmission.

Another type of inline transmission filter is the "spin-on" type. This type is also known as a "remote-type" filter because the adapter is

9.2e Find a mounting location for the cooler in front of the radiator or condenser (if you have air conditioning). Make sure you've thought out the routing of the hoses so they won't obstruct anything, then mount the cooler with the nylon straps provided. Be sure to stick the adhesive pads to the cooler so they will be sandwiched between the cooler and radiator when the straps are tightened

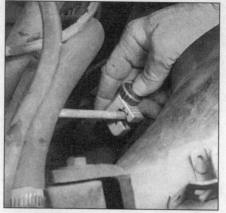

9.2f Find a convenient location to cut off the steel cooler line(s), as close to the cooler as possible. The miniature tubing cutter shown here is very useful in tight spaces. When the lines are cut, fluid will leak out, so place a container underneath to catch the leakage. If you'll be using the existing cooler in conjunction with the auxiliary cooler (recommended in cold climates), only the return line will need to be cut

9.2g Using a flare-nut wrench, unscrew the cut-off ends of the line(s) from the radiator fittings. If you'll be using the existing cooler in conjunction with the auxiliary cooler, install the fitting designed for this purpose - it should be included in the kit

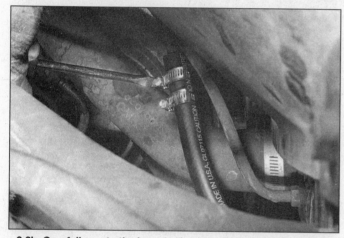

9.2h Carefully route the hose to the cut-off line(s) (and radiator fitting, if you'll be using the existing cooler). Be careful not to kink the hoses or bend them sharply. Make sure the hoses will not be in contact with any sharp surface or near any hot surfaces that could damage them. If possible, secure the hoses to the chassis or other hoses or lines with nylon tie-straps. Attach the hoses with hose clamps, being careful not to overtighten them. Now start the engine and check carefully for leaks. Check the transmission fluid level and add additional fluid, as necessary. After two weeks or so, recheck all hose clamps for tightness

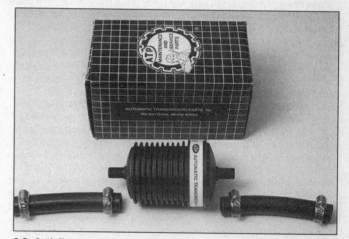

9.3 An inline transmission filter, such as this unit from ATP can be installed in minutes into the transmission cooler lines. This particular filter has dual filtration capabilities that include an internal magnet that attracts loose ferrous particles and a 30 micron paper filter element to trap non-ferrous particles. An internal pressure relief valve assures continuous flow in the event the filter ever becomes clogged

mounted at a remote location, such as a frame rail. A spin-on cartridge filter is threaded on the adapter, much like an oil filter, making this type of filter very easy to service. Most manufacturers of remote mounted spin-on type transmission filters use a common oil filter for replacement purposes, so parts availability is not a problem.

Shift kits

Since the automatic transmissions covered by this manual are used in luxury cars, engineers have designed in a compromise that's unacceptable to people who tow or drive RVs or high-performance vehicles. This compromise is the stock shifting characteristics. The characteristic of shift softness (hardly being able to tell when a stock transmission shifts) is very desirable for luxury cars so owners can enjoy an imperceptible transition from one gear to another. The main way this softness is achieved is through more *overlap*, which is the time during a shift that both the engaging gear and releasing gear are applied at the same time. Obviously, from a performance and durability standpoint, overlap is quite undesirable. Applying two gears at the same time causes slippage, which leads to wear and excessive heat, so the less overlap, the better it is for transmission life. Also, racers claim the time and energy wasted during a heavily overlapped shift can lead to slower quarter-mile times. So, if you can put up with a shift you can feel, there is transmission life and performance to be gained. Most drivers of high-performance cars say they prefer to feel a good, firm shift than to "slide" into the next gear.

Several aftermarket manufacturers produce quality "shift kits" to

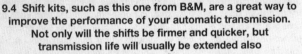

9.4 Shift kits, such as this one from B&M, are a great way to improve the performance of your automatic transmission. Not only will the shifts be firmer and quicker, but transmission life will usually be extended also

re-program the shifting characteristics of the transmissions covered by this manual **(see illustration)**. Generally, the kits require the installer to replace springs and steel balls in the valve body, as well as do some minor drilling to the valve body separator plate and passages. If done as a part of an overhaul, a shift kit takes very little time to install. Shift kits are a bit more difficult to install with the transmission in place, but can generally be installed in a day. Try to do the installation at the same time you change transmission fluid, so you'll save a little work. Since all shift kits use their own unique methods of changing shift characteristics, we will not detail an installation here - the kit will come with complete installation instructions.

Also keep in mind that shift kits come in different versions for different types of driving. There are RV kits designed to keep very high apply pressures for towing. There are also street/strip kits designed for the performance enthusiast and kits designed for competition racing that are usually not practical for use on the street. Many of the "race only" kits convert the transmission to manual shifting, which is undesirable on the street, since coast-down engine braking is also reduced (this will increase brake wear and can be dangerous on long down-hills). Read all manufacturer's literature carefully to pick the kit best suited to your needs, and be honest - you won't be using the family car for Top-Fuel competition, so don't install components recommended for racing use only - you'll be unhappy with the way the car drives on the street.

High-stall torque converters

In street/strip and racing vehicles, a major disadvantage of the stock torque converter is its low *stall speed*. Basically, stall speed is the engine speed (in rpm) at which the fluid coupling in the torque converter achieves a near lock-up condition that is theoretically so efficient that it can stall the engine when the vehicle is at a stop in gear with the brakes applied and the engine is accelerated. In practice, on most high-performance engines, the brakes fail to hold the engine torque during this test and the rear wheels spin, so a better test is to accelerate the car from a stop at full-throttle (on a race track or similar safe area) and note the engine rpm during the launch.

Stock converters have a stall speed of about 1200 to 1500 rpm, which provides good fuel efficiency, since converter slippage is reduced overall. Basically, on a high-performance engine, a higher stall speed will allow the engine to rev higher before the car must move, which improves initial acceleration (launch).

Since you'll usually be replacing your torque converter at overhaul time, it's a good idea to consider a higher stall converter if you have a

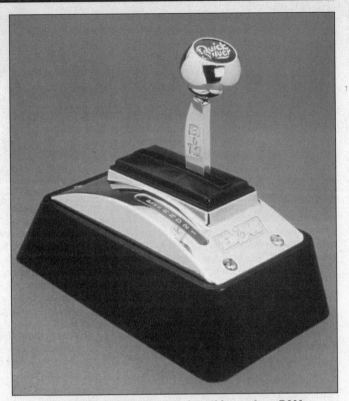

9.5 Aftermarket shifters, such as this one from B&M, add greater precision to manual shifting and can also provide a weight savings

high-performance vehicle. When choosing a torque converter, try to pick one that has an advertised stall speed about 500 to 750 rpm under the rpm at which peak torque occurs. This will allow the vehicle to launch during maximum torque output. But be very careful not to overestimate the rpm where torque occurs on your engine. Too high a stall speed is just as bad (if not worse) than too low a stall speed, since efficiency will be lost during peak torque output, when you want it most. Also keep in mind that torque converter slippage leads to more heat, so a higher stall speed may mean the transmission will have more of a tendency to overheat.

Most street-driven high-performance vehicles will benefit from a torque converter with a stall speed of about 2000 to 2500 rpm. Converters in this range still retain enough efficiency at low speeds that fuel economy will not be significantly affected, if at all.

Some manufacturers also produce torque converters specifically designed for motorhome and RV applications that provide a bit higher-than-stock stall speed (about 1800 rpm) for better torque delivery during hauling and towing. These converters are especially helpful on engines that have an RV-type camshaft in them, since these camshafts will slightly raise the rpm where maximum torque is delivered.

Aftermarket shifters

Quality aftermarket shifters, from companies such as B&M, provide greater shifting precision than stock shifters **(see illustration)**. If you have a racing vehicle that has been converted to fully manual shifting operation, such a rugged and exacting shifter is essential. Even for high-performance street use, if you ever select gears manually, such a shifter can prevent over-shifting into the next higher gear or accidentally shifting into Neutral or Reverse (which could cause major damage). Aftermarket shifters are relatively inexpensive and are generally easy to install. Many of them also offer a weight savings, since they have a lightweight cable that replaces the heavier rod-type linkage often installed at the factory.

Source list

Alto Products Corp.
832 Ridgewood Ave.
North Brunswick, NJ 08902
980-249-3633
Specialty products for automatic transmissions

Automatic Transmission Parts, Inc.
5940 Oakton St.
Morton Grove, IL 60053
708-967-6790
Automatic transmission components and repair kits

B & M Racing and Performance Products
9142 Independence Ave.
Chatsworth, CA 91311
818-882-6422
Automatic transmission repair kits, accessories and complete transmissions

BRYCO
7495 NW 48th St.
Miami, FL 33166
305-592-2760
Automatic transmission components and repair kits

Hayden, Inc.
1531 Pomona Rd.
Corona, CA 91720
800-854-4757
Automatic transmission accessories

Hayden Trans-Tool
110 Connelly
San Antonio, TX 78203
800-531-5978
Automatic transmission repair tools and equipment

OTC Division/SPX Corp.
655 Eisenhower Dr.
Owatonna, MN 55060
507-455-7000
Automatic transmission repair tools and equipment

Rotunda Tools
P.O. Box 1000
Plymouth, MI 48170
800-768-8632
Ford special service tools and equipment

Techpak-Fitzall
730 South Westwood Blvd.
Poplar Bluff, MO 63901
314-785-3303
Automatic transmission cables, solenoids and repair kits

Notes

Glossary

Accumulator - A device that dampens pressure fluctuations within a hydraulic system. Accumulators allow gradual pressure build-up on application of an apply device, preventing fluid shock and resultant vibration.

Apply device - The term used for devices that hold or drive the planetary gearset. Apply devices include bands, multiple-disc clutch packs and one-way clutches.

Band - A thin steel band lined with friction material that is placed around a circular drum, anchored to the case on one side and held by an apply device on the other side. When applied it holds a drum from turning.

Belleville spring - A tapered spring used in clutch pack assemblies to aid in the control of the disc clutch.

Bevel gear - A gear with tapered or angle-cut ends.

Booster valve - A valve that raises hydraulic pressure when loads are high to prevent apply devices from slipping.

Clutch plates - Steel plates or steel plates with friction material attached. Clutch plates are used in multiple-disc clutch packs.

Control valving - Any devices that reduce, govern or manage the flow of fluid in a hydraulic system.

Compound planetary gearset - A planetary gearset that has two sets of planet gears shared by a single sun gear.

Clutch pack - The assembled group of steel and friction plates in a drum that are used to apply a particular gear range.

Coupling phase - The time at which the turbine and the impeller in the torque converter spin at the same speed and no torque multiplication is present.

Direct drive - When the engine, transmission and driveshaft all turn at the same speed (the gear ratio is 1:1).

Downshift valve - A kickdown valve or detent valve that increases throttle pressure to force a downshift under high driveline loads.

Driveplate - See "Flexplate."

Endplay - A measure of axial movement encountered or allowed in an automatic transmission. Endplay is usually measured at the input shaft.

Filter - A filter traps particles of dirt and other contaminants as fluid is drawn across its surface. Screen and paper filters are usually used in automatic transmissions.

Final drive - The final geared assembly in the transmission.

Flexplate - The thin metal plate that attaches the engine crankshaft to the torque converter of a automatic transmission.

Friction modifiers - Additives that help lubricants maintain their properties over a wide range of temperatures.

Gear pump - A pump that uses an inner drive gear and an outer driven gear, separated on one side by a crescent-shaped boss, to produce oil flow.

Gear ratio - The number of revolutions made by a driving gear as compared to the number of revolutions made by a driven gear of a different size. For example, if one gear makes three revolutions while the other gear makes one revolution, the gear ratio is 3:1.

Gear reduction - Is when the drive gear turns faster than the driven gear. The output speed of the driven gear is then reduced, while output torque is increased.

Geartrain - A series of two or more gears. Meshing of the teeth of two gears enables one to drive the other, thus transmitting power.

Governor pressure - A pressure which varies in relation to speed, usually that of the transmission output shaft.

Governor valve - This valve is driven off of the transmission output shaft and varies hydraulic pressure for upshifts and downshifts in relation to vehicle road speed.

Helical gear - A gear on which the teeth are cut at an angle to the center of the gear.

Hydraulic circuit - A series of fluid passages, control valves and an output device that is used to transmit motion from hydraulic pressure which produces movement or work.

Hydraulics - The physical science and technology of the static and dynamic behavior of fluids and their use to transmit force and motion.

Impeller - A component of the torque converter. Its angled fins produce fluid flow inside the torque converter. Also known as the pump.

Internal ring gear - A spur gear in the form of an internally toothed ring.

Land - The stepped outer circumference of a valve that contacts the valve bore.

Manifold vacuum - The difference in air pressure, or pressure drop, between atmospheric pressure and the air pressure in the intake manifold that occurs just below the throttle plate(s); usually expressed in inches of Mercury (in-Hg).

Manual valve - This valve is manually operated by the shift linkage and used to select the drive range in an automatic transmission.

Multiple-disc clutch - A clutch pack, consisting of alternating steel plates and driven friction plates. When hydraulically applied through a servo piston, the plates lock together and apply a gear range.

One-way check valve - A style of valve that allows fluid to flow in one direction only, and only when the pressure is sufficient to unseat the valve.

One-way clutch - A mechanical holding device that locks up when rotated in one direction and free-wheels when rotated in the opposite direction.

Orifice - A small opening or restriction to flow in a line, pipe, passage or valve.

Overdrive - Any arrangement of gearing which produces more revolutions of the driven shaft than the drive shaft.

Pinion gear - A smaller gear which engages a larger geared wheel or toothed rack.

Planetary gearset - A system of gearing named after the solar system because of similarities between its function and the way the planets revolve around the sun. The sun gear is surrounded by an internal ring gear with planet gears in mesh between the ring gear and the sun gear.

Planetary carrier assembly - Carrier or bracket in a planetary system which contains shafts upon which pinions or planet gears turn. The carrier assembly keeps the planet gears evenly spaced.

Planetary pinions - The gears mounted on the planetary carrier assembly in a planetary gearset. The planetary pinions mesh with and revolve around the sun gear. They also mesh with an internal ring gear.

Ported vacuum - A slot-type port located right at the throttle plates, used for controlling various devices that must work in proportion to the throttle opening. When the throttle plates are closed at idle, there's virtually no vacuum signal at this slot. But as the throttle plates open during acceleration, they expose the slot to increasing amounts of manifold vacuum.

Pressure - Force applied over a surface, measured as force per unit of area. Pressure is usually measured in pounds per square inch or kilopascals. Pressure = Force X Area.

Pressure regulator valve - The valve that regulates line pressure by creating a variable restriction.

Pressure-relief valve - A one-way valve that opens above a preset pressure to relieve excessive internal pressure build up.

Reaction member - The part of a planetary gearset that is held so that output motion can be produced. Other members react against the stationary, held member.

Roller clutch - A type of one-way clutch utilizing spring-loaded rollers to lock on an inner cam-type race.

Rotor pump - A mechanical pump that uses an inner drive rotor and an outer driven rotor to produce oil flow. Lobes on the rotors create fluid chambers of varying volumes and eliminate the need

for a crescent, as used in a gear pump.

Servo - A piston-and-cylinder assembly that uses hydraulic system pressure to operate a transmission band.

Shift valve - A valve moved by throttle pressure and governor pressure to allow a shift at a precise point based on vehicle speed and throttle position.

Speed ratio - Designates the output speed divided by the input speed. Turbine (output) speed is divided by impeller (input) speed and indicated as a percentage.

Spool valve - A valve that has raised lands. Spool valves are used in the valve body to control fluid flow and pressure.

Sprag - A figure-eight-shaped locking element of a one-way sprag clutch.

Spur gear - A gear in which the teeth parallel the center line of the gear.

Stall speed - The engine speed in rpm at which the torque converter becomes efficient enough to stall the engine if the rear wheels are held stationary.

Stator - A component of the torque converter. It redirects fluid flow from the turbine back to the impeller in the direction of rotation, thus creating torque multiplication.

Sun gear - The center gear in the planetary gearset. This gear meshes with the planetary pinions in the reaction and output carriers.

Throttle pressure - The transmission hydraulic pressure that varies in relation to throttle opening.

Throttle valve - The valve that controls throttle pressure based on the movement of the throttle opening or manifold vacuum.

Torque - A turning or twisting force, such as the force imparted on a fastener by a torque wrench. Measured in terms of the distance times the amount of force applied. Commonly expressed in foot-pounds (Ft-lbs), inch-pounds (In-lbs), or Newton-meters (Nm).

Torque converter - A fluid coupling that transmits power from a driving to a driven member by hydraulic action. And, because of its design, this turbine-like device multiplies the torque between the engine and the transmission. It consists of a rotary pump or impeller, one or more reactors or stators, and a driven circular turbine.

Turbine - A component of the torque converter. It's splined onto the end of the transmission input shaft and is driven by the impeller.

Two-way check valve - A type of valve that manages fluid flow in two separate hydraulic circuits, through one fluid passage.

Vacuum modulator - A small canister mounted on the outside of a transmission that has a spring-loaded plunger and diaphragm inside. The diaphragm and plunger move a valve in relation to changes in manifold vacuum. It is often used to control a throttle valve.

Valve body - The housing containing the transmission's hydraulic control valves. Also known as the control valve assembly.

Index

Haynes Automotive Manuals

NOTE: New manuals are added to this list on a periodic basis. If you do not see a listing for your vehicle, consult your local Haynes dealer for the latest product information.

ACURA
*12020 Integra '86 thru '89 & **Legend** '86 thru '90

AMC
Jeep CJ - *see JEEP (50020)*
14020 Concord/Hornet/Gremlin/Spirit '70 thru '83
14025 (Renault) Alliance & Encore '83 thru '87

AUDI
15020 4000 all models '80 thru '87
15025 5000 all models '77 thru '83
15026 5000 all models '84 thru '88

AUSTIN
Healey Sprite - *see MG Midget (66015)*

BMW
*18020 3/5 Series '82 thru '92
*18021 3 Series except 325iX models '92 thru '97
18025 320i all 4 cyl models '75 thru '83
18035 528i & 530i all models '75 thru '80
18050 1500 thru 2002 except Turbo '59 thru '77

BUICK
Century (FWD) - *see GM (38005)*
*19020 Buick, Oldsmobile & Pontiac Full-size (Front wheel drive) '85 thru '98
Buick Electra, LeSabre and Park Avenue; Oldsmobile Delta 88 Royale, Ninety Eight and Regency; Pontiac Bonneville
19025 Buick Oldsmobile & Pontiac Full-size (Rear wheel drive)
Buick Estate '70 thru '90, Electra'70 thru '84, LeSabre '70 thru '85, Limited '74 thru '79
Oldsmobile Custom Cruiser '70 thru '90, Delta 88 '70 thru '85,Ninety-eight '70 thru '84
Pontiac Bonneville '70 thru '81, Catalina '70 thru '81, Grandville '70 thru '75, Parisienne '83 thru '86
19030 Mid-size Regal & Century '74 thru '87
Regal - *see GENERAL MOTORS (38010)*
Skyhawk - *see GM (38030)*
Skylark - *see GM (38020, 38025)*
Somerset - *see GENERAL MOTORS (38025)*

CADILLAC
*21030 Cadillac Rear Wheel Drive '70 thru '93
Cimarron, Eldorado & Seville - *see GM (38015, 38030)*

CHEVROLET
10305 Chevrolet Engine Overhaul Manual
*24010 Astro & GMC Safari Mini-vans '85 thru '93
24015 Camaro V8 all models '70 thru '81
24016 Camaro all models '82 thru '92
Cavalier - *see GM (38015)*
Celebrity - *see GM (38005)*
24017 Camaro & Firebird '93 thru '97
24020 Chevelle, Malibu, El Camino '69 thru '87
24024 Chevette & Pontiac T1000 '76 thru '87
Citation - *see GENERAL MOTORS (38020)*
*24032 Corsica/Beretta all models '87 thru '96
24040 Corvette all V8 models '68 thru '82
*24041 Corvette all models '84 thru '96
24045 Full-size Sedans Caprice, Impala, Biscayne, Bel Air & Wagons '69 thru '90
24046 Impala SS & Caprice and Buick Roadmaster '91 thru '96
Lumina '90 thru '94 - *see GM (38010)*
24048 Lumina & Monte Carlo '95 thru '98
Lumina APV - *see GM (38035)*
24050 Luv Pick-up all 2WD & 4WD '72 thru '82
24055 Monte Carlo all models '70 thru '88
Monte Carlo '95 thru '98 - *see LUMINA*
24059 Nova all V8 models '69 thru '79
*24060 Nova/Geo Prizm '85 thru '92
24064 Pick-ups '67 thru '87 - Chevrolet & GMC, all V8 & in-line 6 cyl, 2WD & 4WD '67 thru '87; Suburbans, Blazers & Jimmys '67 thru '91
*24065 Pick-ups '88 thru '98 - Chevrolet & GMC, all full-size models '88 thru '98; Blazer & Jimmy '92 thru '94; Suburban '92 thru '98; Tahoe & Yukon '95 thru '98
*24070 S-10 & GMC S-15 Pick-ups '82 thru '93
24071 S-10, Gmc S-15 & Jimmy '94 thru '96
*24075 Sprint & Geo Metro '85 thru '94
*24080 Vans - Chevrolet & GMC '68 thru '96

CHRYSLER
10310 Chrysler Engine Overhaul Manual
*25015 Chrysler Cirrus, Dodge Stratus, Plymouth Breeze, '95 thru '98
*25020 Full-size Front-Wheel Drive '88 thru '93
K-Cars - *see DODGE Aries (30008)*
Laser - *see DODGE Daytona (30030)*
25025 Chrysler LHS, Concorde & New Yorker, Dodge Intrepid, Eagle Vision, '93 thru '97
*25030 Chrysler/Plym. Mid-size '82 thru '95
Rear-wheel Drive - *see DODGE (30050)*

DATSUN
28005 200SX all models '80 thru '83
28007 B-210 all models '73 thru '78
28009 210 all models '78 thru '82
28012 240Z, 260Z & 280Z Coupe '70 thru '78
28014 280ZX Coupe & 2+2 '79 thru '83
300ZX - *see NISSAN (72010)*
28016 310 all models '78 thru '82
28018 510 & PL521 Pick-up '68 thru '73
28020 510 all models '78 thru '81
28022 620 Series Pick-up all models '73 thru '79
720 Series Pick-up - *see NISSAN (72030)*
28025 810/Maxima all gas models, '77 thru '84

DODGE
400 & 600 - *see CHRYSLER (25030)*
*30008 Aries & Plymouth Reliant '81 thru '89
30010 Caravan & Ply. Voyager '84 thru '95
*30011 Caravan & Ply. Voyager '96 thru '98
*30012 Challenger/Plymouth Saporro '78 thru '83
Challenger '67-'76 - *see DART (30025)*
30016 Colt/Plymouth Champ '78 thru '87
*30020 Dakota Pick-ups all models '87 thru '96
30025 Dart, Challenger/Plymouth Barracuda & Valiant 6 cyl models '67 thru '76
*30030 Daytona & Chrysler Laser '84 thru '89
Intrepid - *see Chrysler (25025)*
*30034 Dodge & Plymouth Neon '95 thru '97
*30035 Omni & Plymouth Horizon '78 thru '90
30040 Pick-ups all full-size models '74 thru '93
*30041 Pick-ups all full-size models '94 thru '98
*30045 Ram 50/D50 Pick-ups & Raider and Plymouth Arrow Pick-ups '79 thru '93
30050 Dodge/Ply./Chrysler RWD '71 thru '89
*30055 Shadow/Plymouth Sundance '87 thru '94
*30060 Spirit & Plymouth Acclaim '89 thru '95
*30065 Vans - Dodge & Plymouth '71 thru '96

EAGLE
Talon - *see MITSUBISHI Eclipse (68030)*
Vision - *see CHRYSLER (25025)*

FIAT
34010 124 Sport Coupe & Spider '68 thru '78
34025 X1/9 all models '74 thru '80

FORD
10355 Ford Automatic Transmission Overhaul
10320 Ford Engine Overhaul Manual
*36004 Aerostar Mini-vans '86 thru '96
Aspire - *see FORD Festiva (36030)*
*36006 Contour/Mercury Mystique '95 thru '98
36008 Courier Pick-up all models '72 thru '82
36012 Crown Victoria & Mercury Grand Marquis '88 thru '96
*36016 Escort/Mercury Lynx '81 thru '90
*36020 Escort/Mercury Tracer '91 thru '96
Expedition - *see FORD Pick-up (36059)*
*36024 Explorer & Mazda Navajo '91 thru '95
36028 Fairmont & Mercury Zephyr '78 thru '83
*36030 Festiva & Aspire '88 thru '97
36032 Fiesta all models '77 thru '80
36036 Ford & Mercury Full-size, Ford LTD & Mercury Marquis ('75 thru '82); Ford Custom 500,Country Squire, Crown Victoria & Mercury Colony Park ('75 thru '87); Ford LTD Crown Victoria & Mercury Gran Marquis ('83 thru '87)
36040 Granada & Mercury Monarch '75 thru '80
36044 Ford & Mercury Mid-size, Ford Thunderbird & Mercury Cougar ('75 thru '82); Ford LTD & Mercury Marquis ('83 thru '86); Ford Torino,Gran Torino, Elite, Ranchero pick-up, LTD II, Mercury Montego, Comet, XR-7 & Lincoln Versailles ('75 thru '86)
36048 Mustang V8 all models '64-1/2 thru '73
36049 Mustang II 4 cyl, V6 & V8 '74 thru '78
36050 Mustang & Mercury Capri incl. Turbo Mustang, '79 thru '93; Capri, '79 thru '86
*36051 Mustang all models '94 thru '97
*36054 Pick-ups and Bronco '73 thru '79
*36058 Pick-ups and Bronco '80 thru '96
*36059 Pick-ups, Expedition & Lincoln Navigator '97 thru '98
36062 Pinto & Mercury Bobcat '75 thru '80
36066 Probe all models '89 thru '92
*36070 Ranger/Bronco II gas models '83 thru '92
*36071 Ford Ranger '93 thru '97 & Mazda Pick-ups '94 thru '97
*36074 Taurus & Mercury Sable '86 thru '95
*36075 Taurus & Mercury Sable '96 thru '98
*36078 Tempo & Mercury Topaz '84 thru '94
36082 Thunderbird/Mercury Cougar '83 thru '88
36086 Thunderbird/Mercury Cougar '89 and '97
36090 Vans all V8 Econoline models '69 thru '91
*36094 Vans full size '92 thru '95
*36097 Windstar Mini-van '95 thru '98

GENERAL MOTORS
*10360 GM Automatic Transmission Overhaul
*38005 Buick Century, Chevrolet Celebrity, Olds Cutlass Ciera & Pontiac 6000 all models '82 thru '96
*38010 Buick Regal, Chevrolet Lumina, Oldsmobile Cutlass Supreme & Pontiac Grand Prix front wheel drive '88 thru '95
*38015 Buick Skyhawk, Cadillac Cimarron, Chevrolet Cavalier, Oldsmobile Firenza Pontiac J-2000 & Sunbird '82 thru '94
*38016 Chevrolet Cavalier & Pontiac Sunfire '95 thru '98
38020 Buick Skylark, Chevrolet Citation, Olds Omega, Pontiac Phoenix '80 thru '85
38025 Buick Skylark & Somerset, Olds Achieva, Calais & Pontiac Grand Am '85 thru '95
38030 Cadillac Eldorado & Oldsmobile Toronado '71 thru '85, Seville '80 thru '85, Buick Riviera '79 thru '85
*38035 Chevrolet Lumina APV, Oldsmobile Silhouette & Pontiac Trans Sport '90 thru '95
General Motors Full-size Rear-wheel drive - *see BUICK (19025)*

GEO
Metro - *see CHEVROLET Sprint (24075)*
Prizm - *see CHEVROLET (24060) or TOYOTA (92036)*
*40030 Storm all models '90 thru '93
Tracker - *see SUZUKI Samurai (90010)*

GMC
Safari - *see CHEVROLET ASTRO (24010)*
Vans & Pick-ups - *see CHEVROLET*

HONDA
42010 Accord CVCC all models '76 thru '83
42011 Accord all models '84 thru '89
42012 Accord all models '90 thru '93
*42013 Accord all models '94 thru '95
42020 Civic 1200 all models '73 thru '79
42021 Civic 1300 & 1500 CVCC '80 thru '83
42022 Civic 1500 CVCC all models '75 thru '79
42023 Civic all models '84 thru '91
42024 Civic & del Sol '92 thru '95
Passport - *see ISUZU Rodeo (47017)*
*42040 Prelude CVCC all models '79 thru '89

HYUNDAI
*43015 Excel all models '86 thru '94

ISUZU
Hombre - *see CHEVROLET S-10 (24071)*
*47017 Rodeo '91 thru '97, Amigo '89 thru '94, Honda Passport '95 thru '97
*47020 Trooper '84 thru '91, Pick-up '81 thru '93

JAGUAR
*49010 XJ6 all 6 cyl models '68 thru '86
*49011 XJ6 all models '88 thru '94
*49015 XJ12 & XJS all 12 cyl models '72 thru '85

JEEP
*50010 Cherokee, Comanche & Wagoneer Limited all models '84 thru '96
50020 CJ all models '49 thru '86
*50025 Grand Cherokee all models '93 thru '98
*50029 Grand Wagoneer & Pick-up '72 thru '91
*50030 Wrangler all models '87 thru '95

LINCOLN
Navigator - *see FORD Pick-up (36059)*
59010 Rear Wheel Drive all models '70 thru '96

MAZDA
61010 GLC (rear wheel drive) '77 thru '83
61011 GLC (front wheel drive) '81 thru '85
*61015 323 & Protegé '90 thru '97
*61016 MX-5 Miata '90 thru '97
*61020 MPV all models '89 thru '94
Navajo - *see FORD Explorer (36024)*
61030 Pick-ups '72 thru '93
Pick-ups '94 on - *see Ford (36071)*
61035 RX-7 all models '79 thru '85
*61036 RX-7 all models '86 thru '91
61040 626 (rear wheel drive) '79 thru '82
*61041 626 & MX-6 (front wheel drive) '83 thru '91

MERCEDES-BENZ
63012 123 Series Diesel '76 thru '85
*63015 190 Series 4-cyl gas models, '84 thru '88
63020 230, 250 & 280 6 cyl sohc '68 thru '72
63025 280 123 Series gas models '77 thru '81
63030 350 & 450 all models '71 thru '80

MERCURY
See FORD Listing

MG
66010 MGB Roadster & GT Coupe '62 thru '80
66015 MG Midget & Austin Healey Sprite Roadster '58 thru '80

MITSUBISHI
*68020 Cordia, Tredia, Galant, Precis & Mirage '83 thru '93
*68030 Eclipse, Eagle Talon & Plymouth Laser '90 thru '94
*68040 Pick-up '83 thru '96, Montero '83 thru '93

NISSAN
72010 300ZX all models incl. Turbo '84 thru '89
*72015 Altima all models '93 thru '97
*72020 Maxima all models '85 thru '91
*72030 Pick-ups '80 thru '96, Pathfinder '87 thru '95
*72040 Pulsar all models '83 thru '86
*72050 Sentra all models '82 thru '94
*72051 Sentra & 200SX all models '95 thru '98
*72060 Stanza all models '82 thru '90

OLDSMOBILE
*73015 Cutlass '74 thru '88
For other OLDSMOBILE titles, see BUICK, CHEVROLET or GENERAL MOTORS listing.

PLYMOUTH
For PLYMOUTH titles, see DODGE.

PONTIAC
79008 Fiero all models '84 thru '88
79018 Firebird V8 models except Turbo '70 thru '81
79019 Firebird all models '82 thru '92
For other PONTIAC titles, see BUICK, CHEVROLET or GENERAL MOTORS listing.

PORSCHE
*80020 911 Coupe & Targa models '65 thru '89
80025 914 all 4 cyl models '69 thru '76
80030 924 all models incl. Turbo '76 thru '82
*80035 944 all models incl. Turbo '83 thru '89

RENAULT
Alliance, Encore - *see AMC (14020)*

SAAB
*84010 900 including Turbo '79 thru '88

SATURN
*87010 Saturn all models '91 thru '96

SUBARU
89002 1100, 1300, 1400 & 1600 '71 thru '79
*89003 1600 & 1800 2WD & 4WD '80 thru '94

SUZUKI
*90010 Samurai/Sidekick/Geo Tracker '86 thru '96

TOYOTA
92005 Camry all models '83 thru '91
*92006 Camry all models '92 thru '96
92015 Celica Rear Wheel Drive '71 thru '85
*92020 Celica Front Wheel Drive '86 thru '93
*92025 Celica Supra all models '79 thru '92
92030 Corolla all models '75 thru '79
92032 Corolla rear wheel drive models '80 thru '87
*92035 Corolla front wheel drive models '84 thru '92
*92036 Corolla & Geo Prizm '93 thru '97
92040 Corolla Tercel all models '80 thru '82
92045 Corona all models '74 thru '82
92050 Cressida all models '78 thru '82
92055 Land Cruiser Series FJ40, 43, 45 & 55 '68 thru '82
*92056 Land Cruiser Series FJ60, 62, 80 & FZJ80 '68 thru '82
*92065 MR2 all models '85 thru '87
92070 Pick-up all models '69 thru '78
*92075 Pick-up all models '79 thru '95
*92076 Tacoma '95 thru '98, 4Runner '96 thru '98, T100 '93 thru '98
*92080 Previa all models '91 thru '95
92085 Tercel all models '87 thru '94

TRIUMPH
94007 Spitfire all models '62 thru '81
94010 TR7 all models '75 thru '81

VW
96008 Beetle & Karmann Ghia '54 thru '79
96012 Dasher all gasoline models '74 thru '81
*96016 Rabbit, Jetta, Scirocco, & Pick-up gas models '74 thru '91 & Convertible '80 thru '92
*96017 Golf & Jetta '93 thru '97
96020 Rabbit, Jetta, Pick-up diesel '77 thru '84
96030 Transporter 1600 all models '68 thru '79
96035 Transporter 1700, 1800, 2000 '72 thru '79
96040 Type 3 1500 & 1600 '63 thru '73
96045 Vanagon air-cooled models '80 thru '83

VOLVO
97010 120, 130 Series & 1800 Sports '61 thru '73
97015 140 Series all models '66 thru '74
*97020 240 Series all models '76 thru '93
97025 260 Series all models '75 thru '82
*97040 740 & 760 Series all models '82 thru '88

TECHBOOK MANUALS
10205 Automotive Computer Codes
10210 Automotive Emissions Control Manual
10215 Fuel Injection Manual, 1978 thru 1985
10220 Fuel Injection Manual, 1986 thru 1996
10225 Holley Carburetor Manual
10230 Rochester Carburetor Manual
10240 Weber/Zenith/Stromberg/SU Carburetor
10305 Chevrolet Engine Overhaul Manual
10310 Chrysler Engine Overhaul Manual
10320 Ford Engine Overhaul Manual
10330 GM and Ford Diesel Engine Repair
10340 Small Engine Repair Manual
10345 Suspension, Steering & Driveline
10355 Ford Automatic Transmission Overhaul
10360 GM Automatic Transmission Overhaul
10405 Automotive Body Repair & Painting
10410 Automotive Brake Manual
10415 Automotive Detailing Manual
10420 Automotive Eelectrical Manual
10425 Automotive Heating & Air Conditioning
10430 Automotive Reference Dictionary
10435 Automotive Tools Manual
10440 Used Car Buying Guide
10445 Welding Manual
10450 ATV Basics

SPANISH MANUALS
98903 Reparación de Carrocería & Pintura
98905 Códigos Automotrices de la Computadora
98910 Frenos Automotriz
98915 Inyección de Combustible 1986 al 1994
99040 Chevrolet & GMC Camionetas '67 al '87
99041 Chevrolet & GMC Camionetas '88 al '95
99042 Chevrolet Camionetas Cerradas '68 al '95
99055 Dodge Caravan/Ply. Voyager '84 al '95
99075 Ford Camionetas y Bronco '80 al '94
99077 Ford Camionetas Cerradas '69 al '91
99083 Ford Modelos de Tamaño Grande '75 al '87
99088 Ford Modelos de Tamaño Mediano '75 al '86
99091 Ford Taurus & Mercury Sable '75 al '95
99095 GM Modelos de Tamaño Grande '70 al '90
99110 GM Modelos de Tamaño Mediano '70 al '88
99110 Nissan Camionetas '80 al '96,
Pathfinder '87 al '95
99118 Nissan Sentra '82 al '94
99125 Toyota Camionetas y 4-Runner '79 al '95

Listings shown with an asterisk (*) indicate model coverage as of this printing. These titles will be periodically updated to include later model years - consult your Haynes dealer for more information.

Nearly 100 Haynes motorcycle manuals also available

5-98

Haynes North America, Inc., 861 Lawrence Drive, Newbury Park, CA 91320 • (805) 498-6703